Cosmopolitan Sex Workers

OXFORD STUDIES IN GENDER
AND INTERNATIONAL RELATIONS

**Series editors: J. Ann Tickner, University of Southern California,
and Laura Sjoberg, University of Florida**

*Enlisting Masculinity: The Construction of Gender in U.S. Military Recruiting
Advertising during the All-Volunteer Force*
Melissa T. Brown

Cosmopolitan Sex Workers: Women and Migration in a Global City
Christine B.N. Chin

*Intelligent Compassion: Feminist Critical Methodology in the Women's
International League for Peace and Freedom*
Catia Cecilia Confortini

Gender and Private Security in Global Politics
Maya Eichler

Gender, Sex, and the Postnational Defense: Militarism and Peacekeeping
Annica Kronsell

The Beauty Trade: Youth, Gender, and Fashion Globalization
Angela B. V. McCracken

A Feminist Voyage through International Relations
J. Ann Tickner

The Political Economy of Violence against Women
Jacqui True

Bodies of Violence: Theorizing Embodied Subjects in International Relations
Lauren B. Wilcox

COSMOPOLITAN SEX WORKERS

WORKERS

Women and Migration in a Global City

Christine B. N. Chin

Oxford University Press is a department of the University of Oxford.
It furthers the University's objective of excellence in research, scholarship,
and education by publishing worldwide.

Oxford   New York
Auckland   Cape Town   Dar es Salaam   Hong Kong   Karachi
Kuala Lumpur   Madrid   Melbourne   Mexico City   Nairobi
New Delhi   Shanghai   Taipei   Toronto

With offices in
Argentina   Austria   Brazil   Chile   Czech Republic   France   Greece
Guatemala   Hungary   Italy   Japan   Poland   Portugal   Singapore
South Korea   Switzerland   Thailand   Turkey   Ukraine   Vietnam

Oxford is a registered trade mark of Oxford University Press
in the UK and certain other countries.

Published in the United States of America by
Oxford University Press
198 Madison Avenue, New York, NY 10016

Library of Congress Cataloging-in-Publication Data
Chin, Christine B. N., 1963–
Cosmopolitan sex workers : women and migration in a global city/Christine B.N. Chin.
p. cm.—(Oxford studies in gender and international relations)
Includes bibliographical references and index.
ISBN 978-0-19-989091-0 (cloth : alk. paper); 978-0-19-024926-7 (paperback : alk. paper)
1. Prostitutes—Southeast Asia. 2. Immigrants—Southeast Asia.
3. Cosmopolitanism—Southeast Asia. I. Title.
HQ241.A5.C45   2013
306.74'20959—dc23   2012046070

For my father who instilled in me the worth of a good heart above all else, and for my mother who raised me to believe that with courage, there is no mountain too high to climb

CONTENTS

LIST OF FIGURES

LIST OF TABLES

ACKNOWLEDGMENTS

When we hold an open book in our hands, or click on a hyperlink to access an e-book, we enter a world to which many voices have contributed, directly and indirectly. The analogy of a symphonic choir comes to mind here: the choir, orchestra, arrangements, back and front stages of the hall, lighting, and acoustics are some of the crucial elements. The conductor has to make and give sense to integrating and coordinating all elements for a successful performance of brand new scores, reinterpretations, or even radical rearrangements of much vaunted classics.

Any single-authored book, then, is an intellectual symphonic choir with the author as conductor. This book is no different: many individuals have contributed to its production, intellectual and physical. First and foremost, I am awed by the choir without which this book could not be written. They are the transnational migrant and local women and men whom I encountered and interviewed in the field. Each soprano, alto, bass, and tenor voice could have sung alone and indeed, as you shall read, many did so in this study. Although their narratives conveyed specific hopes, fears, and dreams, when woven together they elucidated common paths to pursuing meaningful and secure lives in the twenty-first century, despite what they knew others might and did think of them. I owe an immense debt of gratitude as well to the women and men whom I got to know during the production of my first two books and who eventually helped pave the way to some members of this choir.

No symphonic choir is complete without the orchestra: the strings, percussion, and brass and woodwind instruments. Contributors can be found in the bibliography. They come from different disciplines and fields of study such as feminist international relations, critical political economy, geography, transnational migration, sociology, and intercultural communication. Unbeknownst to many of them, they have contributed to the construction of an interdisciplinary conceptual framework. To be sure, my participation on International Studies Association panels, and especially conversations in the past few years with feminist IR colleagues, have helped shape the orchestral arrangement. As always, I am very grateful for their time and intellectual generosity. Among them is J. Ann Tickner, who, once I described the emerging project and related challenges, not only posed incisive questions but persistently reminded me of the project's value and the need to move forward with it.

Here at American University, my deep appreciation goes to James Goldgeier, Dean of the School of International Service (SIS), and Phyllis Peres, Senior Vice Provost and Dean of Academic Affairs, for their unwavering support of me and my work. I also thank my colleagues in SIS, especially James Mittelman for always seizing the opportunity to ask me provocative intellectual questions. Successive SIS doctoral students assisted in keeping track of, and coordinating major components of the project. Kia Hall jumped right in, even as she and I worked on her Fulbright Fellowship to research Garifuna gender relations and development in Honduras. Yelena Osipova, who took over when Kia was awarded the Fellowship to Honduras, spent many hours reading and discussing the different chapters, and working on the maps and charts. Willow Williamson assisted in the final copyediting stage. My dear colleague-friends Fanta Aw and Loubna Skalli Hanna made it a point, during a lonely and at times frustrating process of writing the book, to juxtapose some of my arguments with those from their specific fields of specialization, and notably, to make me laugh with much (unprintable) humor. They were resolute in refusing to let me entertain doubts or to wallow in self pity, even for a moment.

Production of this symphonic choir could not have been completed without the backstage work of Angela Chnapko and the editorial, marketing, and production team at OUP. They were the consummate professionals who made the journey from review to production a painless and smooth experience. To the anonymous reviewers, thank you for your time and effort: I remain heartened by your constructive criticisms and encouragements to help me arrange and conduct the best performance possible. I alone am responsible for the contents and any errors in this book.

My deepest and most abiding gratitude goes to my family. They are my rock: I am, primarily because of them. My sisters and I were born into a never-let-go-of-tradition, extended patriarchal family. Yet our parents, grandmother, and Buddhist teachers deliberately raised us to believe that despite the explicit and implicit privileging of sons and grandsons in the very large family, we were equally worthy of support and respect: our gender was not a handicap at all. We were expected to choose our own paths and to walk them with courage, commitment, and conviction. In the process, we were enjoined never to compromise decency, civility, and kindness.

I am the only one among the daughters and granddaughters who eschewed other opportunities in favor of conducting intellectual symphonic choirs. Still, my sisters are the most fervent champions in their steadfast endorsement of my work and their unconditional love for me. They insist that we must not relinquish the right to ask questions, even if the answers may elicit discomfort for some. If the ultimate goal is to improve the human condition for all, we will have to be able to "hear" while we listen to different voices, and to "look" while we see different peoples as they present to us, and not as we may wish them to be.

Christine B. N. Chin
Washington, D.C.
November 2012

ABBREVIATIONS

ASAs   Air Service Agreements
ATPA   Anti-Trafficking in Persons Act
BCIC   Bumiputera Commercial and Industrial Community
CATW   Coalition Against Trafficking in Women
FT   Federal Territory
GAATW   Global Alliance Against Trafficking in Women
GATS   General Agreement on Trade in Services
GaWC   Globalization and World Cities Research Network
ICT   Information and Communication Technology
IE   International Education
ILO   International Labour Organization
IMF   International Monetary Fund
KL   Kuala Lumpur
KLCC   Kuala Lumpur City Centre
KLIA   Kuala Lumpur International Airport
MAS   Malay Agricultural Settlement
MOHA   Ministry of Home Affairs
MOHE   Ministry of Higher Education
MOU   Memorandum of Understanding
MSC   Multimedia Super Corridor
NEM   New Economic Model
NEP   New Economic Policy
NGOs   Nongovernmental Organizations
OPEC   Organization of Petroleum Exporting Countries
PHEI   Private Higher Education Institutions Act
PRC   People's Republic of China
PTT   Petronas Twin Towers
RELA   Ikatan Relawan Rakyat Malaysia (People's Volunteer Corps or
        Malaysian Volunteer Corps)
RM   Ringgit Malaysia (Malaysian currency: approx RM3 to USD1)

SAPs	Structural Adjustment Programs
STDs	Sexually Transmitted Diseases
SUARAM	Suara Rakyat Malaysia (Voice of the Malaysian People)
UNODC	United Nations Office on Drugs and Crime
USD	US Dollar
USTIP	US Trafficking in Persons Report
VIPs	Very Important Persons
VOA	Visa-on-Arrival
WB	World Bank
WTO	World Trade Organization

Cosmopolitan Sex Workers

CHAPTER 1

Kaleidoscope of City, Creativity, and Cosmopolitanism

It may seem peculiar to offer a study titled "Cosmopolitan Sex Workers" when international journalists, policy makers, and academics typically focus on women and girls trafficked for sex. Sold by families, duped by boyfriends, or tricked by recruiters, these trafficked people are transported in-country and across borders and forced to perform sex work. This book's title, then, may raise some eyebrows, because it calls attention to women who are not sex-trafficked and who, in the process of migration for sex work, may and do exhibit qualities that have been associated exclusively with elite travelers. This is not to deny the empirical realities of sex trafficking that are documented and analyzed by researchers in different regions of the world. Rather, it is to foreground a less often acknowledged phenomenon of nontrafficked women who participate in transnational migration for sex work. Women sex workers of diverse nationalities now are in major cities throughout the world, from Nigerian women in Kuala Lumpur and Chinese women in Paris, to Italian women in Doha and South African women in Dubai.[1] This, too, is an empirical reality.

Women's transnational migration for sex work is occurring within the larger context of economic restructuring processes that interlock the global, regional, national, and local levels to bring about a new global economy. This raises the question: "In what ways and with what consequences do contemporary economic restructuring processes encourage and facilitate women's transnational migration for sex work?"

These economic restructuring processes most often are referred to collectively as "neoliberal globalization" or "economic globalization." Arising from the post–World War II era's "embedded liberalism" and ascendant since the late twentieth century, neoliberal ideology champions selling state-owned firms to private sector interests, removing barriers to the free flow of capital and goods, and opening up protected economic sectors and industries.[2] States implement economic privatization, deregulation, and liberalization policies to bring about or strengthen and integrate free market economies. The state's role henceforth "is to create and preserve an institutional framework appropriate to" national, regional and global free market operations (Harvey 2005, 2).

The contradictory effects of economic restructuring processes on different groups of urban and rural people are well documented all over the world. Although there may be robust economic growth in some sectors, it often is accompanied by unemployment in other sectors, as well as by dependence on "flexibilized" labor in the form of temporary, contractual, outsourced, and offshored work. States help render labor less demanding (or more flexible), for example, by weakening or eliminating workers' rights and benefits, and by encouraging firms to parcel out or subcontract work (Standing 1999, 2011; see also Chin 2003; Van Eyck 2003): "Temporary workers . . . never achieve seniority, are not eligible for fringe benefits, considered to perform menial chores, and have no resources to independent and collective means of redress" (Teodosio 2007, 117). Data on employment, wages, nature of work, and so forth reveal that women continue to be negatively affected by labor flexibilization processes. For example, although the International Labour Organization study "Women in Labor Markets" found a narrowing of the gap in employment rates of women and men,

> There is a clear segregation of women in sectors that are generally characterized by low pay, long hours and oftentimes informal working arrangements. And even within sectors where women dominate, it is rarely women who would hold the upper managerial jobs.
>
> (International Labour Office 2010, 5)

Women's and men's transnational migration for employment exists as a concurrent phenomenon that shapes and is shaped by labor flexibilization processes. Labor-sending states directly and indirectly promote out-migration of their nationals in order to relieve the pressures of underemployment and unemployment, while generating foreign exchange earnings via migrant remittances. Labor-receiving states open their immigration gates to meet the labor demands of their formal and informal economies. However, not all transnational migrant workers enjoy unrestricted mobility: receiving states selectively open their immigration gates based on considerations such as nationality, race-ethnicity, religion, gender, class, education, and occupation. Migrant women and men who fail to qualify for entry via legal channels will often pursue alternative means of entry. Some succeed, while others fall prey to traffickers.

More and more, migrant women pursue "mobile livelihoods" via legal and extralegal channels, participating in intra-regional and inter-regional migration (Briones 2008, 62). In major receiving cities, many work in low-wage jobs in such places as restaurants, homes, factories, hotels, and hospitals. Despite the fact that the range of positions is broad—including domestic workers, nursing home aides, assembly-line workers, restaurant servers, and hotel housekeepers—the common denominator is that these jobs are made available to, and often occupied by, migrant women. The labor is often in line with women's ascribed gender traits:

> As the service sector grows, many "female" tasks, such as child care and food service, are incorporated in the market economy. The affinity of many of these new service sector jobs to women's traditional domestic roles may broaden the gender division of labor into the sectoral and occupational spheres.
>
> (World Bank 2011b, 214)

According to the ILO, women account for 83% of all domestic workers worldwide (Simonovsky, and Luebker 2011, 8). In London, for example, women constitute 82% of all Slovakian and 71% of all Filipino migrants, and the majority of them are employed in domestic and health-related service jobs (Vertovec quoted in Dyer, McDowell, and Batnitsky 2010, 640). There are migrant women, to be sure, who exchange their sexualized labor for wages as well. Migrant women who perform gendered or even sexualized labor in cities rarely receive affirmative recognition in public discourse or in national and international accounting registers.

On the other hand, as regularly reported by global newsprint media such as the *Financial Times*, the *Wall Street Journal* and *Forbes*, men "expatriates" or "highly skilled" transnational migrants and local professionals are seen to "organize and lead the drive to global control and the opening of markets to international competition" (Acker 2004, 29). They represent the "global talent" symbolized particularly by bankers, corporate managers, accountants, lawyers, and information technology experts who travel from major city to city all over the world, sharing their much in-demand knowledge and skills.

In these ways, there is a gendered and classed dimension to neoliberal globalization. Valorization of masculinized global talent in popular and academic literature obscures what is called "shadow globalization" or "activities made possible by global flows of information, technology, finance and people, that are taking place in informal and illegal ways, but in the shadows in terms of otherness" (Penttinen 2007, 7). Given the illicit status of sex industries in many labor-receiving contexts, migrant women sex workers then are quintessential participants of shadow globalization. Beyond the dominant dyadic schema of exploited victim–criminal trafficker, the structural forces that directly and indirectly promote the migration of nontrafficked women sex workers—and the ramifications of these forces—remain inexplicably obtuse.

Therefore, this phenomenon of nontrafficked women's participation in transnational migration for sex work within the larger context of neoliberal globalization calls for a more comprehensive and nuanced framework of analysis. Below, I present an interdisciplinary "3C" framework—of city, creativity, and cosmopolitanism—to organize and analyze complex interlocking forces on the global, national, local, and individual levels. The framework interweaves neoliberal economic restructuring processes that have given rise to networks of global cities and interconnected migratory pathways; "creative" responses of receiving states, migrant women, and facilitating groups to structural constraints and contradictions; and the cosmopolitan attitudes, practices, and worldviews emerging from migrant women's encounters with difference in global cities.

This book applies the 3C framework to the empirical case of transnational migrant women sex workers in Kuala Lumpur (KL), the capital of Malaysia. Unlike its Asian counterparts, such as Bangkok, Manila, and Seoul, KL did not host foreign military bases (around which thrived "military" or "base" prostitution) in the twentieth century; nor is it internationally renowned as a destination for sex tourism, as are Bangkok's Patpong district, Singapore's Geylang neighborhood, and Tokyo's Shinjuku ward. KL has served, since the 1970s, as the country's gateway and destination city for low-wage Southeast Asian migrant workers in key economic sectors. By the 1990s, however, and as KL ascended to the club of "global" or "world" cities, it also had become a destination and transit city for migrant women sex workers from within and beyond the region.

CITY

One major outcome of global economic crises in the mid- to late twentieth century was the retreat of states from their respective economies. While those in the Global North voluntarily did so, the World Bank and International Monetary Fund's structural adjustment programs (SAPs) ensured that many states in the Global South followed suit. Free-market competition was considered the engine of economic growth, if not a panacea for improving the human condition. Privatization, deregulation, and liberalization policies, in effect, "deterritorialized" or freed capital to flow freely around the world (Scholte 2000).

New spatial configurations began to emerge with the "reterritorialization" of capital: one example is the so-called global city (others are offshore tax havens, free-trade zones, export processing zones, and regional growth triangles). As transnational firms extend their coverage and operations globally, these cities offer one-stop sites with access to specialized services, such as accounting, advertising, legal, finance, and research and development services. These cities "possess capabilities for servicing the global operations of firms and markets, for organizing enormous geographic dispersal and mobility, and for maintaining centralized control over that dispersal" (Sassen 2008, 57). The most renowned global cities of London, New York, and Tokyo are located in the Global North (Sassen 2001).

What of cities in the Global South? The Globalization and World Cities Research Network (GaWC) ranks world cities according to "economic function and the presence of global headquarters and producer service firms" (Shatkin 2007, 2). New York, London and Tokyo are hailed as archetypal or alpha world cities, followed by beta and gamma world cities located in different regions. However, Sassen (2005, 2009) and others (Shatkin 2007; Robinson 2002; Schiller and Cağlar 2009), caution against assuming that these three global cities offer the template for development of other global cities. Doing so is tantamount to adopting a linear developmental trajectory in which the archetypal cities are made to become the mirror of all other cities' future. The emergence of global cities elsewhere need not follow strictly established economic criteria or perform the same financial functions.[3] The characteristics and functions of a global city are shaped by its experiences with economic globalization, its negotiations of global forces, and the agency of local actors, that is, "differences rooted in cultural, geography, and institutional dynamics" (Shatkin 2007, 2). Despite states' retreat from their own economies, they remain deeply implicated in the rise of their global cities.[4]

As command posts or centers for the new global economy, global cities are connected to one another within and beyond regions via electronic infrastructure made possible by innovations in new information and communication technologies (ICTs), and complemented by infrastructural expansion of freeways, railways, ports, and airports for the transport of passengers and cargo (Derudder et al. 2008; Shin and Timberlake 2000; Grubesic, Matisziw, and Zook 2008; Fu, Oum, and Zhang 2010). States sign "open skies" bilateral air service agreements (ASAs) that vitally link cities cross-regionally and globally (Forsyth, King, and Rodolfoc 2005; Sheller 2010).

Metaphorically, these interconnections represent multilane global and regional highways. Ongoing competition and collaboration among global cities for capital and human resources have the effect of continuously adding new lanes to the highways, for example lanes for commodities and goods, and lanes for financial and other services.

It is important to note that bilateral ASAs strengthen global cities' relationships to transnational migrant labor. As firms relocate key functions to global cities, labor demands increase in many categories of work. Global cities' so-called advanced producer services (such as financial, advertising, management, and consulting services) are performed by local and international knowledge workers or global talent. Global cities' personal services (such as domestic work, gardening, and dry cleaning) are provided by low-wage local and transnational migrant workers.

In the more established cities of the Global North, empirical research demonstrates that the in-migration of knowledge workers continues to be accompanied by the in-migration of low-wage workers. While migrant flows to the "immigrant gateway" cities such as New York and Toronto are extremely diverse, other global cities such as Tokyo and Mexico City, have significantly lower but growing percentages of low-wage transnational migrant labor (Price and Benton-Short 2007, 103; see also Price and Benton-Short 2008).

Notably, the growing interconnectedness of global cities facilitates migrants' ability to move from one region to another:

> It is . . . a mistake to think of these destinations as sites of permanent settlement. A more accurate metaphor may be that of a turnstile, where immigrants enter for a period of time and then leave for other cities in a transnational network. Thus a Nigerian immigrant may migrate to Seville, then to London or New York, and then return back to Lagos. . . . Urban economies are increasingly reliant upon new and large flows of foreign-labor for distinct segments of the labor market.
>
> (Price and Benton-Short 2007, 104)

In this way, global and regional highways connecting cities also serve as formal and informal migratory pathways for migrant workers all over the world.[5]

Nonetheless, the overemphasis on specialized services and professional workers has tended to obscure pathways taken by other categories of migrants (Sassen 2000, 82). Since global cities surreptitiously affirm the "masculinized worlds of finance, banking, insurance and law, seeing these as more 'skilled occupations' and more important in driving the world economy" (Hubbard 2011, 1), the concomitant expansion of sex industries and migrant women's participation in them remain in the shadows, as if tangentially or unconnected to the rise and expansion of the cities (Agathangelou 2004; Altman 2002). Whenever a connection is made, the presumption is that women are sex-trafficking victims or that they have no other option but to perform sex work. Although such cases do exist, there also are women who, despite options available to them, make the decision and subsequent arrangement to migrate for sex work.

The past three decades of research on transnational migration for employment in different regions of the world show that there are no neutral pathways for migrant women and men. Depending on (1) labor demands of receiving economies; (2) interstate relations; and (3) immigration policies and regulations, officially sanctioned or authorized migrant pathways practice "differential inclusion" (Andrijasevic 2009, 391). Since pathways are not unconditionally open, how do migrant women enter and participate in what many host states and societies consider an immoral and illegal activity?

More and more, competition and collaboration among global cities is creating new and different opportunities and modes of migration that have come to include women's migration for sex work. To ascertain this more clearly, we turn next to specific ways in which states maintain their global cities' "brand"—their distinctiveness—in order to attract transnational capital and human resources (Anholt 2009a).

In the late twentieth century, states borrowed a key practice from the corporate arena to help create and maintain their distinctiveness in a hypercompetitive era.[6] Global cities are one of the foremost sites of states' branding projects, because they exemplify the reasons for, and legitimize outcomes of, urban (re)development projects, while serving as gateways to the hinterlands and the world. Urban space planning and imaging strategies are expected to attract firms and to offer a host of services for residents and visitors alike, generating employment, revenue, and positive images of the place, culture, people, and services (Hall and Rath 2007, 9–10).[7] The lines are further blurred between corporate and public sectors as states adopt management principles based on efficiency, transparency, productivity, and assessment metrics that promise more hospitable environments for transnational capital and residents.

Still, branding practices alone cannot reveal specific ways in which competition and collaboration among global cities forge additional migratory pathways. To better capture what states are trying to do in the twenty-first century, Anholt (who originally introduced the concepts of city and nation branding) proposed the concept of "competitive identity": basic channels or activities by which states construct and accordingly manage their respective city and nation brands (2009b). Among the channels are those increasingly considered by states as integral to restructuring and strengthening free-market economies. Most notably, the channels of tourism promotion, investment and foreign talent recruitment, and cultural exchanges coincide with the two major sectors of tourism and education listed under the General Agreement on Trade in Services (GATS). As discussed below, they also create additional pathways on which women migrate for sex work.

GATS: Servicing the World

Implemented in 1995 following the Uruguay Round on trade agreements, GATS is one of the main treaties of the World Trade Organization (WTO). This treaty focuses on trade in services per se, and not goods or products. It covers twelve service sectors: business; communication; construction and engineering; distribution; education; environment; financial; health; tourism and travel; recreation, cultural, and sporting; transport; and other services. Exempted are "services in the exercise of governmental authority and air traffic rights."[8]

GATS was expected to eliminate all domestic or discriminatory barriers to trade in services by progressively lowering restrictions or barriers to foreign investments. Recognizing multidirectional movements of capital and people, this treaty is comprehensive in its coverage, addressing consumption abroad, cross-border trade, commercial presence in foreign markets, and temporary migration of service providers. Succinctly put, GATS broadens and deepens the integration of local, national, regional, and global economies. Of the twelve service sectors, liberalization policies in tourism and education establish and institutionalize additional migratory pathways.

Tourism

Women's relationship to sex work and migration is not unique to the present time. During the European imperial era, women migrated (voluntarily and involuntarily) internally and across borders to perform sex work in ports, towns, and military outposts of colonies (Pratt 2008; Stoler 1992; Tagliacozzo 2008). By the mid-twentieth century, women sex workers again were key to meeting demands of soldiers stationed in allied countries during the Cold War. The end of the Cold War transformed military prostitution into renowned sex tourism sites in several Asian global cities (see especially Enloe 2000; Moon 1997; Phongpaichit 1982; Robinson 2006; Trương 1990). Meanwhile, tourism development in the Caribbean created the four S's (sun, sea, shopping, and sex) of island destinations for international tourists (Cabezas 2004; Brennan 2004; Taylor 2001).

One of the major differences between the imperial past and the present is that contemporary processes of liberalizing tourism under GATS are institutionalizing women's migration for sex work in major cities all over the world—not just those that are internationally renowned for sex tourism—throughout Europe, the Middle East, Latin America, and the Asia-Pacific region (see, for example, Agustín 2007; Wonders and Michalowski 2001; Spanger 2002; Mahdavi 2010; Kim and Fu 2008). Migratory lanes or pathways created by liberalization of tourism sectors offer women at least two institutionalized modes of migration: they may enter as workers for tourism-related industries, and they may enter as tourists or visitors.[9]

Beyond the fortunate few who are able to secure managerial positions, migrant women are often hired to perform low-wage gendered work, for example as hotel housekeepers or restaurant servers (Equitable Tourism Options 2000; Sinclair 1997). Some supplement their monthly incomes with sex work. Migrant women also can enter global cities as tourists or visitors and then engage in sex work. ASAs connecting far-flung cities are designed to provide more direct routes for movements of goods, services, and tourists. Categorized as hospitality workers or as tourists, women can participate in global cities' sex industries alongside those who augment their authorized employment with sex work and those who are sex-trafficked.

Arguably, these additional pathways on which women migrate for sex work are an unintended outcome of liberalizing tourism sectors. However, resilient patriarchal and racial-ethnic ideologies implicitly shape economic restructuring processes:

> Women in the sex industry become—in certain kinds of economies—a crucial link supporting the expansion of the entertainment industry and thereby of tourism as a development strategy. This in turn becomes a source of government revenue. These tie-ins are structural, not a function of conspiracies.
>
> (Sassen 2002, 270)

Phrased differently, although policies are not designed explicitly to bolster sex industries, cities' and states' responses to global competition for resources and revenue are nurturing and strengthening "the foundation for globally structured, though geographically localized, sex tourism" (Wonders and Michalowski 2001, 565).

Despite the passage of time, what has not changed much is that women's transnational migration for sex work can affirm or reconfigure "ethnosexual frontiers" in destination sites, that is to say, "erotic locations and exotic destinations that are surveilled and supervised, patrolled and policed, regulated and restricted, but are constantly penetrated by individuals forging sexual links with ethnic 'others' across ethnic boundaries" (Nagel 2000, 159). Racialized-ethnicized and sexualized hierarchies of the European imperial era hence will find twenty-first-century expression in the racial-ethnosexual frontiers of global cities.

Transnational migrant women sex workers' presence in global cities that have little or no historical linkages to their home countries highlights the growing web of interconnectedness. As states continue to sign bilateral ASAs expanding the practice of open skies for transporting people and cargo, migrant women also are able to identify and travel to new destinations that demand their racialized-ethnicized and sexualized labor. As will be discussed later, migrant women's selection of global cities depends on a host of factors including a city's reputation, the ease of entry/immigration regulations, and local access and support for sex work.

Education

The second additional pathway on which women migrate for sex work is not as obvious as the tourism pathway. In part, this is due to education's status as a relatively new sector being liberalized under GATS. At the Seattle-Millennium round of meetings of the World Trade Organization, education was elevated as an "internationally traded service" (McBurnie and Ziguras 2001).[10] Processes of liberalizing education services are leading to new products and services, such as corporate funding of academic initiatives in public and private universities, education via the Internet or other means of long-distance teaching and learning, as well as dual-degree cross-border programs, short-term educational exchanges, programs in language certification, and international vocational education programs.[11] The last three programs are key indicators of internationalizing higher education. In such international education (IE), new international programs, as well as corporate-owned and -managed universities and colleges, are created to attract cross-border movements of students and faculty.[12] New types of providers are corporate universities, for-profit institutions, media companies, and education brokers that also specialize in cross-border delivery of education services, such as branch campuses, distance learning, virtual universities, and franchise and twinning arrangements. The multi-directional mobility of students then is matched by the multidirectional mobility of academic-vocational programs and providers: students have many more opportunities and sites from which to pursue full-time degree programs, study-abroad exchanges, foreign language training and certification, and vocational skills acquisition.

In the Global North, recruitment of international students has become an important strategy of local, national, and regional economic development, because the students are expected to help increase knowledge bases or improve human capital, while addressing issues related to receiving countries' aging populations, declining fertility rates, and skill shortages (Gribble 2008, 26).[13]

Over time, organized schemes for international student recruitment have emerged in such countries, because these are seen as the quickest way to recruit and nurture highly skilled labor: "In the long term, the ageing of the population in developed countries may mean that the labour force advantages of international education will outweigh the direct economic benefits from tuition fees and living costs of international students" (Ziguras and Law 2006, 61).

Concurrently, some states in the Global South are pursing IE as another major way in which to (1) generate much-needed revenue; (2) educate the next generation of international students; and (3) pursue "cultural diplomacy" while strengthening the competitive identity of their global cities.[14] Examples are Doha's Education City and Singapore's Global Schoolhouse initiative with partnerships and branch campuses established by renowned institutions of higher education from the Global North. Traditional higher education hubs based in cities of the Global North now are competing against nonprofit and for-profit universities and colleges based in global cities from East Asia to the Middle East.

IE programs are premised largely on the assumption that students or their families can afford them. International students must meet immigration regulations for student visas, and many do not qualify for in-country educational aid, grants, and loan programs. Although the cost of education may be relatively less expensive in the Global South, financial pressures can encourage some women and men to turn to sex work. In Singapore, the state's long-term visa issued to mothers who accompany their student children—has elicited the phenomenon of *peidu mama* "(literally, a 'study mother'), a mainland Chinese woman working, usually in a massage parlor, to support her young children studying in Singapore" (Lim 2004, 71).[15] In

Kuala Lumpur, international students have been detained for unauthorized work, including sex work.

This additional migratory pathway created by states' liberalization of education offers at least two entry modes for migrant women sex workers: they enter legally as international students and then participate in sex work to help finance their studies; and they enter legally as international students mainly to pursue sex work. A third entry mode emerges from the intersection of tourism and education; that is, women enter as tourists with the intent to pursue sex work and then enroll in part-time certification courses (for example, English language or computer programming).

Global cities, thus, are not just sites that offer advanced producer services. They also offer personal services performed increasingly by transnational migrants. In light of intensifying competition among global cities, states are implementing liberalization policies especially in tourism and education to generate revenue and to enhance their cities' competitive identities. These liberalization policies simultaneously open migratory pathways for women to offer personal sexual services in the cities.

Chapter Two presents the global city of Kuala Lumpur. The discussion focuses on KL's origins as a nineteenth-century colonial trading settlement, and its late twentieth-century ascendance to the global arena. Colonial state policies in KL indelibly shaped Malays' relationship with Chinese and Indian migrant workers. In the effort to address colonial legacies, the postcolonial state implemented a social engineering policy that gradually shifted to a neoliberal development path. As the city and citizens move toward a knowledge-based economy and society while hosting many more international tourists and students, the labor of migrant women and men from a range of nationalities and in a range of state-approved jobs remains indispensable to sustaining KL's regional and global competitive identity.

CREATIVITY

Ongoing economic restructuring processes generate different kinds of constraints and opportunities for receiving states, migrant women, and groups that facilitate women's migration and employment. This section discusses the creative strategies deployed by these three sets of actors to mitigate constraints, and to identify and take advantage of opportunities. How do state authorities in receiving countries manage migrants who seek entry into, or who already are present in, their global cities? Why do women migrate for sex work, particularly when they have alternative employment opportunities either in sending or receiving countries? Who facilitates their migration and employment as sex workers? How do migrant women make sense of their encounters with difference in the global cities? In this section, I employ the word *creativity* to emphasize the complex and even contradictory ways in which the exercise of human agency shapes and is shaped by structural forces.

State Privatization of Security

Global cities encourage potential investors, tourists, corporate executives, international students, and other approved categories of transnational migrants to appear at their gates for entry. At the same time, the cities also attract those in search of employment, refuge or asylum, but who do not or cannot meet entry requirements. As welcome mats are laid out by receiving states for some because of the promise of their skills, knowledge base, or purchasing power, detention centers await others: the right to travel or move (as enshrined by the Universal Declaration of Human Rights, Articles 13 and 24) is not accompanied by the right of entry.

Herein lies a major contradiction emanating from neoliberal globalization's promotion of globally integrated free markets within the existing framework of nation-states. The global flow of information, capital, and even goods is unrestricted relative to the flow of people. Migratory pathways linking global cities may be fully open to some—but they are conditionally open or even completely closed to others. Traditional border-control checkpoints, nevertheless, have not been able to stem all irregular migration.

Compounding this is public discourse on the presence and activities of regular and irregular transnational migrants, which explores the issue of who rightly belongs to the nation or can make claims to do so. As outsiders, migrants' relationship to the receiving nation is evaluated along societal, criminological, economic, and political axes (Karyotis 2007). Migrants can be represented and treated as if they pose socioeconomic or political threats, or as if they pose threats to others' identity or security (Ceyhan and Tsoukala 2002). In major receiving countries of the Global North and South, migrant men and women are said to be the causes of higher crime rates, as well as higher rates of unemployment among citizen workers. They also are held responsible for declining traditions and diluting a community's gene pool. Politicians, security forces, and the news media are key actors complicit in these processes, framing and fueling public discourse: migrants are said to destabilize economies, polities, and societies. The discourse justifies state strategies devised to enforce the "originary distinction" between insider-citizen and outsider-foreigner at the external and internal borders (Rajaram and Grundy-Warr 2004, 34).

One of the most obvious examples can be found in the control exercised by consulates that issue visas. Approvals often enforce selectivity based on a variety of factors, such as gender, race-ethnicity, nationality, and the needs and demands of the receiving society (Dobrowolsky 2007; Bigo and Guild 2005). Highly skilled workers, global talent, or expatriates are welcomed for their expertise and contributions to the receiving economy and society. As briefly discussed earlier, the prominence of the dimensions of occupation, education, and class tends to obscure the gender dimension. Prevailing assumptions of immigration authorities and sending corporations are that women tend mostly to follow their spouses, and that women executives' perceived gendered sensitivities and sensibilities tend to dissuade them from overseas corporate assignments (see especially Kofman 2004; Mathur-Helm 2002; Westwood and Leung 1994).

"Unskilled" migrant workers (often called "guest workers") also can obtain official approval, provided they meet entry and employment requirements. Depending on the receiving country, approvals are given based not just on demands from various economic sectors but considerations of race-ethnicity, religion, gender, and so forth (Calavita 2006; Kaur 2010). States depend on immigration regulations to strategically select migrants, and to practice "complexity reduction" by conceptualizing away wide-ranging conditions in which migrant men and women seek entry or become "illegal" while in-country (Trappolin 2005, 341).[16] Responses of many receiving states are encapsulated in the so-called 3D approach of detaining, disempowering and deporting irregular migrants (United States Department of State 2010).

State efforts to secure the nation from migrant incursions along external borders are evident: for example, in the construction of Fortress Europe, culminating in the 1985 Schengen Agreement and 1997 Amsterdam Treaty; in naval patrols along the Malaysian and Thai coastlines; in the French and Australian states' leasing of offshore detention sites; and in US negotiations to establish immigration clearance facilities at overseas airports. Significantly, state strategies of protecting external borders echo neoliberal thought and practice in calling for the state's retreat from the economy. A salient example can be seen in the transfer of some aspects of border security operations to firms in the private sector (Wakefield 2003; van Munster 2005). Since the September 11, 2001, terrorist attacks in the United States and subsequent attacks from Western Europe to Southeast Asia and Australia, firms have rushed to develop, sell, or operate technologically advanced surveillance tools for external border control on behalf of receiving states. Meanwhile, air- and sea-based carriers (in some cases, travel agencies) are held responsible by states for ensuring travelers' eligibility. Carriers then purchase liability insurance from insurance firms that in turn build databases with biographical information, travel profiles, arrest records, and so forth (Muller 2004). Security functions, such as monitoring and vetting travelers, are now everyday business responsibilities.

More and more, processes of securitizing migration stretch the meaning and practice of protecting territorial and maritime borders to places and spaces *within* the nation. Most notable is the involvement of civilian-citizens with tacit or direct state approval. Key examples are vigilante groups, such as the Minuteman Project in the United States, which conducts "border defense" and an "internal vigilance operation that monitors businesses and governments (Vina, Nunez-Neto, and Weir 2006, 1); and state deployment of Ikatan Relawan Rakyat Malaysia (RELA), the Malaysian citizen volunteer corps (Chin 2008b). Depending on the receiving context, efforts to secure the nation from within commonly involve immigration raids by state authorities as well as paramilitary groups that surveil public spaces and business establishments; passing legislation at the municipal level to rid communities of irregular migrants by denying housing, employment, education, and social services; and everyday practices of "petit apartheid" by local residents and the police in their signaling of an unwelcome environment for migrants (see especially Georges-Abeyie 2001; Milovanovic and Russell 2001).

While some might argue that the privatization of security in varied ways is yet another indication of declining state sovereignty, such a perspective misses the point of expanded roles for the private sector and citizenry. Receiving states are "neither losing control nor abdicating their sovereignty; rather, states seek to reduce the costs of immigration and to control migration at the same time that they allow the free flow of trade and goods" (Lahav 2000, 216).

The symbolic extension inward of territorial borders to, and the de facto or de jure privatization of security for, monitoring such spaces as homes, schools, hospitals and workplaces, render irregular migrant workers and even some regular migrants and immigrants as political, economic, social and cultural outsiders who are perceived to threaten the receiving nation. Anti-migrant and anti-immigrant perspectives in public discourse easily equate and even conflate a state's defense of the nation with its citizens' defense of public and private spaces. In these spaces, which have become miniature versions of the securitized nation, migrants who are easily distinguished by their physiognomic features, accents, or cultural practices then become "figurative borders" (Chang quoted in Romero 2006, 449). Ongoing state efforts to protect the nation by securing and extending the borders paradoxically lead to a milieu of insecurity for migrants and citizens alike. So-called cultures of security are created, in which states promise to protect citizens against major sources of threats including the onslaught of migrants, so long as citizens "comply with the ideological, political, and legal frames of regulation and control" (Hesford and Kozol 2005, 4).

Chapter Three focuses specifically on how state authorities in the receiving country of Malaysia attempt to secure internal boundaries of the nation against migrant workers. The state pursues two unique strategies, based on neoliberal tenets of diversification and privatization for internal border management, especially in the global city of KL. One strategy diversifies migrant nationalities in order to prevent dominance by a few nationalities. The other strategy transfers some key security operations to RELA, the civilian-citizen volunteer corps. This chapter's analysis outlines the racialized-ethnicized, gendered, and class dimensions of both strategies devised for state surveillance and control of migrants, including that of "foreign prostitutes." Implemented concurrently with migratory pathways established by state liberalization of the tourism and education sectors, the strategies feed into an already vicious cycle of policies by broadening the conditions in which many more migrant men and women from many more nationalities are represented and treated as illegal aliens.

Despite state securitization of migration in major receiving countries such as Malaysia, migrant women and men persist in seeking entry for employment or refuge. Paradoxically, stricter immigration regulations and heightened external-internal border patrols help drive migration further underground. Put simply, migrants and their facilitators are as innovative in their strategies as are receiving states in trying to curb them. The next two subsections discuss why women migrate for sex work and how they are assisted by others in doing so. Together, migrant women's and facilitating groups' actions reveal creative strategies devised and pursued at the conjuncture of structural constraints and opportunities brought about by competition among global cities and collaboration in the midst of state securitization of migration.

Transnational Migrant Women Sex Workers

Women's employment opportunities are shaped by four major trends occurring within the larger context of neoliberal globalization: the shift to free-market determination of economic outcomes; economies' reliance on export-oriented production; transnational firms' globalizing networks in manufacturing, commodities and services; and SAPs dictating reductions in public spending and subsidies (Pyle and Ward 2003, 463–465). These trends are gendered because they disproportionately limit the scope of women's economic participation. In many sending or home economies, even though women overwhelmingly are in the four "gendered production networks" of sex work, domestic work, export work, and microfinance, their contributions remain largely invisible in national accounts despite and because of states' reliance on these networks as buffers against economic restructuring processes (Pyle and Ward 2003, 470). Similarly, in receiving economies, migrant women tend to find authorized and unauthorized work based on their ascribed gender traits.

Women's decisions to participate in transnational migration for employment are influenced by sending state policies, personal factors, individual household and family strategies, and social networks. While some women migrate via formal channels, others pursue informal channels for a variety of reasons, including their inability to meet entry and eligibility requirements, the high costs of fees, and the length of time taken to process applications. Informal channels are characterized by profit- or revenue-generating "counter-circuits," which operate mostly in the shadows beyond the reach of formal laws and regulations. Nonetheless, these counter-circuits of shadow globalization emerge from neoliberal economic restructuring processes. Put simply, neoliberal globalization creates "an institutional infrastructure that facilitates cross-border flows and represents, in that regard, an enabling environment for these alternative circuits" (Sassen 2002, 256).

Women's transnational migration for sex work from one global city to another constitutes such a counter-circuit: it is an extralegal profit-generating circuit enabled by the interlocking network of global cities. However, not all migrant women sex workers are fairly described as truly disadvantaged, nor are all of them tricked and forced into sex work. In light of the overwhelming global focus on combating sex trafficking, empirical research is crucial in ascertaining nuances among sex workers and their counter-circuits.

The abolitionist perspective dominating anti–sex trafficking discourse and policies asserts that migrant women largely are duped, sold, kidnapped, and coerced into sex work by criminal groups, many of which operate on the transnational level. Even though some women may voluntarily migrate for sex work, their consent is deemed irrelevant because prostitution inherently is exploitative and abusive toward women (see especially Jeffreys 1997; Barry 1984). The abolition of prostitution thus is considered integral to the abolition of sex trafficking.

This perspective is not without controversy. Its proponents are challenged on a variety of fronts. For example, they are criticized for resurrecting an outdated "crusade ideology," which is guiding, but unsuited to, contemporary policy, legislation, and enforcement practices (Weitzer 2007; Soderlund 2005); for failing to "distinguish between trafficking for forced prostitution and voluntary migration (regular or irregular) for sex work" (Gozdziak and Bump 2008, 44); and overall, for the totalizing assumptions, problematizations, generalizations, methodologies, and proposed solutions (Brunovskis and Surtees 2010; Kelly 2005).[17]

The pro-rights or sex worker perspective takes a different stance. Proponents assert that while some women are sex-trafficked, others migrate willingly to perform sex work for a variety of reasons, although some may not be fully aware of working conditions elsewhere (Agustín 2005, 2007; Kempadoo, Sanghera, and Pattanaik 2005; Agathangelou 2004). This perspective calls for delinking migration prostitution from sex trafficking, and for decriminalizing prostitution while combating sex trafficking and forced prostitution.[18] Key goals include redress of the conditions in which migrant women work, such as reform of immigration legislation that criminalizes them, standardization of workplace regulations, and enforcement of laws against sexual violence. By drawing nuanced distinctions between trafficked and nontrafficked women sex workers, this perspective makes the argument for analyzing women in sex work from the perspective of migration, not trafficking per se. Both the abolitionist and sex worker perspectives helped shape the United Nations' Protocol to Prevent, Suppress, and Punish Trafficking in Persons, especially Women and Children, that affirmed the "3P" approach: preventing trafficking, protecting victims, and punishing traffickers (Capous-Desyllas 2007; Andrijasevic 2010).

Given the mutually reinforcing forces of combating sex trafficking and securitizing migration today, the sex worker perspective is vulnerable to accusations of "normalizing men's prostitution abuse of women" (Jeffreys 2006, 203), or even encouraging and supporting irregular migrant women's "dangerous" and "unsavory agency" (Nyers 2003, 1071) because of their unauthorized entry, stay and sex work in the receiving country. As illegal-criminal-immoral aliens, nontrafficked migrant women sex workers become prominent targets of receiving states' 3D approaches.

To examine migration for sex work as a key strategy adopted by women is not to celebrate prostitution as an inherently liberating form of work for women, nor does it entail "denying the vast structural changes that push and pull them . . . [or] making them over-responsible for situations largely not of their own making" (Agustín 2006, 39). Rather, it is to shed light on why and how "women have found a way to navigate networks of migration for their own benefit" in the context of neoliberal globalization (Berman 2003, 46; Mahdavi 2011).

Women's transnational migration for sex work need not be driven exclusively by an economic survival imperative, that is, it need not be the job of last resort. Their decisions range from the need to provide financially for their families and to escape highly restrictive patriarchal home environments, to the desire to travel and see the world. Some may and do combine sex work with other activities, such as being a tourist, hospitality worker, part-time student, or small business owner. Most times, women knowingly engage in sex work even though they may not always be able to fully anticipate working conditions (see, for example, Kitiarsa 2008; Aoyama 2009; Andrijasevic 2009; Parreñas 2011).

Migrant women's participation in sex work—whether as their major economic activity or as one among other economic activities—potentially reveals the coexistence of their "enduring self" and "situated self" (Spindler and Spindler 1992). The former refers to "the deep-seated sense of continuity that one has with one's past," that is, a clear, strong, and abiding sense of self. The latter refers to "the adaptive capabilities manifested in goal-oriented, context-specific aspects of the person" or the immediate exigencies of daily life in foreign environments (Schram 1994, 466; see also Geoffroy 2007). Some empirical research has already revealed that from migrant women's perspectives, participation in sex work does not define their enduring self: how they see themselves as women and as human beings in general (see, for example, Agustín 2007; Andrijasevic 2010). For them, sex work is work.

The contemporary phenomenon of women's transnational migration for sex work reflects their "imagination or mind work," that is, women's responses to the meanings, images, and values associated with gender, work, modernity, and consumption in an era that attaches exchange values to nearly all dimensions of life (Mahler and Pessar 2006, 44). To be sure, neoliberal globalization espouses and endorses individual responsibility and requisite participation in free-market exchange relations to better one's life (Chin 2008a; Martin 1998). Women who migrate for sex work realize neoliberal globalization's promise of free markets as the sites from which people can and should be authors of their own destinies, because of and despite inequities and inequalities circumscribed by their gender, class, and so forth. Unpalatable as it may be, given the global imperative to combat human and sex trafficking, some migrant women do view the exchange of sexual services for money as a life enhancement strategy, as the means to what they plan as a better end.

Legitimacy, nevertheless, is persistently denied this form of work and worker: sex work is treated as a moral issue, but this sense of morality is at odds with the ways in which morality is being reconfigured in an era of globalized free markets. The irony here is that if and when women take responsibility to better or improve their lives via transnational migration for sex work, they bear the wrath of moral indignation and legal sanctions by receiving states, societies, and even their own families. At the other extreme is the argument that women, regardless of consent, must be protected from prostitution because of its inherently exploitative and abusive nature. We are left with a deafening silence on why and how women come to want and are able to migrate for sex work from global city to global city. The silence also absolves those who unconditionally accept and celebrate neoliberal globalization of their culpability in minimizing or even refusing to acknowledge and address contradictions that fuel women's transnational migration for sex work.[19]

Chapter Four begins with a brief history of prostitution in KL and of Malaysian women's gradual displacement by transnational migrant women sex workers. Following this is an analysis of migrant women from various nationalities, why and how they migrate for sex work, and their views of such "mobile livelihoods" (Briones 2008, 62). Compared with other kinds of jobs open to them, an overwhelming majority of the women consider sex work to be a relatively quicker and less exploitative way of earning more income and improving their socioeconomic positions. Their goals may include gaining an education or vocational skills, establishing a business, financially assisting family members, finding a husband, or seeing the world. The women's decisions and perspectives are shaped by their understandings and experiences of structural forces, that is, by their social locations in multiple intersecting and mutually constituting hierarchies of nationality, gender, class, and race-ethnicity.

Facilitating Groups or Syndicates

Arising alongside state regulation of migration are "migration industries": state agencies, licensed labor brokers, employment agencies, transportation firms, and so on, which organize and manage the in-migration of workers via formal channels (Massey et al. 2005; Chin 1998). Since the "prostitute" is a prohibited category of migrant in many receiving countries, women must therefore enter under other immigration-labor categories. To reiterate, they do so via the two additional migratory pathways established by ongoing liberalization of services in global cities: the tourist and student categories. While some women migrate and seek work on their own or with the help of individuals, others do so by contracting with groups. More often than not, the perception is that these are transnational criminal groups specializing in the smuggling or trafficking of human beings, especially given that they manage and control the entire migratory process. Human and sex-trafficking groups are distinguished in general by harboring and exploiting migrants.

Published empirical research on human smuggling and trafficking groups indicate that the groups are organized and operate in accordance with their specific political-cultural contexts (Shelley 2003; Zhang, Chin, and Miller 2007; Turner and Kelly 2009). Of late, there has been a shift from hierarchically structured groups—such as those associated with the Mafia, Triads, or Yakuza—to loosely connected or horizontally based networks comprised of alliances among groups of different nationalities (United Nations Office on Drugs and Crime 2010b). This development mirrors the decentralization processes characteristic of transnational corporations: the networks have become flexible and adaptive to changing market and regulatory conditions in ways similar to their legal counterparts.

Depending on the context, there are different organizational structures with varying degrees of overlap between businesses in the formal and informal economies (Sanders 2008). Still, there are gaps in knowledge with regard to the origins, structures, and memberships of the groups; linkages with their counterparts overseas as well as legal businesses; and the presence or absence of women participants (United Nations Office on Drugs and Crime 2010a, 2010b). The dominant assumption is that loose and horizontally based transnational networks are entirely illegal or criminal in their operations and that they are managed wholly by men.

Chin and Finckenauer's study of Chinese sex workers in eight Asian and two American cities highlights nontrafficked women's diverse modes of migration shaped by the specific political-cultural contexts of receiving countries. Depending on the city, women may be aided by labor brokers, escort agencies, "mommies," or big business owners. The study reveals that "organized crime," most commonly thought to be involved in the triadic activities of money laundering, drugs and human trafficking, is not involved in migration prostitution: "What our data suggest is more akin to this being a crime that is organized rather than organized crime" (Chin and Finckenauer 2011, 480). Notably as well, the researchers stress,

In our opinion, the word "traffickers," as is often utilized in the sex trafficking literature to refer to the key person who is recruiting, transporting, exploiting female victims, is a misnomer. In fact, in the course of our fieldwork and field interviews, we encountered a diverse group of facilitators, but none of our subjects use the word "trafficker" in referring to any of these facilitators.

(Chin and Finckenauer 2011, 482)

How then are facilitating groups different from those involved in human smuggling and trafficking? Do the groups consist exclusively of men or are women involved as well, and in what capacity? What is the nature of migrant women's relationships to these groups?[20]

Chapter Five examines "Syndicate X," which is a pseudonym for one of the largest facilitating groups or syndicates in KL that specializes exclusively in nontrafficked migrant women sex workers. The analysis demonstrates why and how the syndicate has morphed over time from the organization of a hierarchical Chinese Triad or secret society controlling on-street Malaysian sex workers to a more horizontal, corporate-like enterprise, specializing in up-market sexual services performed by transnational migrant women. This transformation came in response to clean-up campaigns by state authorities in the mid- to late 1990s that sought to remove all on-street sex workers, pimps, and known brothels in KL. The syndicate's emergence signifies "an entrepreneurialism borne out of opportunism and necessity, as options for making money in the 'normal' mainstream economy are not options for all" (Sanders 2008, 712). Syndicate X brings in women of different nationalities and provides them with board and lodging, personal security, and clientele. Transnational migrant women, in return, pay a monthly fee and "taxes" for services rendered by the syndicate. Shaped by KL's history of race relations, the racialization of syndicates and their migrant sex workers also will be examined in the chapter.

Thus far, the discussion highlights the types and expressions of human creativity that appropriate key neoliberal principles in the identification, pursuit, and management of opportunities. Receiving states "privatize" or transfer some security functions to private sector firms and citizens groups as part of external and internal border management. Migrant women, who express their right to move and earn a living, consider sex work as another form of work for economic survival or life enhancement. While some migrate on their own, others do so with the assistance of individuals and groups that have emerged or transformed to organize, manage, and profit from the growing business of transnational sex work.

Transnational migrant women's presence in global cities raises an important but rarely examined issue concerning the nature of encounters and resultant outcomes between migrant women and residents.

Until the past decade or so, the concept of a "cosmopolitan" or "cosmopolite" rarely if ever was applied to unskilled transnational migrant workers. Rather, the category has been and largely continues to be employed in relation to elites whose frequent travels, exposure to, and encounters with people from different cultures are said to distinguish them in outlook and conduct from the rest of the population.[21] Cosmopolitans are presumed to have the qualities of "tolerance, flexibility, and openness" that signal their transcendence of particularized national-cultural loyalties (Molz 2006, 2). In theory, the category should be open to anyone who exhibits such qualities. In practice, it has been reserved almost exclusively for specific categories of elite travelers.

From the European imperial era through most of the twentieth century, cosmopolitans were mostly elite men of the Global North (for example, colonial administrators, explorers, corporate executives, diplomats, and academics) because they had the "resources to travel, learn other languages, and absorb other cultures" (Cohen 2004, 143–144). Since the end of the twentieth century, women from the Global North and elite men and women from the Global South also are considered cosmopolitans. Expansion of the middle classes, followed by the development and liberalization of tourism and education, create many more opportunities for people to travel—and encounter and appreciate other cultures.

Despite and because of this, four sets of binaries persist in informing dominant conceptualizations of the cosmopolitan: parochial versus global; home versus away; immobile versus mobile; and nonelite versus elite (Kothari 2008). Cosmopolitanism's historical origins or its birth in opposition to parochialism retains what is a seemingly "irreducible duality" (Abdelhalim 2010, 64).[22]

Of late, scholarship is beginning to challenge cosmopolitanism's Eurocentric origins, that is, the ways in which the rise of the cosmopolitan European self was achieved via "asymmetrical and racialized" encounters with the Other (Abdelhalim 2010, 83), and for the failure to consider nonelite mobility and related emerging cosmopolitan attitudes, practices, and worldviews. Dominant conceptualizations of the cosmopolitan have denied legitimacy to nonelites; at the same time, they uphold and normalize a largely racialized-ethnicized, classed, and implicitly masculinized notion of a single humanity without critically examining the causes and consequences of unequal historical encounters.[23]

Consequently, the focus is shifting to account for "actually existing cosmopolitanisms" (Robbins 1998) that can include migrant workers as well as nonmobile persons living in culturally diverse contexts. This is readily evinced from adjectives used to qualify cosmopolitanism: for example, the "abject" cosmopolitanism of refugees whose actions are read as a demand to be included as part of humanity, especially in relation to exclusionary practices of receiving states (Nyers 2003); the "rooted" cosmopolitanism of individuals attached to local communities but who are accepting of cultural differences and who espouse toleration and openness to the world (Appiah 1997); the "strategic" (Datta 2009; Kothari 2008) or "tactical" cosmopolitanism of transnational migrant workers (Landau and Freemantle 2010) who must negotiate oppressive and repressive host environments; the "vernacular" cosmopolitanism in which the local and parochial can coexist with the translocal and transnational (Diouf 2000; Werbner 2006); the "discrepant" cosmopolitanism that arises from violent dislocations of individuals who then are compelled to migrate (Clifford 1992); and "everyday" or "ordinary" cosmopolitanism of the nonmobile working classes in culturally diverse environments (Lamont and Aksartova 2002; Skrbis and Woodward 2007; Brett and Moran 2011).

Many of the variants above can be placed under the larger category of "cosmopolitanism from below" in their respective attempts to establish the conceptual and empirical imperative for understanding and examining cosmopolitan worldviews and practices of nonelites. Nonelite cosmopolitanism does not assume an immediate detachment of the individual from her original rootedness: "[it is] a simultaneous rootedness and openness to shared human emotions, experiences and aspirations rather than . . . a tolerance for cultural difference or a universalist morality" (Schiller, Darieva, and Gruner-Domic 2011, 399). In fact, some studies of elite cosmopolitans show that they, too, do not fully transcend the local or national, despite their journeys all over the world and constant exposures to and encounters with cultural differences (Chan and Chan 2010; Yeoh and Huang 2011; Gustafson 2009).

To be sure, research on the emerging cosmopolitan subjectivities of transnational migrant workers and working-class residents in global cities have to account for contexts of unequal power relations. Global cities are not just strategic sites or command posts for managing the new global economy; they are contemporary contact zones or "social spaces where disparate cultures meet, clash, grapple with each other, often in asymmetrical relations of domination and subordination" (Pratt 2008, 4). Encounters between migrants and residents are shaped by and shape intersecting racialized-ethnicized, gendered, and classed hierarchies. The postcolonial era does not necessarily eliminate colonial-like situations: "cultural, political, and economic oppression of subordinate racialized ethnic groups by dominant racial/ethnic groups [may persist], with or without the existence of colonial administrations" (Grosfoguel 2004, 320).

Cosmopolitanism signifies an "embodied way of being in and moving through the world" (Molz 2006, 2), and much empirical research remains to be conducted on how transnational migrant women and men perceive and relate to different cultural environments and people. As Molz points out, not all bodies travel well: people of color, for example, have different experiences. They may fit in more readily in the Global South than whites. Women are treated differently from men, and they cannot be invisible strangers especially if they travel alone. Color and passports also make a difference (2006). This is an especially pertinent point in relation to women who migrate for sex work. In global cities, migrant women sex workers encounter people from other cultures, classes, nationalities, religions, and racial-ethnic groups. These encounters can strengthen, affirm, or modify migrant women's worldviews and practices toward the Other, and vice versa. One challenge is to ascertain the extent to which such encounters affirm or modify stereotypes based on ascribed national-cultural, gendered and/or racialized-ethnicized traits.

Chapter Six analyzes migrant women's and Syndicate X members' emerging cosmopolitan subjectivities in KL. The discussion begins with migrant women sex workers' views of living and working in urban spaces that, at the outset, are multiracial and multicultural but upon closer exam- ination, are claimed by residents from specific intersections of class, race- ethnicity, and nationality. The focus then shifts to syndicate members (Malaysian men and women) who provide support services to the migrant women. Despite the centrality of earning income, the women's and syndi- cate members' encounters with difference are not entirely based on utili- tarian need. From views on humanity to acts of reciprocity, many of them genuinely desire to know, understand, and appreciate alternative ways of living, being, and doing by people born and raised in communities other than their own. Still, some endorse deprecating stereotypes premised on racial-cultural superiority. In KL's stratified contact zones, migrant women and syndicate men evince emerging cosmopolitan subjectivities, and paradoxically, affirm colonial-like ascriptions and ensuing worldviews and treatments of the Other.

Chapter Seven concludes this study by discussing the findings and their implications. The key argument is that women's transnational migration for sex work occurs in and is fueled by structural constraints and opportu- nities born from the marriage of patriarchal power and free-market econo- mies. Until and unless structural forces are acknowledged and addressed comprehensively, policies based explicitly on either-or positions relating to sex trafficking, migration prostitution, illegal aliens, and so forth, may and will perpetuate the contradictions that elicited them.

But to the extent that all writing must be autobiographical, even where it takes shelter behind
the appurtenances of footnotes and learned quotations, this is also my own account of a very
complex and problematic set of relationships which could be told in many ways.
—Dennis Altman (2002, xii)

The era of neoliberal globalization raises compelling challenges: How is knowledge (or how should it) be generated, given the dynamic flows of capital, goods, information, and people that reconfigure places, spaces, and relationships? As described by Burawoy et al. (2000), global ethnography is appropriately positioned to meet these challenges. This methodology is designed to generate knowledge in three identified sets of "experiences of globalization": global-supranational forces that modify or reshape the local; global-transnational connections between individuals and communities; and global-postnational imaginations that galvanize collective actions (Burawoy 2001, 149). Global ethnography "still locates itself firmly in places but . . . conceives of those places as themselves globalized with multiple external connections, porous and contested boundaries, and social relations that are constructed across multiple spatial scales" (Gille and Ó Riain 2002, 291). Global ethnographic studies can employ different qualitative methods to focus on a single site or multiple sites with regard to any one of the three sets of experiences.

Poster, nevertheless, argues that since the 1980s, feminists have conducted what might be considered global ethnographic studies even though they did not (and many still do not) identify them as such (2002, 128).[24] Although feminist ethnographers share key assumptions on global forces, connections, and imaginations, a major difference is that they focus on the gendered and, when appropriate, the racialized-ethnicized and sexualized dimensions. Hence, Poster calls for a "gendered global ethnography" that, aside from examining new forms of women's and men's incorporation in the global economy, also explicitly grapples with the insider-outsider distinction, and with the power differentials between researchers and participants that affect the generation of knowledge (2002, 148–150).

In 2010 and 2011, I conducted field work for this study in KL. Retrospectively, it took many years to lay the groundwork for doing so. I could not have known when I first started conducting research on Filipina and Indonesian domestic workers in the early 1990s that the initial path for this later work was being laid. At that time, there was not a visible presence of sex workers from different nationalities in the city. On occasion, there were newsprint reports of some migrant domestic workers who moon-lighted, or who ran away from employers to become sex workers.

As transnational migrant women sex workers' numbers began to grow during the late 1990s and early 2000s, my attention shifted to migrant workers in the global cruise industry. I did not anticipate, even when I interviewed labor brokers who recruited Southeast Asian women and men to work on cruise ships, that many more contacts developed in the field would take me further along the path to migrant women sex workers and syndicate members.

By the mid-2000s, it became very clear to residents, workers, business owners, and state authorities that "foreign prostitutes" were in the city and its suburbs. While some migrant women blended easily into different com-munities, others simply could not do so: their foreignness, signified by dress, demeanor, accent, and physiognomy gave them away. Then, as now, persistent newsprint reports of raids on businesses, together with patrol-ling RELA, immigration and police officers, created an overall atmosphere of fear and anxiety among the women. Although some women stay indoors (or are advised to do so by their syndicates) to escape detection, many in the city are seen in public spaces not for the purpose of soliciting clients, although some do, but to take a walk, to shop, or to enjoy a meal. Taxi driv-ers, *mamak* (Malaysian Indian-Muslims who own and operate halal food and drink stalls) and employees of beauty salons, boutiques, restaurants, coffee shops, and hawker stands know of the women. They also know that many of the women are protected by local syndicates.

In time, I would come to know this as well. What began as side conversa-tions, for example, with sales representatives in shopping malls, labor bro-kers, hotel employees and employment agents led to a sharpened focus on transnational migrant women sex workers in the city. I came to know at least two versions of KL. One is visible on the surface, to be enjoyed by tourists, locals and migrants alike. The other is hidden in plain sight. Even though it overlaps with the visible KL, it is a world not readily accessible to the majority of outsiders. This is the world in which my access had to be vetted, as intermediaries informed me, by individuals whom I did not meet and probably will never know, but who conducted the necessary "back-ground checks" to ensure that indeed I was an academic and not an under-cover police officer. My prior research foci, background, and field contacts seemed to have been key to securing access.

As a scholar of Malaysian Chinese ancestry who lives and works in the United States conducting fieldwork in the global city of KL, I was acutely aware of the fluidity of contextual conditions in which I am considered an insider or an outsider. From syndicate men's perspectives, despite the fact that I have lived overseas for more than two decades, I am considered an insider or a member of the Malaysian Chinese community. The fact that I achieved the right to wear a "four-cornered cap" (the cap of commencement regalia, signifying learnedness) told them that I sought to study what they did, instead of suppressing their activities. The gender dimension was not a concern to them: eventually I was treated as an honorary male in whose presence many of the lower-level syndicate men comfortably smoked cigarettes, drank beer, and swore vociferously.[25] Higher ranking syndicate men were more polite, reserved, or professional—and cautious in their interactions with me: as one said, "This is a business." They tended to speak in generalities to ensure anonymity of their identity and business operations. No discussions were allowed to be tape-recorded, and I was asked to listen and recall later. Whenever discussions became too specific, they simply would stop mid-sentence and change the topic.

My interactions with women in the syndicate as well as transnational migrant women sex workers were more varied. Among the few known women members in the syndicate, only one agreed to speak with me directly. Another answered my questions via an intermediary. Although the syndicate approved my requests to speak with its members and also migrant women who contracted with them—passing on my messages and leaving it to the women to decide if they wanted to speak with me—some of the women simply refused to meet with me despite my assurances of anonymity for them (all names in this study are pseudonyms). The women feared surveillance by authorities, and especially the threat of inadvertent exposure. To the Malaysian women syndicate members, I was a "suspicious insider" (Kusow 2003, 595); they did not know me and could not fully understand why I would be interested in them. To some of the migrant women, either I was a suspicious insider (when gender is used as the definitive criterion) or a suspicious outsider (when nationality is used as the definitive criterion). Sometimes appointments were made, but the women did not show up or offer any explanations. As informants explained, the women were not interested in being interviewed, but they did not want to explicitly and rudely decline my request. Other migrant women came by way of intermediaries such as taxi drivers, labor brokers, *mamak*, concierges, and parking valets in luxury hotels and apartments.

My interactions with the thirty-nine migrant women interviewed for this study were influenced by their varying emphases, for instance, on the nexus of gender-race as a common bond, or the nexus of nationality-race as a dividing line (see especially Chapters Four and Six). Nigerian women sex workers' experiences with racism in KL strongly influenced how they viewed Malaysians and daily life in the city. Even though they agreed to speak with me because of my gender and occupation, they were wary initially of the race-nationality nexus, associating me with the oppressor group of Malaysian Chinese (Soni-Sinha 2008, 532). On the other hand, some Asian women sex workers, particularly those from the People's Republic of China, considered me a westernized insider at best, or an outsider both to Malaysian and Chinese cultures. Some women even took it upon themselves to teach me the meanings of certain Chinese proverbs, or inform me about the latest happenings in the city.

The strictly dichotomous insider-outsider distinction did not hold at all during fieldwork in KL in which "different kinds of knowledge [were] gained through different positionalities" (Widerberg 2007, 13). My multiple positionality as a woman, an academic of Malaysian Chinese ancestry who lives and works in the United States, and a perceived member of the middle classes, led to very fluid contextual experiences of being an insider *and* an outsider (Soni-Sinha 2008; see also Narayan 1993). It should be said that gendered global ethnography conducted in global cities such as KL is affected not only by the politics of positionality but, equally significant, these contact zones accentuate "the politics of intercultural perception and interaction" (Ong 1995 quoted in Henry 2003, 236) not only in researcher-participant relations but also among participants (see Chapters Four, Five, and Six). As presented in this study, the luxury of time and reflection has turned what were the chaos of "logic-in-use" during fieldwork into the "reconstructed logic" of why, how, and with what consequences transnational migrant women sex workers are in the global city of KL.

CHAPTER 2

Making of a "World-Class City"

The State and Transnational Migrant Labor

Situated at the juncture of two rivers, Kuala Lumpur means "muddy confluence" in Malay, but this fast-rising city has redefined itself. With its looming skyscrapers, stellar cuisine, and thumping night life, the Malaysian capital has emerged as one of Southeast Asia's most alluring metropolises, offering all the amenities of a major city but on a friendlier scale.
—New York Times (December 20, 2009)

On any given day in what is commonly referred as to KL's Golden Tri-angle, Malaysian workers and residents navigate busy sidewalks beside European backpackers, Arab families with their domestic workers, and tour-guide led groups of domestic and Asian tourists.[1] Located in the north and northeast quadrant of the Triangle are the Petronas Twin Tow-ers (PTT), Kuala Lumpur City Centre (KLCC, including Suria KLCC, the premier shopping center), high-rise luxury hotels, short-term furnished apartments and condominiums, and upscale shopping malls with security guards inside glass-enclosed boutiques.

The intersection of Jalan Bukit Bintang and Jalan Sultan Ismail marks the Triangle's entertainment and shopping area. Standing at attention along both roads are hotels belonging to world-renowned chains. At the southwest end of Jalan Bukit Bintang, women sales representatives encour-age passersby to view their range of low-priced luggage for sale; women and men hold testimonial photographs and sing the health praises of head-foot-body massages outside of their shophouse spas; and workers relax with cigarette breaks as they await instructions from supervisors in budget hotels. In this area, many of the employees are transnational migrant men and women.

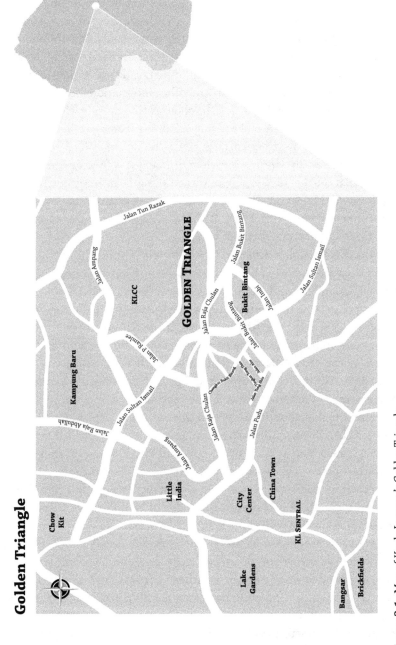

Figure 2.1: Map of Kuala Lumpur's Golden Triangle

This similarly is the case on Jalan Alor that runs parallel to the back of Bukit Bintang's shophouses. Jalan Alor is distinguished by *kopi tiam* (coffee shops), restaurants, and hawker stalls. It often is considered the "Malaysian restaurant row." Myanmarese men, and Malaysian women and men fill orders that are served mainly by Indonesian women. Jalan Alor is bookended by Changkat Bukit Bintang and Jalan Tong Shin. Changkat Bukit Bintang's post–World War II low-rise apartments and shophouses now are home mostly to bed-and-breakfast establishments, small restaurants, and bars. Locals, expatriates, and tourists alike have their choice of Moroccan, Italian, South American, and other international cuisine in the ambience of renovated colonial-era shophouses side-by-side with *kopi tiam* and within walking distance of lodging. Claiming frontage when possible, and tightly nestled at street corners along this international restaurant row, are hawker stalls offering a variety of Malaysian (Malay, Indian, and Chinese) food-on-the-go. The neighborhood along Jalan Tong Shin remains predominantly Malaysian Chinese: its oldest pre–World War II medium-rise apartment complex, the Blue Boy Mansion, seems out of place with three-star hotels and budget inns.

The Golden Triangle's never-ending traffic congestion encourages competition between imported luxury cars that try to outmaneuver made-in-Malaysia automobiles, only to be bested by seemingly suicidal motorcyclists as traffic police blow their whistles and gesticulate wildly to keep vehicles moving along the thoroughfares. Malaysian and transnational migrant men workers stand on each side of garbage trucks for quick on-off pickup of trash as the trucks navigate congested main roads and narrow side streets. At KL Sentral, trains drop off and pick up passengers arriving from and departing for different parts of the metropolitan area, including the twenty-minute nonstop fifty-seven km trip to Kuala Lumpur International Airport (KLIA). Every Friday afternoon, the buzz of city life is interposed by calls to prayers emanating from loudspeakers of mosques: traffic congestion is heightened as nearby roads become semi–parking lots.

Punctuating KL's skyline are high-rise structures made of concrete, steel, and glass. As if a stubborn reminder of the past, unoccupied old single-story mansions with for-sale signs and overgrown grass—including those mansion grounds that are temporarily converted into makeshift parking lots—randomly dot the valleys. Huge electronic billboards announcing the latest Hollywood movies, weather forecasts, and news help illuminate apartments, condominiums, and hotels flanking the landmark PTT and KLCC.

A few short kilometers in all directions from the city's historic-geographic center near Chinatown yields pockets of gentrification. Tree-lined roads

Figure 2.2: Kuala Lumpur skyline. Photo by Christine B. N. Chin

bordering older residential communities and colonial-era shophouses are interspersed with newly gated communities, construction sites, and small makeshift homes made of plank wood and adorned by satellite dishes and connected to the rest of the world via crisscrossing electrical wires pulled in from poles on main roads.

Twenty-first-century KL has far surpassed its nineteenth-century birth as a colonial trading settlement. Today, it is a global city—an "alpha" world city—or in the words of Dr. Mahathir Mohamad, the former prime minister who largely guided its transformation from 1981 to 2003, "a world-class city" (Morshidi 1997, 2000).

KL, the capital of Malaysia, is located in the state of Selangor on the west coast of the peninsula. Administratively, it is a federal territory (FT) or Wilayah Persekutuan, under control of the federal as opposed to state government. This FT covers only 243 km^2 with a population of approximately 1.8 million. The global city of KL, however, is a large conurbation encompassing much more territory and space as it extends mostly westward, southward and northward into the state of Selangor. Unless specifically referred to as an FT, "KL" is used interchangeably with Greater KL, the KL metropolitan area, or Klang Valley, covering an area of nearly 3000 km^2 with an approximate population of seven million.

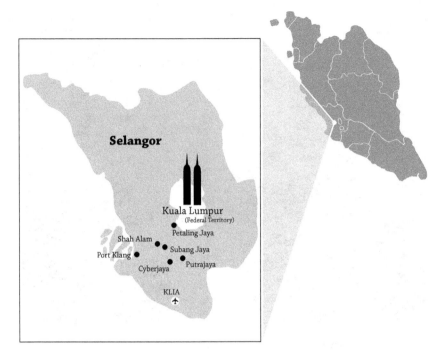

Figure 2.3: Map of Selangor State

Similar to global cities elsewhere in the world, KL's transformation indicates a new spatial reconfiguration emerging from global economic restructuring processes. As firms seek to extend their operations globally, they outsource key functions to other highly specialized service firms (for example, those specializing in law, accountancy, public relations, and new information and communication technologies), which are attracted to and located in such cities. Collectively, these functions distinguish global cities for their advanced producer services. In other words, global cities are strategic sites for the agglomeration of specialized firms that perform centralized functions for the management and coordination of the new global economy. They symbolize the reterritorialization of deterritorialized capital in the twenty-first century.

Even though New York, London, and Tokyo frequently are represented as the referent or archetypal world cities through which to assess all others, global cities necessarily will be different from one another because of contextual, historical, cultural, and geographical specificities (see, for example, Bishop, Phillips, and Yeo 2003; Robinson 2002; Sassen 2009). States have and continue to play integral roles in their cities' transformation: the primacy attached to the type and intensity of advanced producer services, nonetheless, tends to mask state policies that "bring about pro-found social and cultural change" in the cities (Shatkin 2007, 3). Depending on the context, transnational migrant workers are integral as well to sustaining cities' formal and informal economies (May et al. 2007; Schiller and Cağlar 2009).

Likewise, KL's colonial history and legacies shaped opportunities and constraints as the postcolonial state assumed a central role in the city's ascendance to the regional and world stage: the state continues to negotiate between external and internal forces to maintain KL's position as a competitive global city. Transnational migrant workers, to be sure, remain integral to the city's everyday life and identity.

MIGRANT LABOR AND THE ESTABLISHMENT OF A COLONIAL TOWN

What visitors to KL may not discern immediately is that the city was born from British colonial attempts to manage socioeconomic relations between Malays, who were considered the original inhabitants and heirs of the country, and the Chinese, who migrated to the peninsula in search of economic wealth. During the early 1800s, Malay rulers employed Chinese migrants to mine tin ore in the Klang region. The discovery of rich deposits in jungle areas of Ampang, for example, encouraged the establishment of migrant mining shacks next to Malay *kampung* (villages). By the 1850s, Chinese migrants settled in Kuala Lumpur at the muddy confluence of the Klang and Gombak Rivers.

KL's origin was that of a "trade settlement to serve outlying mines [Ampang to the northeast; Pudu to the southeast; and Petaling to the southwest]" (Gullick 2000, 8). Business enterprises—such as brick-laying, tin-mining, trading, and brothels—owned by Yap Ah Loy, one of KL's most powerful *Kapitan Cina* ("captain" or head of the Chinese community from 1868 to 1885), fueled growth of the settlement, initially composed of Chinese migrants and Malay villagers.

When the sultan of Selangor moved his capital from Klang near the coast to the town in 1880, the British administration followed suit. The colonialists then sought to "protect" Malays from being overrun in what was perceived as "a Chinese town with a colonial overlay" (Rimmer and Dick 2009, 62). Stipulated by the Malay Agricultural Settlement (MAS) of 1899, Malay villages were relocated to ninety-one hectares of land north of the town center, which was set aside for exclusive Malay settlement and ownership.[2] Today, this Malay settlement, called Kampung Baru, is situated next to PTT and is the site of continued struggles between its Malay residents, the Selangor state government, and the federal government over proposed commercial development of the area.[3]

As the colonial town expanded, it took on a distinctive ethos nurtured directly and indirectly by colonial policies that naturalized the construction and association of race with place, space, class, gender, and occupation (Chin 1998). Colonial trusteeship of the Malays, expressed in the form of residential-occupational segregation and immigration regulations, was justified by the perceived need to protect them against a burgeoning population of Chinese migrants, as well as the smaller community of migrants from India. The British's self-designated role of managing relations between Malays and migrant communities constituted and affirmed what King calls a "culture of suspicion" or surveillance (2008, 56).

At the initial stages of colonial rule, the British did not regulate Chinese migration. Instead, Chinese secret societies organized and managed the population of mostly indentured single migrant men (see Chapter Five). They were recruited from southern China to work in the mining and other urban industries. In order to reduce the numbers of indentured Indian workers, the British set up a fund to pay for the passage of workers as part of the colonial regulation of migration from South Asia (Chin 1998, 36). Indian migrant plantation workers were provided with on-site housing: "plantations were more permanent fixtures and workers a 'captive' community, unlike mining enterprises. Workers' accommodation was also contingent on workers remaining employed and cessation of employment meant eviction, destitution and subsequent repatriation" (Kaur 2008, 5–6).

Key legislation such as the Malay Reservation Enactment 1913 and Rice Lands Act of 1917 kept Malays primarily in the rural areas and prevented the emergence of a Malay capitalist class during the colonial era. Rooted in precolonial-era trading and ethnoreligious networks, people from the archipelago (for example, Javanese and Sumatrans) traveled freely between the many islands and the peninsula (Kaur 2008).

Chinese and Indian migrant women did not have a significant presence in the early phases of colonial rule. This changed toward end of the nineteenth century in response to the overwhelming migrant population of single men. Despite and because of imperial restrictions placed on Chinese women's out-migration, secret societies recruited women and girls for work in British Malaya. Some migrated knowingly and willingly, while others were sold, tricked, deceived, or kidnapped. In the colonial town of Kuala Lumpur, women and girls either were placed in brothels or sold as wives, or girl-slaves (*mui tsai*) for housework (Chin 1998, 37).

The British initially permitted Chinese women who self-declared as prostitutes to enter for work. In time, however, this practice had to be abolished because of public and political pressure back in the UK (see Chapter Four). Meanwhile, the British encouraged Indian women's in-migration for plantation work, and to help "stabilize" the population of migrant men. Even so, some women were kidnapped from India to perform forced sex work on plantations and estates. Malay women's roles in their rural communities were largely left intact (Chin 1998, 37–41).

Global economic depression in the 1930s prompted colonial implementation of the Aliens Ordinances of 1930 and 1933, which banned the in-migration of Chinese migrant men. Chinese women still could enter for work, but the immigration doors were closed to sex workers. The colonial state did not restrict the entry of Indians, however, because they were considered British subjects.

Colonial policies in the town of Kuala Lumpur had the effect not only of strengthening the occupational but the residential segregation of Malays, Chinese, and Indians. While British residences were built to the west of town (in Damansara Heights and Kenny Hills) and to the east (Ampang), Malay settlements dotted the northern, western, and southern quadrants (Wong 1991). Sandwiched between Malays in the Chow Kit area to the north, and the Chinese town center to the south (now known as Chinatown), was an Indian settlement along Jalan Masjid India (now known as Little India). Another Indian settlement, Brickfields, originally was the site of Yap Ah Loy's brick-making industry. In time, the area became home to Indian migrants who were brought in specifically to construct the main railway depot: "In Kuala Lumpur, as in other towns, the Indian population preferred to congregate in certain sections of the town, such as Brickfields, Bangsar and Sentul" (Gullick 2000, 199; see also Baxstrom 2008). During the so-called Emergency in the 1950s, British concern about the Malayan Communist Party (MCP) and the related labor unrest led to the forced relocation of approximately 500,000 to 600,000 Chinese to "new villages" or MCP-free "white [as opposed to red] areas" such as Jinjang and Salak South, which were located to the north and south of town, respectively (King 2008, 68).

A few years prior to Malaysian independence, the British implemented the Immigration Ordinance of 1953 that clarified approved categories for specific occupations:

Permanent entry was restricted to, first, persons who could contribute "to the expansion of commerce and industry"; second, to persons who could provide "specialised services not available locally"; third to "families of local residents";

and fourth to other persons on "special compassionate grounds" (Saw 1988, 17). Overall, this legislation was designed to appease Malay nationalists and underlined the connections between race, occupation, and economic role in the country. Intending immigrants were also required to hold a contract of at least two years duration with a Malayan firm and earn a salary of not less than M$400 a month.

(Kaur 2008, 6)

The postcolonial state kept immigration gates open to select "skilled" migrants, while halting completely the in-migration of low-wage workers.[4]

A key legacy of colonial rule was racialization of the population according to specific intersections of place of origin, physiognomy, cultural practices, class, occupation, place, and space (see especially Alatas 1977). Over time, it became a naturalized way to perceive and classify people into the three categories of Malay, Chinese and Indian (Hirschman 1986, 1987; Lee 2004). At independence, the country's population was composed of 50% Malay, 37% Chinese, 11% Indian, and 2% other (for example, Eurasians who did not fit neatly into any of the categories). In the town of Kuala Lumpur, however, the Chinese constituted a majority at 62% of the population, with 15% Malay, 18% Indian, and about 5% other (Hamzah 1965, 128). The Chinese economic dominance in KL would come into sharp focus soon thereafter.

Independence in 1957 came after lengthy nonviolent negotiations, in which Malay special rights were enshrined in the Federal Constitution. The special rights—such as Malay reservation land, Malay as the national language, Islam as the national religion, and Malay royalty's symbolic roles as protectors of Islam and leaders of the people and country—clearly defined Malay identity and hegemonic status in the country. The Chinese and Indians were granted citizenship in return for their acknowledgment and acceptance of these rights.

The postcolonial state did not address the colonial-era legacy of constructing and naturalizing race with place, space, and occupation until the end of the 1960s. By then, persistent and intersecting issues of race and class found violent expression in post–national election clashes between Malays and Chinese. The race riots of May 13, 1969, occurred in major racialized spaces of Kampung Baru, Jalan Tuanku Abdul Rahman (Chow Kit), and Jalan Tong Shin in Kuala Lumpur. The state responded first by declaring martial law that then was followed by the introduction of a policy designed to disassociate race from occupation, place, and space. This policy transformed Kuala Lumpur and, in the process, reopened the immigration gates to low-wage transnational migrant labor. Race, nevertheless, remains "an inclusive term that covers both physical and cultural characteristics" (Lee 2004, 120).

The May 13 conflict initiated an era of an unabashed, overtly state-led social engineering program called the New Economic Policy of 1971–1990 (NEP). The NEP had a two-pronged objective of eradicating poverty regardless of race, and restructuring society to eliminate the identification of race with economic function and geographic space. Financial and nonfinancial public enterprises led the way in nurturing growth of a Bumiputera Commercial and Industrial Community (*Bumiputera* means "sons of the soil" and generally refers to Malays).[5] The NEP stipulated quotas for Malay employment in the private sector as well as for representation on boards of directors. Other policies included urban in-migration as a major way of disassociating Malays from their agricultural past and identity, or to "indigenize (to increase the number of Malays in) urban areas and employment sectors that previously were 'sinicized' (or made Chinese) during colonial rule" (Chin 1998, Chapter Two passim).

In 1970, Malaysians of Chinese descent still dominated the town of KL's population at approximately 67%, while there were 14% Malays, 17% Indians and about 1% other. By end of the NEP period in 1990, KL's population distribution reflected a significant shift: Malays at 41%, Chinese at 46%, and Indians at 11%. One decade later, Malays became the dominant group at 41% of the population, whereas Malaysians of Chinese descent comprised 39%. Numerically, the playing field had been leveled between the two largest communities. Moreover, a new census category was introduced to enumerate and highlight the presence of non-Malaysian citizens or foreigners: within the FT, this category constituted 6.7% of the 1.4 million people (Malaysia Economy 2010).

The postcolonial state's pursuit of NEP objectives within a context of export-oriented economic growth led to increased job opportunities for Malaysians in the public and private sectors: unemployment rates averaged 5–6% as labor participation of all three major groups increased to more than 50% (Chin 1998, 63–4). Between the 1970s and the mid-1980s, the NEP reopened the country's immigration gates, albeit without official recognition or management of low-wage migrants. Gradual transformation of the base of the Malaysian economy, from the export of commodities to manufacturing, led to unceasing demands for low-wage agriplantation workers. At the same time, households of the emerging Malaysian middle classes complained of the inability to employ domestic workers. Malaysian women preferred factory work conditions and salaries over the unregulated environment of employers' homes, as urbanization and employment policies heightened expectations of rural people, especially Malays, for higher paying white-collar jobs in urban areas. Agriplantation and household employers filled low-wage labor demands by hiring migrant men and women from neighboring Indonesia and the Philippines. Equally significant was the construction industry's demands for low-wage workers. These demands emanated most visibly from firms based in the FT and suburbs.

In 1972, the town of KL was granted city status as the NEP proceeded to expand urban economic activities along the western corridor of Petaling Jaya, Subang Jaya, Shah Alam and Port Klang in Selangor, in addition to "planned townships" such as Bangi in the south (Bunnell, Barter, and Morshidi 2002, 360-1).[6] Whereas older neighborhoods were racially segregated, new places and spaces such as townships created by deforestation were racially integrated with heightened material consumption as a common denominator (see especially Khoo 2008).

Two years later, on February 1, 1974, the state designated KL as an FT when the sultan of Selangor formally transferred control to the federal government. The city's mayor reported to the minister of federal territory who, in turn, reported directly to the prime minister's department. The department's Economic Planning Unit was put in charge of city planning: "By the 1980s, KL was recognizable as the commercial and political core of Malaysia's primary metropolitan region" (Bunnell, Barter, and Morshidi 2002, 361). In return for the city, the sultan of Selangor was given land for a new capital west of the city. The Federal Highway stretched from Selangor's new capital, Shah Alam, to the city's center as it linked suburbs of Petaling Jaya, Subang Jaya and so forth. Mixed-use real estate development projects continue to be built along this western corridor.

Rapid urban development brought about a construction boom in the KL metropolitan area that encouraged further the in-migration of workers from Indonesia. Until the early 1980s, Malaysian Chinese men dominated the construction industry. Even prior to this, Malaysian construction firms began employing Indonesian migrant men (and to a lesser extent, women) as Malaysian workers demanded higher wages. Public discourse on the growing population of Indonesian migrants in KL and other urban areas finally culminated in official acknowledgment and regulation by the state. The Medan Agreement of 1984 was the first bilateral agreement on migrant labor signed between Malaysia and a major labor-sending state.

Indonesian migrant workers increased in numbers despite the mid- to late-1980s economic recession, because of the vacuum left by Malaysian Chinese who migrated for higher wages offered by construction industries in East Asia (Narayanan and Lai 2005), in addition to Malaysian women's persistent refusal to engage in paid live-in and day housework (Chin 1998). Indonesian women domestic workers lived in employers' homes, while

Indonesian men and women construction workers with established social networks stayed in areas such as Chow Kit and Kampung Baru, or were housed in *kongsi* (makeshift on-site accommodations) built by construction firms. The numbers of regular and irregular Indonesian migrants in construction work continued to grow in response to Greater KL's megastructural and other construction projects. Over time however, Indonesian migrants' presence and reported activities created a rift with Malaysian Malays (see next section).

In 1991, as part of the Sixth Malaysia Plan (1991–1995) and the Privatization Master Plan, Prime Minister Mahathir Mohamad introduced Wawasan 2020—or Vision 2020—as a blueprint for the country to reach "developed" status (Nambiar 2009). Introduced on the heels of the 1980s economic downturn, Vision 2020 laid out the rationale and plan for bringing about a knowledge-based economy and society.

KL's achievement of world-class city status was central to the material and symbolic dimensions of this vision. The Kuala Lumpur Structure Plan 1984 and its successor, the Kuala Lumpur Structure Plan 2020 specified changes such as changes in land use, public-private sector joint ventures and private sector–led projects, new housing for the expanding middle classes, low-cost housing in place of squatter settlements, and other commercial activities (Kuala Lumpur City Hall 2002; King 2008; Rimmer and Dick 2009).

The state acquired property within the FT for construction of the PTT and KLCC. Subsequently, plantation land south of the FT was acquired for construction of the world-class international airport, KLIA. The stated aim of these multibillion-dollar projects (completed in 1998) was to place the city on the world map, capped by PTT-KLCC at the north end and KLIA at the south end (Bunnell, Barter, and Morshidi 2002, 362). These multibillion-dollar megastructural projects were the state's responses to "new 'global' ways of seeing . . . and being seen" (Bunnell and Nah 2004, 2455): they symbolized "global connections while promoting nationalist sensibilities" by providing KL with the physical and virtual infrastructure expected of a global city (Yeoh 2005, 947).

Within the Golden Triangle, old residential houses, several primary and secondary schools, and an open-air wet market were among structures that gave way to construction projects culminating in luxury hotels, short-term furnished apartments, condominiums, and shopping malls:

> The business heart of the city is the area around Sungei Wang Plaza, Jalan Rajah [sic] Chulan and Jalan Sultan [sic]. Jalan Sultan [sic], a pernicious stretch of snail's pace, has been designated the thoroughfare of five-star hotels, either already built and long in operation or in various stages of construction and

completion. Five-star is the status Prime Minister Mahathir sought for everything, budget tourists not really wanted or needing to apply. Five-star tourists
require five-star shopping complexes to service their place in the scheme of
things, making Kuala Lumpur a premiere shopping holiday destination.

(Sardar 2000, 107)

Public and private construction projects vertically and horizontally stretched KL's skyline. At the north end, the PTT advertises KL's symbolic
arrival into the exclusive club of global cities. At the south end, KLIA and
its facilities compete with Singapore and Bangkok for inter-and intrare-
gional flows of goods and passengers: "Like a spider, the world city sits in
the center of a transport web" (Shin and Timberlake 2000, 262; Bowen
2000). KL has become a major gateway, or "staging post" connecting the
hinterlands and country to the global economy and the world (Bunnell,
Barter, and Morshidi 2002, 362).

Constructed near KLIA are the planned townships of Putrajaya and
Cyberjaya. Since 1999, Putrajaya, with its Islamic motif buildings, serves as
the administrative seat for the federal government (it is designated as a FT
as well), and Cyberjaya is Malaysia's answer to Silicon Valley, replete with
transnational firms, factories, residential homes, and private higher educational institutions (for example, Limkokwing University of Creative Technology, Malaysia Multimedia University, and Cyberjaya University College
of Medical Sciences).[7] The Multimedia Super Corridor (MSC), with its
underground fiber optic cables, stretches from KLIA, Putrajaya, and Cyberjaya to PTT. While the MSC provides a virtual network connecting KL to
rest of the country and the world, the North-South highway and North-
South railway link KL to Singapore and Bangkok.

By the late 1990s, tertiary or advanced producer services had become
second only to manufacturing in terms of activities and revenue. The services sector in KL contributed 83% of the total value-added activities, growing at an annual average of 10%. Four major service industries marked
this rapid growth: financial, insurance, real estate and business services;
estate and business services; wholesale and retail trade, hotels, and restaurants; and transport, storage, and communications. At that point,
however, KL was ranked a "gamma" world city with a major global banking
service center and a minor global accountancy and advertising service
center (Morshidi 2000, 2221–3). Within approximately one decade, KL
achieved the "alpha" world-city rank with its advanced producer services
in accountancy, advertising, banking-finance and law, linking "major economic regions and states into the world economy" (Globalization and
World Cities Research Network 2011). The state's strategic policies

successfully transformed KL into a regionally and globally competitive city with respect to its types of infrastructure and the range of its advanced producer services.

In becoming a world-class city, however, the state's urban development and economic diversification policies marginalized different groups of people. An outcome of the NEP's success was a lack of affordable housing for urban in-migrants (particularly Malays) who, over time, established urban villages. They joined the non-Malay urban poor with their settlements on undeveloped state and private parcels of land.[8] The sale of public land for private commercial and residential development projects, together with state appropriation of privately owned land for megastructural projects, displaced older and newer squatter settlements that had expanded during the NEP era.[9]

Collectively, these unauthorized settlements symbolized disarray within the planned orderly urban expansion and transformation of KL. State authorities identified and targeted many for demolition. As residents' homes were torn down, state promises of relocation to low-cost housing seldom materialized. Even though the state required all new housing development projects to include 30% low-cost units, smaller firms in pursuit of profits contravened this by "building one short of the minimum number of houses so as to avoid having to set aside 30 per cent of their scheme for low-cost housing" (Yeoh 2001, 114). In any case, many squatter residents could not even afford low-cost housing.

Despite grass-roots organization to oppose the state (including NGOs that assisted in residents' legal actions to prevent forced eviction and razing of the settlements), many settlements were forced to give way to new construction projects. Similar to its colonial predecessor, the postcolonial state continues to view these settlements, at best, as economically unproductive spaces and, at worst, as disorganized unruly sites that harbor crime and disease.[10] The razing and clearance of squatter settlements then render the land "legible" (Scott 1999) and "commodified" (Lefebvre 1991) for capitalist expansion and life in the twenty-first century world-class city.

Although KL's successful ascendance onto the world stage has been made possible by infrastructure that supports and facilitates growth of advanced producer services, it also is distinguished by the simultaneous processes of dislocating the working poor and incorporating low-wage migrant labor from the Philippines and Indonesia. By the first decade of the twenty-first century, migrant men and women entered jobs in more economic sectors and industries: Table 2.1 shows the growth in migrant numbers from major labor sending countries, while Table 2.2 shows the growth in numbers by economic sector.

Table 2.1. TRANSNATIONAL MIGRANT WORKERS IN MALAYSIA
BY COUNTRY OF ORIGIN, 2000–2010

Country Of Origin	2000		2005		2008		2010	
	Total	%	Total	%	Total	%	Total	%
Indonesia	603,453	74.8	1,211,584	66.7	1,085,658	52.6	967,100	50.9
Bangladesh	158,149	19.6	55,364	3.0	316,401	15.3	330,600	17.4
Thailand	2,335	0.3	5,751	0.3	21,065	1.0	n/a	
Philippines	14,651	1.8	21,735	1.2	26,713	1.3	n/a	
Pakistan	3,101	0.4	13,297	0.7	21,278	1.0	n/a	
Others	25,407	3.1	507,507	28.0	591,481	28.7	602,300	31.7
Total	807,096	100	1,815,238	100	2,062,596	100	1, 900,000	100

Source: Economic Planning Unit, Prime Minister's Department (2011a), except for 2010 data. The estimated data for 2010 come from *The Malaysian Insider* (May 20, 2010). Please note that data for 2010 were
not officially published at the time of this writing, and therefore the latest estimates were taken from a
news source in which data of migrants from Thailand, Philippines, and Pakistan appeared to be subsumed
in the category of Others.

Table 2.2. TRANSNATIONAL MIGRANT WORKERS IN
MALAYSIA BY ECONOMIC SECTOR, 2000–2010

Sector	2000		2005		2008		2010	
	Total	%	Total	%	Total	%	Total	%
Domestic Work	177,546	22	320,171	17.6	293,359	14.2	228,000	12.0
Manufacturing	307,167	38.1	581,379	32.0	728,867	35.3	741,000	39.0
Plantation	200,474	24.8	472,246	26.0	333,900	16.2	266,000	14.0
Construction	68,226	8.5	281,780	15.5	306,873	14.9	361,000	19.0
Services	53,683	6.7	159,662	8.8	212,630	10.3	190,000	10.0
Agriculture					186,967	9.1	114,000	6.0
Total	807,096	100	1,815,238	100	2,062,596	100	1,900,000	100

Sources: Economic Planning Unit, Prime Minister's Department (2011b), except for 2010 data. The estimated data for 2010 come from *The Malaysian Insider* (May 20, 2010).

As Table 2.1 shows, numerically, Indonesians remain the dominant
nationality of migrant workers in Malaysia. Yet, their percentage share of
the total regular migrant population has declined, primarily because of a
deliberate state strategy to diversify migrant nationalities (Chin 2008b).
Historically, Indonesians and Malaysians of Malay descent enjoyed overall
strong formal and informal ties (despite the 1960s Indonesian policy of

konfrontasi that challenged the inclusion of Sabah and Sarawak on the island of Borneo into the Federation of Malaysia). These ties were shaped by their ethnoreligious networks originating from intra-archipelagic travel and trade during the precolonial era. Negative newsprint reports and portrayals of Indonesian migrant activities in KL and other parts of the country, however, gradually caused a radical shift in Malay perceptions and treatment of Indonesians, from "insiders" to "outsiders."

As early as 1981, Indonesian petty traders reportedly fought with enforcement officers in KL's Chow Kit area (Kassim 1987, 270). In the years following this, news media continued to report Indonesian migrants taking over economic activities and residences in some Malay neighborhoods and squatter settlements, as well as committing crimes such as rape, murder, and robbery. The seemingly unceasing numbers of regular and irregular Indonesians and their reported activities gradually fueled a crisis: they were perceived as having taken over what used to be Malay spaces and livelihoods.

By the early 2000s, a conjuncture of geopolitical and socioeconomic forces cemented the growing divide when Indonesians were identified with Islamic militancy in Southeast Asia, and with migrant riots (regardless of causal factors) at worksites and hawker stalls in KL and elsewhere (Liow 2003, 2006). These culminated in state implementation of the 2002 Hire Indonesians Last policy that had the effect of reconstructing Indonesian migrants as outsiders to the Malay community and the Malaysian nation. Indonesians no longer were to be considered ethnoreligious kin. Although Indonesians are Muslims (that is, members of a larger *ummah* or pan-Islamic community), they were recast as foreign Muslims, or poor and dangerous citizens from a neighboring Muslim country (Spaan, van Naerssen, and Kohl 2002; Liow 2003; Crinis 2005; Liow 2006).

The 2002 policy heightened labor demands from the service sector, which led to the opening of immigration gates for workers from other countries.

STAYING COMPETITIVE: ENHANCING KL'S
REPUTATION AND REVENUE SOURCES

What began as a 1970s state-led development effort to reengineer society in the midst of export-oriented growth shifted in the post-1980s economic crisis to a neoliberal trajectory (qualified by maintenance of specific Malay special rights) overseen by a "competition state" (Cerny 1997). The state, without external pressure, voluntarily pursued this development path:

"Malaysia's record is particularly remarkable in that it entirely reflects unilateral and voluntary policy choices, not a result of influence by a major trading partner . . . conditionality imposed donor agencies, or multilateral negotiations under the auspices of the GATT/WTO" (Athukorala 2005, 32).

One year after Prime Minister Dato' Sri Mohd Najib bin Tun Abdul Razak took office in 2009, he emphasized the need to continue work toward realizing Vision 2020. Introduced in 2010, the New Economic Model's (NEM) overall promotion of private sector–led growth is to be pursued further via the 10th Malaysia Plan 2011–2015 (New Economic Advisory Council 2010). Together, they are expected to elevate Malaysia into the high income and high productivity club of countries with the state acting as a competitive corporation subject to performance metrics (Najib 2010, 11). To quell dissent from within the Malay community, the prime minister promised to maintain the NEP's Malay quotas or set-aside policy for their employment in the private sector, albeit "at [the] macro level" (Najib 2010, 20).

KL's competitive identity as a global city, to be sure, is a central focus of state elites. In his speech on the 10th Malaysia Plan to Parliament, the prime minister acknowledged that

> Global competition is no longer just between countries but increasingly between cities. Economic activities will naturally concentrate in cities, where the density of firms and talent drives productivity and innovation. Cities are therefore at the frontline in the drive towards high income.
>
> (Najib 2010, 42)

To make KL even more attractive, proposed projects include turning Lake Gardens into a botanical garden, and establishing a cultural tourism park called "Malaysia Truly Asia Centre" in 2014 (not to be confused with the Malaysia Tourism Centre, a one-stop tourist center with a physical building in Ampang as well as an e-portal). The public transportation system also will be strengthened via a Mass Rapid Transit System that "[w]hen completed . . . is expected to cover a radius of 20 km from the city centre with a total length of about 150 km, and when fully operational, will serve up to two million passenger trips per day from 480,000 trips on current urban rail systems" (Najib 2010, 42–4). At the same time, the "Talent Corporation" is charged with attracting and retaining foreign and Malaysian-born professionals: it is "a one-stop centre to coordinate with relevant government agencies, including immigration matters, for the entry of skilled workers into the country" (Najib 2010, 40).

In addition to strengthening KL's advanced producer services, the state has targeted tourism and education as essential components of generating income (per the "National Key Results Areas"). Tourism and education are part of the twelve service sectors identified for liberalization under GATS as well: "In our effort to restructure the nation's economy, in line with global trends, the focus will be on the services sector as it has potential to continue expanding and contribute significantly to economic growth" (Harun 2010). These two service sectors not only generate revenue and enhance the city's regional and global standing; they also create additional migratory pathways for workers from all over the world.

Calling International Tourists and Even More Transnational Migrant Workers

According to the KL Structure Plan 2020,

> As with other major cities, tourism plays an important part in the economic life of Kuala Lumpur, providing income, employment, and expanding business opportunities. The tourism industry is very wide ranging in the services and facilities where it requires and provides employment across all sectors of the population.... Foreign visitors gain a greater understanding and appreciation of the culture and achievements of the City and its people. The impressions that are taken back to their home countries can do much to raise the profile of the City and the country.
>
> (Kuala Lumpur City Hall 2002)

The Malaysia Tourism Promotion Board, also known as Tourism Malaysia is charged with promoting domestic and international tourism. Introduced in 1999, the agency's "Malaysia—Truly Asia" campaign has proven so successful that it still is in effect: symbols of nature are targeted primarily to North Asian and North American markets, whereas shopping malls target Middle Eastern and Southeast Asian markets. For the domestic tourism market, the slogan *"cuti cuti Malaysia"* (vacation in Malaysia) headlines many advertisements that prominently feature PTT and KLCC. These advertisements have copy such as this:

> As a land blessed with a variety of cultures, traditions, and attractions, Malaysia definitely serves up an exciting variety of unique experiences. Savor new culinary delights, explore nature's wonders on land and in our waters, feel the soothing breeze of our highlands or take a trip down memory lane—each experience promises a world of memories to treasure forever.
>
> (Malaysia Tourism Promotion Board 2011a)

Similar to other global cities in Asia, tourism in KL is fueled by megastructural projects, world-class hotels, newly designated cultural sites, and even global sporting events (Douglass 2006; Yeoh 2005). The city is marketed as the destination and main gateway for mass tourism or packaged tours catering to large groups and conventions. For example KL aggressively competes with other global cities to host "MICE" tourism: meetings, incentives, conventions, and events (Bernama April 23, 2010). In the past few years, KL has been ranked at the top tiers of Asian destinations, especially for health tourism, because of the quality of private hospitals and medical personnel, relatively low cost, and strong healthcare infrastructure.[11] Total tourism receipts nearly doubled from RM32 billion in 2005 to RM57 billion in 2010 (Malaysia Tourism Promotion Board, 2011b). The state's target is thirty-six million tourist arrivals with total receipts of RM168 billion by 2020 (New Straits Times October 19, 2010).

Tourism therefore is integral to maintaining KL's regional and global competitiveness. In 2000, the total number of tourism arrivals in Malaysia was 10.2 million. At the end of 2010, the total number had jumped to 24.5 million with annual growth averaging 7% (Malaysia Tourism Promotion Board, 2011b). Although neighboring Singapore is the top sending country, tourists from the PRC, India, Saudi Arabia, and Iran have increased markedly since even the mid-2000s (see Table 2.3). This is due to the state's

Table 2.3. TOURIST ARRIVALS IN MALAYSIA
BY SELECTED COUNTRY, 2000–2010

Country of Residence	2000	2005	2010	2011
Singapore	5,420,200	9,634,506	13,042,004	13,372,647
Thailand	940,215	1,900,839	1,458,678	1,442,048
People's Republic of China (including HK & Macau)	501,590	432,570	1,130,261	1,250,536
India	132,127	225,789	690,849	693,056
Australia	236,775	265,346	580,695	558,411
UK	237,757	240,030	429,965	403,940
USA	184,100	151,354	232,965	216,755
Iran	4,514	12,309	116,252	139,617
Saudi Arabia	27,808	53,682	86,771	87,693
Russia	5,799	8,386	32,075	38,918
South Africa	11,540	16,381	26,395	31,441
Others	562,626	712,440	778,723	792,024

Source: Malaysia Tourism Promotion Board, (2011b, 2012)

gradual shift in orientation from the West to countries in Asia and the Middle East.

Sustained stronger bilateral trade relations with the PRC, in particular, have led to substantially improved bidirectional flows of executives, investors, tourists, and students (Lim 2009; Chin 2000; Ku 2008). Tourist arrivals from Iran have increased exponentially since 2005 because of improved political, economic, and cultural relations between the two states. Malaysian firms are leading the way in helping Iran develop its gas fields and liquefied gas plants (Vaughn and Martin 2007), while Iranian students are attracted to institutions of higher education in KL (see Table 2.5). Tourist arrival numbers from Central Asian states are relatively small (and not even noted separately in official data) compared to countries listed in Table 2.3 because bilateral ties were established only in the early 2000s. Nevertheless, trade relations (for example, related to oil-gas joint ventures and import-export of goods) already have led to direct air routes between KL and Central Asian capital cities such as Tashkent and Almaty (Stark 2006).

In marketing campaigns, the state's hegemonic discourse of "unity out of diversity" has had the effect of glossing over, erasing, or decontextualizing histories of racialized-classed contestations over rights, use of space, and so forth in KL (see especially Hoffstaedter 2009; Sardar 2000):

> In Bukit Bintang there is no marker to remind shoppers and revelers that Jalan Tong Shin was a focus of the May 13, 1969 "Incident," nor are there markers indicating the mob's progress along Jalan Tuanku Abdul Rahman . . . KLIA does not mark the history of its site (plantation, settlement, eviction) nor does Putrajaya on its symbol-laden Dataran Putra. The National History Museum displays images of the Emergency, but no reminders of the dangers of ignoring class and its (re)production.
>
> (King 2008, 194)

Meanwhile, the Islamicized architecture of some major structures symbolizes the Malaysian state's efforts to affirm membership, if not leadership, in the pan-Islamic world (Fujita 2010; Goh and Liauw 2009; King 2008). Embedded in a dominant Malay-Muslim ethos, these structures are designed and expected to attract tourists from Muslim countries in the Middle East, North Africa, and Central Asia.[12] For instance, along Changkat Bukit Bintang, there are

> gentrifying lorong (laneways) with small galleries, graphic design firms . . . into Ain Arabia offering small hotels and restaurants to an "alternative" Middle-Eastern

clientele. Ain Arabia's focal point is a small park that was "Arabised" in 2005, presumably to attract a different sort of tourist and perhaps to counter the otherwise Chinese ambience of Bukit Bintang.

(King 2008, 42)

Ain Arabia's park was a small plot of land used as a children's playground by Malaysians, primarily of Chinese descent, who lived in surrounding apartments. With approval from City Hall, Islamic structures were erected along the park's boundaries. The neighborhood soon was likened to and marketed as "little Arabia" with an anchor restaurant, mini-markets, and laundromats catering to Muslim tourists and workers from the Middle East and West Asia. Gradually, the low-rise buildings, with shops on the ground floor and apartments above, began hosting new tenants: transnational Muslim migrants. Their presence in the neighborhood and city resulted from rising demands for low-wage service workers in the wake of the state's Hire Indonesians Last policy.

In the context of heightened educational and employment opportunities alongside state efforts to upgrade human resources for higher value-added activities, many Malaysians refused low-wage, low-status work in service industries related to tourism. Consistent pressure from employers culminated in state approval of the service sector employing transnational migrant workers. To lessen the concentration of and dependence on any one migrant nationality, the state approved a list of sending countries for each economic sector and corresponding industries. At the time of this writing, migrant workers are approved for six major sectors: manufacturing, construction, plantation, agriculture, services, and domestic help. Within the service sector, there are eleven subsectors: restaurant, cleaning services, cargo handling, launderette, caddy, barber, wholesale/retail, textile, metal/scraps/recycle, welfare homes, and hotel/resort islands (Malaysian Investment Development Authority 2011).

Table 2.4 is a visual representation of the state's direct incorporation of low-wage transnational migrant workers into the economy. It should be emphasized that migrant countries of origin listed in the table are not permanent. That is to say, countries can be added or removed based on bilateral relations, public pressure, and so forth (Chin 2002, 2008b; Kaur 2008). For example, Bangladeshi men had been approved for all sectors except for domestic work until the state banned their in-migration in 2009, because many of them had overstayed their work permits. Two years later, the state proposed an amnesty program of regularization, including a no-penalty return to Bangladesh (see Chapter Three).

Table 2.4. EMPLOYMENT OF TRANSNATIONAL MIGRANT
LABOR BY APPROVED SECTOR AND COUNTRY OF ORIGIN, 2011

Sector	Migrant Country of Origin	
Agriculture	Cambodia	Philippines (men only)
Construction	Indonesia	Sri Lanka
Manufacturing	Kazakhstan	Thailand
Plantation	Laos	Turkmenistan
Services	Myanmar	Uzbekistan
	Nepal	Vietnam
	Pakistan	
Services	India	
Domestic Work (women only)	Cambodia	Philippines
	India	Sri Lanka
	Indonesia	Thailand
	Laos	Vietnam

Sources: Malaysian Investment Development Authority (2011) and Immigration Department of Malaysia (2011).

With the exception of domestic work, permits for low-wage migrants are not renewable beyond the limit of five years, and migrants cannot be accompanied by their spouses or children. People categorized as highly skilled professionals or global talent are subject to different rules that facilitate ease of entry and their stay in the country. Thus, state management of transnational migrants transforms the country, and particularly the world-class city, into a massive turnstile: migrant workers enter via formal and informal channels for some duration of stay before leaving for another destination or their home countries (Price and Benton-Short 2007, 103).

What Table 2.4 cannot reveal is the predominantly gendered placement and employment of migrant workers in the service subsectors related to tourism. For example, migrant men are parking valets in hotels and baggage and cargo handlers at KLIA; migrant women are chambermaids in hotels; migrant men are cooks and migrant women are servers in restaurants; and migrant men are barbers, whereas migrant women are beauticians and masseuses. Domestic work is the only subsector officially restricted to migrant women between the ages of twenty-one and forty-five. The migrant sex worker is not an approved category, so women can and do enter on work permits for approved sectors, or on tourist and student visas. On the whole, migrant women are employed in different types of labor that draw on their ascribed gender traits.

Depending on the economic sector and size of the firm, migrants may be housed in employer-provided accommodations, or rent on their own. There have been reports of substandard on-site or near-site accommodations given to those in construction, manufacturing, and agriplantations (see, for example, Crinis 2010; Robertson 2008). According to labor brokers interviewed for this study, migrants in the service sector live in apartments in KL's neighborhoods and suburbs, which they either rent themselves or which are recommended by employment agencies or provided by employers. Workers from Myanmar, Vietnam, and the Philippines tend to live among Malaysian Chinese; non-Muslim Indians reside in Malaysian Indian neighborhoods; and Bangladeshis live in Malaysian Indian-Muslim or Malay neighborhoods.

By their provision of personal services, transnational migrant women and men in the service sector help underwrite KL's competitive identity as a global city. As Sassen puts it, "We are witnessing the return of the so-called 'serving classes' in globalized cities around the world" (2002, 262). Migrant women sex workers, to be sure, are part of the serving classes: trafficked and nontrafficked women provide sexual services to a host of clientele ranging from migrant workers to tourists, businessmen, and expatriates. The world-class city's provision of advanced producer services for the command and control of the global economy then finds its equivalent in the informal economy inclusive of the sex industry (see Chapters Four and Five).

Migrant women and men who cannot qualify for authorized employment, or who do not wish to do so, are able to enter via another pathway created from state liberalization of education.

Calling International Students: Come to Study, but Don't Work

Positioned at the intersection of the NEM, 10th Malaysia Plan, and GATS, education in Malaysia is a major service sector deemed crucial to the global city's and country's competitive identity. The state's objective is to transform Malaysia into a regional educational hub with KL at its center:

> The Malaysian education sector has enjoyed tremendous growth in recent years as a result of the government's liberalised policy of encouraging the growth of the private education market. The private education sector has grown more than 10 per cent a year since 2003 and is estimated to reach RM14 billion in 2015. It is also one of the 12 National Key Economic Areas under the 10th

Malaysia Plan, in line with the government's strategy to make Malaysia a regional education hub.

(New Straits Times November 6, 2010)

The NEP, by setting aside the majority of seats at public universities for Malay students (and providing full scholarships for select Malay students' overseas studies), had encouraged the non-Malay middle and upper classes to send their children overseas to the traditional education hubs of the UK, Australia, and New Zealand. By the late 1990s, the combination of annual currency outflows related to overseas studies that averaged USD1.2 billion (McBurnie and Ziguras 2001, 92), and the recognition of a "brain drain" (especially that of Malaysians educated abroad), prompted the state to reevaluate its policy on higher education (Ziguras and Law 2006).[13]

In response to internal and external forces, the state implemented the Private Higher Education Institutions Act 1996 (PHEI), which opened up space for private-sector participation in higher education. PHEI was the state's solution to alleviating pressure on public institutions that did not have the capacity to educate the younger generations, in the hopes of mitigating massive currency outflows. The Act was amended in 2003 to cover branch campuses of foreign universities as well as the upgrading of private universities and colleges (Morshidi, Abdul Razak, and Koo 2009, 1).

One year later, the Ministry of Education was split into two: the Ministry of Education and the Ministry of Higher Education (MOHE). MOHE's core mission included the internationalization of higher education in part by attracting foreign institutions and skilled labor. Among MOHE's main responsibilities are vetting applications from institutions and issuing licenses to them, and working with the national accreditation office to assess courses, faculty, and curricula. One objective is to ensure KL's ability to compete against Asian global cities such as Tokyo, Hong Kong, and particularly Singapore with its Global Schoolhouse initiative and its initiative to build world-class universities, which aimed to transform the city-state into the academic "Boston of the East" (Olds 2007; Mok 2008).

The Malaysian state's pursuit of progressive liberalization in services does not formally include that of the education sector. The state has not fully committed to GATS in the education sector, choosing instead "autonomous" liberalization, because this allows the state to discriminate in favor of local courses over transnational programs (Gill 2005; Ziguras 2003). It does not mean, however, that public universities are protected from liberalization processes. For example, MOHE requires public universities to restructure curricula in order to meet the needs of businesses, and to raise a certain percentage of their operating budgets from corporations. Higher education per se increasingly is free market driven in Malaysia (Morshidi, Abdul Razak, and Koo 2009, 17).[14]

By 2010, there were approximately twenty-one public universities and 476 private institutions of higher education in the country, with the majority in Greater KL (Ministry of Higher Education 2011). More and more Malaysian and international students are enrolled in foreign branch campuses of UK and Australian universities (for example, University Nottingham Malaysia and Monash University Malaysia); for-profit universities (for example, Multimedia University); and public universities (for example, Universiti Islam Antarabangsa Malaysia). Prospective students can apply for entry while overseas, or they can enter on social visit passes, gain acceptance by a private college or university, and then apply via the institution's E-Student Pass System.[15] Depending on the institution, students can reside on campus or rent rooms, houses, and apartments in surrounding areas.

International students come from all regions of the world. The majority, however, are from Muslim countries in the Middle East, North Africa, and Central Asia. The state's goal is for the country and KL, by virtue of its prominence as home to many institutions of higher education, to serve as the regional hub of, and academic leader for, the pan-Islamic world (Gribble 2008, 30; Bernama March 31, 2010). Table 2.5 offers a list of the six largest international student-sending countries: PRC is the only large non-Muslim sending country on a list that is led by Iran.

Aside from the anticipated public-cultural diplomacy benefits of liberalizing higher education in Malaysia, international students represent an

Table 2.5. ENROLLMENT OF INTERNATIONAL STUDENTS BY TOP SENDING COUNTRIES, 2009–2011

Country	2009	2010	2011
Iran	10,932	11,832	9,898
Indonesia	9,812	9,889	8,569
People's Republic of China	9,177	10,214	7,394
Nigeria	5,969	5,817	5,632
Yemen	4,931	5,866	3,552
Sudan	2,443	2,837	2,091

Source: Ministry of Higher Education (2011), except for 2011 data, which were calculated based on the latest statistics available from the Ministry of Higher Education regarding enrollment of international students in public and private higher educational institutions (see Ministry of Higher Education 2012a, 2012b). These numbers might not include other kinds of institutions (community colleges, nonaccredited schools, and so forth), for which the 2011 data were unavailable at the time of this writing.

important source of foreign exchange. In 2009, the approximately 70,000 international students generated RM1.5 billion for entertainment, food, health care, and related businesses. The total doubled to RM4 billion with the inclusion of tuition revenue (New Straits Times June 26, 2009).

Nevertheless, MOHE is challenged to implement a comprehensive regulatory framework while fending off allegations of inconsistently approving and registering institutions (Morshidi, Abdul Razak, and Koo 2009, 15). There are reports of fly-by-night "shophouse" colleges that, in privileging profits, do not fully vet student applications, offer quality instruction, or monitor student attendance. For migrants seeking to bypass cumbersome bureaucratic red tape and the associated costs of obtaining work permits, education offers an alternative pathway into the global city. As we shall see in Chapters Four and Five, migrant women sex workers and syndicates have taken advantage of this pathway.

Some migrants indeed enter legally under the pretext of pursuing programs of study. They then work without authorization in hotels, restaurants, supermarkets, golf clubs, gas stations, and so forth. In KL,

> Every year Tenaganita [an NGO that promotes migrant workers' rights] uncovers several cases where colleges are used as fronts for foreign students to enter Malaysia before moving on to working without permits. Its director Florida Sandanasamy said over the past 10 years, there was a steady increase of foreigners who misused their student visas. "Yearly, we handle some 20 cases of foreigners working on tourist and student visas, and the number of people caught working with student visas is steadily rising."
>
> (New Straits Times November 28, 2009; see also New Straits Times January 31, 2010)

MOHE has responded to unscrupulous institutions by deregistering them, while demanding that all private universities and colleges strictly monitor their international students (New Straits Times June 6, 2010).

To be sure, there also are students who enter with the intent of pursuing programs of study but who are compelled to seek unauthorized part-time or full-time employment to subsidize their living expenses or school fees. With the exception of MOHE's Malaysia International Scholarship program, which fully funds a select number of international students from twenty-seven countries for postgraduate and postdoctoral studies in designated "critical fields," many international students do not qualify for in-country subsidies, scholarships, or loans.[16]

Public institutions that are governed by more restrictive quotas for international students face a different challenge. In the post-9/11 era, the state's courting of students from Muslim countries appears inadvertently to elicit a national security threat:

> Muslim international students engaged in militant activities were said to be from Nigeria, Syria, Jordan and Yemen. One of them, Aiman Al-Dakkak from Syria, was an Al-Qaeda operative. He studied at the International Islamic University, Universiti Sains Malaysia and Universiti Teknologi Malaysia during his six years in the country.
>
> (The Straits Times June 26, 2010)

Even as the state's policy of liberalizing higher education serves the dual purpose of enhancing KL's competitive identity and subsequently increasing foreign exchange earnings, it also comes with key challenges. The establishment of this new pathway for the entry of prospective students also facilitates the entry of those considered socioeconomic and security threats to the nation. The net effect is that while international students are welcomed, their activities on and off campus must be surveilled constantly.

CONCLUSION

In less than half a century, postcolonial state policies transformed a town dominated by Malaysians of Chinese descent into a world-class city hosting local and transnational firms, Malaysians from all classes and communities, expatriates, international tourists, and students. The impetus for reconfiguring the usage of places and spaces in KL came from a conjuncture of domestic and global forces. What began as a state-led social engineering program in the 1970s to redress legacies of British colonial rule eventually gave way to the adoption of neoliberal policy tools (for example, economic privatization and liberalization) designed to capture deterritorialized capital freed by global economic restructuring processes. Since the late twentieth century, the state has legitimized a mainly neoliberal path toward realizing the knowledge economy and society of Vision 2020.

KL's centrality to this vision belies a relentless dependence on low-wage transnational migrants. This dependence has its historical roots in the colonial era, when low-wage Chinese and Indian migrant men and women arrived to helped build an extractive economy. Demands for transnational migrant labor resurfaced during the NEP and persists in the contemporary era, as Malaysians refuse low-wage and low-status jobs in many economic sectors.

Postcolonial state management of migrant labor has led to an expanded list of sectors, industries, and migrant nationalities. Those who do not qualify to migrate via formal channels, as well as those who do not wish to do so, pursue other channels. Ongoing liberalization of services, particularly tourism and education, offer two additional migratory pathways. What should have been a short-term answer to low-wage labor demands from agriplantations, construction firms, and Malaysian households has blossomed into a long-term dependence on low-wage migrant labor.

Transnational migrant workers' incorporation into the formal and informal economies exposes the underside of KL even as it serves as one of the "staging posts" for the new global economy. From this perspective, the world-class city's contact zone is exemplified not only by the constant flow of people, but by those people's encounters in contexts of radically asymmetrical power relations. The next chapter examines public anxieties elicited by the presence of regular and irregular transnational migrant women and men, and the state's creative strategies to clarify and protect the nation's perceived boundaries.

CHAPTER 3

Reestablishing Internal Borders of the Nation

Creatively Repressive State Strategies

Man hat Arbeitskräfte gerufen, und es kamen Menschen.
—Max Frisch (quoted in Banderet and Weder 2004, 10)

Global cities are supposed to be the main gateways through which capital, goods, information, and people flow freely. Receiving states, however, do not welcome all people regardless of their occupations and backgrounds. Despite and because of labor demands from the formal and informal economies, states try—with varying degrees of success—to prevent the entry of some, while welcoming others. To paraphrase Max Frisch, "We asked for workers, but in came people"—who may be physiognomically different, with different worldviews, memories, and cultural practices.

Although global cities' contact zones symbolize regional-global recognition, they also encapsulate certain threats that accompany such recognition. This has led to very creative state "strategies of containment and exclusion" that are deleterious principally to unwelcomed migrant workers, refugees, and asylum seekers (Obi 2010, 131). The 9/11 terrorist attacks on the United States, followed by successive attacks in various regions of the world, imbued state strategies with an even greater sense of urgency (Pickering 2001; Chin 2008b).

To secure the nation from migrant infiltration, receiving states in the Global North and South focus not only on external but internal borders as well. Encased within and informed by the larger context of neoliberal globalization, some receiving states in the Global North apply privatization principles to external border management by transferring some security functions (such as designing and managing databases, vetting traveler eligibility) to firms in the private sector. Ostensibly, internal border control still takes the form of "traditional institutions of spatial regulation for political ends" such as prisons, detention centers, and other modes of entrapment that restrict the in-country mobility of unwanted migrants (Turner 2010, 243–4; see also Ibrahim 2005; Lahav 2000). More and more, however, states are outsourcing management of these institutions, too. Collectively, state securitization of migration that involves privatization strategies are eliciting contradictions between liberal political governance, with that of punitive and exclusionary measures taken against migrants (see, for example, Bigo and Guild 2005; Hughes 2006; Wakefield 2003).

The case is somewhat different with regard to Malaysia in the Global South: the state is not encumbered by a liberal tradition of protecting civil and political rights. Malaysia is one of the largest Southeast Asian labor-receiving countries with 1.8 million regular transnational migrant workers, and roughly the same number of irregular migrants. Of a workforce, then, of about twelve million, approximately one in three workers are transnational migrants (New Straits Times October 5, 2011). Although the state has not transferred many external border control functions to private security firms, it has infused internal border management strategies with unique reinterpretations of neoliberal diversification and privatization principles. Implemented concurrently with the establishment of tourism and education pathways, the internal border management strategies exacerbate an already vicious cycle broadening the conditions in which many more migrants from many more nationalities are represented and treated as illegal foreign or alien workers. In this way, the state (re)produces migrant illegality while amplifying a variety of threats that migrants are perceived to pose to the nation (Garcés-Mascareñas 2010). The world-class city of KL and its multiple overlapping contact zones are a focal point of state efforts to reestablish and maintain what are considered internal borders of the nation.

A VICIOUS CYCLE

Since the Malaysian state officially began regulating transnational migrant labor flow in the mid-1980s, the economy's unstoppable and insatiable demands for low-wage workers are paralleled by a dizzying array of policy shifts and rules informing migrant recruitment, entry, employment, and repatriation. In 1992, the state approved migrant labor from specific countries for the manufacturing sector, but then implemented a ban within less than a year—only to reverse course shortly thereafter. During the Asian financial crises of the late 1990s, the state banned new recruitment of migrants for plantation and construction sectors, only to lift the ban within a few months because of employer demands. Again, in the global financial crises that occurred late in the first decade of the twenty-first century, the entry of migrant workers for the manufacturing sector was halted but then allowed to resume within six months when firms could not fill overseas orders because of labor shortages (Devadason and Chan 2011, 7). State declarations and retractions of migrant-worker bans are accompanied by immigration crackdowns and raids in search of irregular migrants. Punctuating these are occasional amnesty and regularization programs, one of which occurred in 2011: "[The] 6P programme—which includes the registration, legalisation, amnesty, deportation, supervision, and enforcement of foreign labour—registered 2,320,034 illegal and legal foreign workers using the biometric system as of August 31" (New Straits Times October 5, 2011). Approximately 1.3 million who registered were irregular migrants and there remained nearly a million who did not participate in the program.

State regulation of recruitment and employment agencies follows a similar pattern. In 2006, for example, employment agencies were allowed to directly recruit, mainly from South Asia, and subsequently hire out migrants to small and medium enterprises in the country. Three years later, state issuance of licenses had to be halted in response to rising rates of exploited and trafficked migrants:

> The outsourcing system has effectively become a brokerage system, whereby the labour hire firm has become the de facto employer. The labour hire firm, which is obliged to have specific jobs for the workers it brings in, acts as a contractor, moving workers around to get the best deal for itself. The system has consequently transformed these workers into bonded labour . . . horror stories of their exploitation have been reported in the media.
>
> (Kaur 2010, 13–4)

Although policy decision-making processes and data with regard to migrant labor are considered politically sensitive and not disclosed fully by the state, there appears to be an intent to maintain flexibility in the midst of economic crises and transformation. As the economy shifted from one primarily based on agriplantation to manufacturing, followed by the present emphasis on strengthening knowledge-based or tertiary services, the state is challenged to delicately balance internal forces (especially sectoral demands and public perceptions of migrants) and external forces. This has resulted in significantly noticeable policy flip-flops. The state's characteristic stop-go, ad hoc, or erratic regulation of migration exposes the persistent absence of a comprehensive and coherent policy on transnational migrant labor (Kaur 2008; Liow 2003; Chin 2002).

To have longer-term viability and effectiveness, the state's policy responses require meaningful and sustained consultation and coordination among state agencies; nonstate actors, such as interest groups in different economic sectors; and NGOs. However, the pattern of instituting a ban or a freeze on migrant labor intake, only to lift it shortly thereafter in response to complaints from employers, cannot but reflect the state's failure to do so.

State enforcement of existing legislation has elicited contradictory effects as well. Two key pieces of legislation govern low-wage transnational migrant workers: the Employment Act 1955 (amended in 1998) and the Immigration Act 1956/1963 (amended in 1997 and 2002). Together, these acts ensure that migrants cannot participate in organized labor, and they are prohibited from working or changing employers without prior state approval. Although migrants have the right to file complaints against their employers, some employers retaliate by terminating their contracts. Migrants can thus immediately be rendered "illegal" by their employers' action.

Migrants have the right to apply to the Immigration Department for a special 30-day pass that allows them to remain in the country while they await police investigation or the Labour Court's adjudication of their cases. The special pass can be renewed for a total of 90 days, after which they must leave the country. Immigration regulations, however, prohibit migrants from working during this time. An official explains, "I cannot allow them to use the special pass to work and stay for as long as their case is being heard because there are hundreds of thousands of illegals in the country." Moreover, the state will not take any responsibility for ensuring migrants' welfare while their cases are being adjudicated because "the worker's family, good friends, nongovernmental organizations, embassies, high commissions or any other person would support him during this period" (New Straits Times April 27, 2008). Basically, migrants who pursue legal recourse end up substituting one set of vulnerabilities for another: they must bear the financial and social costs of lodging complaints against employers, under the threat of deportation.

Taken together, the policies and legislation affirm neoliberal labor flexibilization processes in which migrant workers are rendered less demanding to capital (Chin 2003, 2008b; Standing 1999, 2011). Transnational migrants are low-wage foreign workers who can be hired and fired at will, and with little viable recourse to labor protection and benefits. To ensure that migrants are temporary or guest workers (with the exception of domestic workers who are not subjected to the stipulated limit), their work permits are limited to a total of five years. Prior to 2001, work permits were valid for six years. In 2001, the maximum length of existing migrant work contracts was decreased from six to three years (many migrants became "illegal" overnight), before it was changed again to a maximum of five years (Liow 2003; Chin 2002).[1] In order to ensure that low-wage migrants do not settle in the country, immigration regulations prohibit the entry of their spouses and children. Migrants also are not permitted to marry Malaysian citizens or to apply for permanent residency.[2]

The absence of a minimum-wage system in Malaysia strengthens flexibilized migrant labor: unless specified by Memorandum of Understanding (MOU) between the Malaysian and sending states, wages are determined by labor market competition in the supply of transnational migrant workers. In 2011, and despite employer resistance, the National Wages Consultative Council Bill was tabled in Parliament. The bill provides for establishing a National Wages Consultative Council to determine minimum wages for different sectors and jobs. The bill also mandates fining employers RM10,000 for every employee who is not paid the minimum wage (New Straits Times July 7, 2011). It remains unclear how a minimum wage system (standardized or sectoral-based), when implemented, will affect employer demands for transnational migrant workers, as well as the overall costs incurred by migrants who enter via formal channels.

The cost for migrants to work legally in Malaysia includes initial fees of several thousands of ringgit charged by employment agencies and a host of one-time and annual state-stipulated fees. Until 2009, migrants were responsible for paying annual levies: since then, the state requires employers to pay them instead. Depending on the sector, levies successively increased from several hundred ringgit to more than RM1,000 per migrant.[3] Given the nearly two million regular migrants in the country, state revenues from levies and visa fees exceed RM1 billion annually.

Transnational migrants who enter via formal channels have to maneuver a bureaucratic maze, contend with fluctuating policies, and pay associated fees. The time, documentation, and costs involved in migration via formal channels encourage some migrants to pursue informal channels. These channels are less restrictive and demanding of migrants' time and money, while potentially offering relatively more control over the nature and environment of their work:

In Malaysia, the resort to illegality, both by people who entered the country illegally and those who became illegal immigrants on leaving their employers, has made it possible for people to "escape" the restraints imposed by the state-regulated migrant labor system. To be more concise, illegal immigrants, unlike "legal" immigrants, can change jobs, can to some extent negotiate their salary and working conditions, do not have to pay extra to enter or remain in the country, and can prolong their stay independently of the economic situation or their state of health, or beyond the 5 years stipulated by law. . . . In this regard, and in contrast with what has been observed in Europe and the United States, illegality can also constitute a form of resistance.

(Garcés-Mascareñas 2010, 84)

This phenomenon can be seen in some regular migrants' responses to the 6P programme. By running away from employers in manufacturing, construction, and services, migrants automatically became "illegal." This, however, made them eligible for the program that allowed them to try to switch employers or work in another sector for higher wages (New Straits Times October 5, 2011).

Such migrant resistance has not gone unnoticed by the state. In 2007, the Ministry of Home Affairs announced its drafting of a Foreign Workers' Bill that authorized the ministry to control every aspect of migration, from designation of quotas to migrant induction courses and surveillance.[4] This administrative move signaled that the issue of transnational migrant labor would fall under the aegis of national or internal security. Other ministries and, in particular, the Ministry of Human Resources publicly questioned, albeit unsuccessfully, the efficacy of this proposal that concentrated power under Home Affairs (New Straits Times February 24, 2007).

In 2010, Home Affairs announced the establishment of a "management laboratory" comprised of eight ministries and fifteen government agencies. The laboratory is distinguished by a clear division of labor in accordance with respective sectors. For example, the Ministry of Human Resources oversees services, the Ministry of International Trade and Industry oversees manufacturing, and the Ministry of Tourism oversees tourism. Thus, each ministry is tasked with "foreigner management and monitoring" in its respective sector, with Home Affairs responsible for overall security (BBC February 24, 2010). This mode of "centralized decentralization" with Home Affairs at the helm effectively securitizes every ministry's operations and policies with regard to transnational migrants. Marginalized in the process is the need for state elites to engage in sustained consultation and coordination with industry representatives and NGOs to understand and anticipate the nature and changing sectoral demands for migrant labor. Centralization under Home Affairs also has the effect of diminishing the need to grapple with contradictory effects of policy shifts and new rules on migrants.

Such state securitization of transnational migration is accompanied and reinforced by reinterpretations of two neoliberal principles, which are applied to manage the large population of regular and irregular migrants: diversification of migrant nationalities and privatization of some security operations. Nowhere are these strategies more obvious than in the world-class city of KL.

Diversification of Migrant Nationalities

As discussed in Chapter Two, state diversification of migrant nationalities came in direct response to reports of Indonesian migrants' illegal and criminal activities in KL and elsewhere. Even before 2002, state regulation of transnational migration for employment already was shaped by the legacy of British colonial rule. During the 1970s, tacit state approval of Philippine and Indonesian migrants' presence in the country was evident in the refusal to acknowledge or regulate their entry and employment conditions. Non-Malay-controlled labor unions and opposition parties led the public outcry for state regulation. The prevailing perception was that fragile relations among the three major Malaysian communities could not withstand (alleged) proselytizing by Filipino Christians in Malay Muslim communities of East Malaysia; nor could they withstand state-sanctioned assimilation of Indonesians into Malay communities on the peninsula so as to surreptitiously strengthen the latter's demographic and political power vis-à-vis the Malaysian Chinese and Indian communities (Sadiq 2005). Since then, explicit state diversification of migrant nationalities has emboldened a specific notion of the Malaysian nation, while compounding anxieties and insecurities for citizens and migrants (Healey 2000; Hing 2000; Chin 2008b).

In 1995, Prime Minister Mahathir's concept of *Bangsa Malaysia*, variously interpreted as the Malaysian nation or the Malaysian race, was introduced to reinforce Vision 2020.[5] As state elites called on Malaysians to unite while upgrading their skills and contributing to higher value-added economic activities, demands for low-wage transnational migrants did not abate: migrant workers were needed to sustain the competitiveness of export-based industries in manufacturing and agricultural sectors; construct new buildings and infrastructure; liberate Malaysian women to work outside their homes; and serve residents and visitors in the world-class city. Following its 2002 policy on Indonesian workers, the state signed a series of MOUs that brought in migrant workers from other sending countries. The push for economic diversification in the name of growth and prosperity found its classed, racialized-ethnicized, and gendered expressions in state regulation of transnational migrant labor.

The state's migrant diversification strategy assisted in delineating and affirming *Bangsa Malaysia*'s material and symbolic boundaries. Whether *Bangsa Malaysia* was interpreted as the Malaysian nation or Malaysian race, when juxtaposed against a growing population of low-wage transnational migrants, nationality became synonymous or was conflated with culture and race. The economy's persistent low-wage labor demands, together with real and perceived migrant activities in and beyond their workplaces, infused *Bangsa Malaysia* with specific meaning: "The everyday presence of foreign workers, both in person and in the media, helps emphasize the comparative safety and power of simply being Malaysian" (Williamson 2002, 413). Current Prime Minister Najib's slogan of "1Malaysia" may have removed any explicit assignation of race but the concept of national unity remains the same: Malaysians united in opposition to a range of others. To be Malaysian is to be the antithesis of the poor backward outsider, be they low-wage migrants, victims of human and sex trafficking, or refugees and asylum seekers. As one commentator for the *New Straits Times*, a leading English-language newspaper in the country asserts,

> How do we know Malaysia is the Promised Land? Simple. Ask the millions of Indonesians, Filipinos, Bangladeshis, Chinese, Indians, Nepalese, Myanmars, Africans, and yes, even Mongolians, who made Malaysia home inspite [*sic*] of grave risk to life, limb and nationality. . . . In fleeing the poverty, oppression, repression, disease, catastrophes, ravages, depression, and unending feuds and bloody wars of their respective homelands, the alien horde perceived, correctly, that Malaysia is a sanctuary, a haven that shields them from being discriminated, downtrodden, exploited, enslaved and murdered.
>
> (New Straits Times February 20, 2010)

Nowhere is the diversity of migrant nationalities more glaring than in Malaysia's world-class city. At KLIA, the main port of entry, transnational migrant men are in the low-wage frontline positions of trolley pushers, baggage handlers, and cleaners. In 2008, this prompted the deputy prime minister to make clear that Malaysia Airports (in charge of managing KLIA) was not allowed to employ migrant workers: "Tourists feel they are in a foreign land when they arrive in Malaysia. The government wants a Malaysian face to greet tourists at the airport, not a foreign face" (Associated

Press January 8, 2008). Despite the tourism minister's pronouncement, "We do not allow hotels to employ foreigners as frontliners for the simple fact that we want locals to be employed as many of them are jobless," many Malaysians refuse to occupy these positions (New Straits Times February 12, 2008). Migrant men continue to be placed in low-wage frontline positions, such as that of parking valets and bellhops, while migrant women are housekeepers and servers in the city's hotels.

The economy's dependence on the low-wage labor of migrant men and women from diverse nationalities provokes much ambivalence and anxiety in Malaysians. While the continued in-migration of workers signifies the rise of a prosperous Malaysian nation, their physical presence also informs "an apocalyptic vision of a Malaysia overrun by outsiders" (Williamson 2002, 413). As the deputy prime minister's statement implies, migrants' physical characteristics and conduct constitute "figurative borders" that necessitate their removal from frontline positions in favor of those who look and act as if they belong to the nation (Chang quoted in Romero 2006, 449). Processes of racializing migrants are based on the nexus of physiognomy, culture, and nationality.

In the world-class city's contact zones, "a Kuala Lumpur obsession is to guess the national origins of the servants, waiters, factory workers, and bus conductors laboring in the tremendously porous Malaysian labor force" (Williamson 2002, 412). This "obsession" is an unanticipated outcome of the state's migrant diversification strategy. A text message that made the rounds to mobile phones in KL succinctly captures the public's association of specific threats with specific migrant nationalities:

> Get Vietnamese workers, dogs missing;
> Get Bangladeshi workers, Malay girls missing;
> Get Indonesian workers, money missing;
> Get Indian workers, jewellery missing;
> Get Chinese workers, husbands missing.
> (The Star September 28, 2007)

Newsprint reports and neighborhood rumors of Vietnamese migrant men kidnapping and eating household pets, for example, became such a perceived problem that a member of Parliament urged employment agents to "educate migrant workers not to cook cats and dogs" (Associated Press February 26, 2007). Absent were discussions on why the migrant men would eat Malaysian household pets, if indeed they did: the assumption is that they simply were predisposed to do so. The physical embodiment of a Vietnamese person then signifies specific national-cultural traits.

Bangladeshi migrant men workers, on the other hand, have been accused of "charming" Malay women into marrying them, so much so that the state was compelled to ban their in-migration for two years (some migrants then entered on student visas and proceeded to work without state approval). The Home Affairs minister rationalized it this way: "They have blue eyes and look like Hindi film actors and they create social problems here" (New Straits Times March 13, 2006). Public discourse on Pakistani migrant men elicited similar reactions:

> A while ago, there were debates within the Malay community on the plan to bring in Pakistani workers. Often lulled by Hindi movies, there were many in the community who were concerned that the Pakistanis' movie star looks may compromise the virtue and modesty of Malay girls.
>
> (New Straits Times June 6, 2007)

As racial-cultural bearers of their community and by default the nation, Malay women have to be protected from their perceived weaknesses that leave them vulnerable to these men.

In 2008, the state's explicitly paternalistic stance toward Malaysian women was articulated by the foreign minister's proposed solution to reports of Malaysian women being used as international mules by drug traffickers. His proposal prohibited single women from travelling out of the country if they had not secured prior approval from their families:

> Foreign Minister Datuk Seri Dr. Rais Yatim said the letter would be a declaration which stated clearly the reason the woman was travelling. . . . "Many of these women (who travel alone) leave the country on the pretext of work or attending courses and seminars. With this declaration, we will know for sure where and for what she is traveling overseas."
>
> (New Straits Times May 4, 2008)

The proposal was withdrawn amid highly vocal criticisms from the public and NGOs.

Transnational migrant women also have not escaped state and public scrutiny. For the past few years, there are newsprint reports of migrant women's "rent-a-Malaysian-husband" scheme: they offer cash to Malaysian men who will marry them so that they can stay legally to pursue sex work. In 2009, migrant women reportedly offered Malaysian men RM1,500 to do so. The fees increased in 2011 to anywhere between RM3,000 and RM20,000 for men willing to marry women from the PRC, Vietnam, and other Asian countries (New Straits Times March 23, 2010; The Star February 20, 2011).

With the exception of a brief period in the late nineteenth century when the colonial state approved the in-migration of "self-declared prostitutes," the state's immigration regulations prohibit migrant women's entry for participation in what is considered an illegal and immoral activity (see Chapter Four). Migrant women who do not or cannot enter on valid work permits may elect to "rent-a-Malaysian-husband" or travel on migratory pathways created by state liberalization of the tourism and education sectors. In any case, transnational migrant women engaged in full- and part-time sex work are seen to threaten the social and moral fabric of the Malaysian family and nation, in addition to sullying the global city and country brands.

In 1998, the minister of National Unity and Social Development publicly questioned the accuracy of data on prostitution in KL and Malaysia in the ILO's publication of *The Sex Sector* that examined thriving sex industries in Southeast Asia (Deutsche Presse-Agentur August 20, 1998). Since then, state authorities have identified and arrested women from Southeast Asia, South Asia, as well as the PRC, Russia, and Central Asia for engaging in sex work (see, for example, The Straits Times July 17, 2001; New Straits Times March 21, 2009). It appeared that migrant women sex workers' nationalities diversified together with the nationalities of migrant workers in approved economic sectors and industries.

Given women sex workers' many different circumstances—working for a syndicate versus independent; trafficked versus nontrafficked—and the illicit nature of sex work, there are no accurate data on the total number of migrant women sex workers or a percentage breakdown according to nationality in KL or the country. Arrest records of migrant women may shed some light, but even so, the state does not consistently release annual arrest records according to migrant nationality. Between 2004 and 2006, state authorities arrested 15,500 migrant female sex workers in the country, and 61% of them were from the PRC (South China Morning Post December 9, 2006). In KL, a five-year security operation known as "Ops Noda" led to the arrest of 8,893 sex workers, of whom 6,357 were migrant women (Bernama November 25, 2008). The Anti-Corruption Agency's director-general, upon discovering the involvement of high-ranking state officials (such as immigration officers who helped syndicates modify some migrant women's tourists visas into work permits), acknowledged that "it is a national security problem now" (South China Morning Post July 14, 2008). By 2011, data released on arrests of sex workers revealed a multitude of nationalities, including Thai, Chinese, Indian, Austrian, Russian, Uzbek, Ukrainian, and Nigerian. Women from the PRC dominated the list, followed by women from Southeast Asian countries (Malay Mail February 21, 2012).

Chinese sex workers' presence in KL and the country parallels the strengthening of bilateral ties between Malaysia and the PRC. In the early 2000s, the director-general of immigration responded to rising cases of Chinese women arrested for prostitution by insisting that young women tourists between the ages of eighteen and twenty-five had to be accompanied by their fathers or husbands in order to enter Malaysia. Formal complaints lodged by the PRC ensured his proposal's demise (The Straits Times July 4, 2004). When the state proposed approving the recruitment and entry of Chinese migrant women as domestic workers, middle-class Malaysian women employers vehemently objected out of fear that their husbands would succumb to these "sirens":

> There are also many stories of Chinese nationals who came here on dubious grounds twirling Malaysian males around their little fingers, or Malaysian businessmen having mistresses in China. The newspapers are often filled with reports of raids on karaoke joints, restaurants and massage parlours hauling Chinese nationals involved in vice.
>
> (New Straits Times June 6, 2007)

In the world-class city's Golden Triangle and suburbs, state authorities periodically raid business establishments and revoke licenses if they are found to harbor migrant women sex workers. Some of the raids have promoted "petit apartheid," or micro practices of racialized-ethnicized and gendered profiling, by business owners in the effort to minimize disruptive raids of their establishments:[6] "It is easy to pick them out [Chinese migrant women sex workers]. They are tall and slim, dress differently, and speak with an accent. Their manners are also polite compared to local Chinese women." One establishment went so far as to post the sign, "No women from China allowed," while others asked for proof of identification before they permitted some women customers to enter their shop (South China Morning Post December 9, 2006). Some of these practices have negatively affected Malaysian Chinese women who are perceived to look, act, and speak in a manner similar to Chinese women: the latter also have been denied entry by some business owners. Such petit apartheid practices indicate that "while branding and tattooing, or other forms of 'writing on the body,' are not used to distinguish between aliens and citizens, the practice of racial [and gender] profiling demonstrates that [presumed] citizenship status is inscribed on the body" (Romero 2008, 28).

Nevertheless, the authorities have practiced a form of "writing on the body" of migrant women sex workers, albeit not in the world-class city. In 2011, the police chief on the island of Penang responded to NGOs' criticisms of how his officers had treated migrant sex workers during a raid: "Some of them even ran into shops and tried to buy new clothes to blend in with female members of the public. Because of this, we were forced to mark X's on their bodies." Although he welcomed suggestions on how police ought to treat irregular migrant sex workers, he also insisted that "the NGOs should not just concentrate on what the police had done, but also look into the problems created by the prostitutes . . . they had wrecked many marriages and police had received numerous complaints from wives of men who seeked [sic] their services" (New Straits Times June 4, 2011). For him and other Malaysians, the sex workers are the issue, not their male clients.

In the same year, spouses of Malaysian men reported to the authorities that a prestigious Johor golf club employed Indonesian migrant women golf caddies who also offered sexual services for cash: "Enforcement officers raided the golf resort after they were alerted of 'suspicious activities' there by the golfers' wives who were unhappy that their husbands were spending longer than usual hours at the greens." Upon their arrest, the women caddies

> claimed that they were cheated by their employment agencies who had promised them a handsome salary with perks for working at the resort. Some of them had said that they were paid only RM500 a month as caddies and this had forced them to offer sexual services to the golfers as they had to fork out RM400 per month for their work permits.
>
> (New Straits Times April 17, 2011)

As the state diversifies migrant nationalities for many more approved service subsectors, some traditionally masculinized jobs gradually are opened to women, but at the same time, women's labor can be tacitly sexualized, as the golf caddies' was.

In light of extensive documentation (in newsprint, in academic research, in NGO reports) of unscrupulous and deceitful practices by employment agencies, the women caddies' claims of being cheated by their agencies are not unusual. At the same time, their claims also highlight a murky relationship between migrant women and sex trafficking in Malaysia.

On the one hand, some migrant women make false claims of sex-trafficked status when they are arrested in order to elicit sympathy from the authorities and to mitigate harsh punishments: "The irony is that willing sex workers confess to being trafficked women when they are caught in police raids while the real trafficked women deny their status" (New Straits Times September 27, 2009b; see also Agustín 2005; Aoyama 2009; Andrijasevic 2010; Mahdavi 2010). Police officials assert that sometimes migrant women also claim sex-trafficked status in order to break their contracts with syndicates (New Straits Times September 27, 2009b). In 2010, the authorities "rescued" 1,656 women from nineteen countries but only 484 were found to be "genuine sex-trafficking victims" (BBC August 9, 2010).

On the other hand, "the sex slaves from other regional countries are often ignorant women who are coerced or beaten into submission by members of the trafficking syndicates and readily 'confess' to police that they are sex workers" (New Straits Times September 27, 2009b). Irene Fernandez of Tenaganita, an NGO specializing in service delivery and advocacy on behalf of transnational migrants, has argued that

> most sex workers especially foreign ones are forced or tricked into it. [Fernandez] says while some do come into the country using social visit passes and stay on to work voluntarily as sex workers, those numbers are minimal as the syndicates that control the sex industry will try to force them out.
>
> (The Star July 26, 2009)

According to sex workers in this study as well as syndicate members (who draw the distinction between syndicates that participate in sex trafficking and those that do not), there are nontrafficked migrant women who work under syndicate protection as well as those who work independently in KL. The illicit nature of sex work and the larger repressive context in which transnational migrants live and work pose tremendous challenges in ascertaining who and how many migrant women are sex-trafficked, and at what stages.

The state's main response has been the 3D approach of detention, disempowerment, and deportation. More recently, it is being accompanied by the 3P approach of protection, prevention, and prosecution toward trafficked migrants. Arguably, state efforts to combat human and sex trafficking have been shaped more by pressure from the United States' Trafficking in Persons Report (USTIP) than by the domestic and international advocacy work of NGOs. In 2001, Malaysia was ranked in the bottom Tier 3 countries by the first USTIP. Passage of the Anti-Trafficking in Persons Act 2007 (ATPA) elevated the country to Tier 2. However, state authorities' failure to consistently enforce ATPA, in addition to persistent reports of migrant victimization at the hands of authorities, employers, and labor brokers, relegated the country back to Tier 3 in 2009. An amendment to the ATPA in 2010, together with periodic announcements of arrests of traffickers and the rescue of some victims, elevated the country back to Tier 2.

By and large, the 3D approach remains the state's preferred response to irregular migrants. This approach is reinforced by what are identified as migrant abuses of the tourism and education pathways. Some migrant women and men try to bypass bureaucratic red tape and the fees of legal work permits by seeking entry as tourists or students. Prior to August 2010, they were able to do so easily via the state's visa-on-arrival (VOA) facility, in which travelers could apply for their visas upon arrival in Malaysia. VOA was designed to attract desired categories of travelers. In 2007, and despite officially released data identifying "tourists" who had overstayed as those primarily from labor-sending countries such as Bangladesh, Myanmar, India, Nepal, and the PRC, the deputy prime minister insisted,

> There is no review, visa on arrival remains. We want to make it as convenient as possible for people to visit Malaysia, particularly the genuine tourist, the businessmen and investors so obviously it is a facility which makes us very open and sends a right signal to the world that we invite people to visit Malaysia.
>
> (Agence France Presse November 22, 2007)

At that point, the official rationale for retaining VOA was based on a need to cast the net widely to attract potential investors and tourists. The state's refusal to review VOA when confronted with data on visa overstays amounted to constructing and tacitly approving a back-door entry for transnational migrant workers, while retaining the coercive power to detain and deport "illegal" foreigners when deemed necessary. Hence, the immigration gates were left open for some to enter legally as visitors and fall out of status once they began working without state approval. By August 2010, however, the state abolished VOA because of rampant abuse by transnational migrant workers (Malay Mail August 13, 2010).

Even though Asian migrant workers dominated VOA's list of abusers, migrants from African countries have gradually become a major source of insecurity for KL residents. In the early 2000s, a security operation named Ops Gagak Hitam—"Operation Black Crow"—which specifically targeted irregular African migrants, found that men from West African countries (such as Benin, Mali, Liberia, Nigeria, and Cote D'Ivoire) worked as petty traders selling counterfeit goods in Chow Kit, and as pimps to Uzbek and Thai women sex workers. Many had entered as tourists, via KLIA and the Malaysian-Thai border. According to a high-ranking police official, African migrants somehow were able to draw on existing social networks in the city:

> These immigrants know exactly where to go and what to do . . . they all live around the Pudu and Sentul areas in apartments that cost RM1,000 a month to rent. There must be someone here setting things up—it could even be locals

renting out places from the owner of the premises and subletting it to African immigrants. It is organised to the extent that when we raid their rented apartments, each room has the same stove!

(New Straits Times February 10, 2002)

Immigration officers admitted that irregular African migrant men and women entered not only on tourist visas but also student visas with the intent to work and overstay:

We also found that large groups of Africans are staying in several parts of the country, especially in Kuala Lumpur, and their presence is causing uneasiness among locals. Most of them were found to have come in with student visas. Sometimes, those who come in with a tourist visa will switch to a student visa.

(New Straits Times November 19, 2009)

Newsprint reports elicit public anxieties that are then "confirmed" by KL residents' social networks, which tell of African men and women engaged in the drug trade, sex work, and other kinds of illegal-criminal activities in the Golden Triangle and suburbs such as Bangsar, Cyberjaya, and Puchong. Such anxieties, to be sure, are compounded by cultural misinterpretations. Some residents were quoted as saying

"It's extremely intimidating, because they [Africans] go about in large groups, talking loudly and drinking alcohol."

"The way they speak and stand can be very intimidating. Even the way they look at you."

"You can see that some are serious in their studies. But many others leave their apartments everyday [sic] wearing 'bling-bling.' The girls are no different—you can't help but wonder whether they are here to study or party."

(New Straits Times May 23, 2010)

The overall negative perceptions of African migrants have affected some tourists' experiences in KL. An African-American tourist recounted what had happened to him:

I was walking in Chinatown . . . when a gentleman in very scruffy type clothes, nothing that you would associate with police or anyone in authority, walked up to me and asked me, "Can I see your passport?" [I] was then taken, shackled, through Chinatown and put into a caged truck used by the Malaysian immigration department.

(BBC January 3, 2007)

He was joined in the truck by another African-American tourist. According to the two tourists, they were detained by plainclothes security officers who refused to show identification. Given the public discourse on African migrants in the city, anyone who resembles a black African is susceptible to racial profiling practices: "It became abundantly clear to [the two tourists] they had more in common than their nationality. Both they and every one of the 30 or so other people arrested in the same raid were black" (BBC January 3, 2007).

From the public's perspective, regular and irregular migrants are the main cause of rising crime rates, even though statistically they are responsible only for a very small percentage of crimes: "Many Malaysians blame the influx of migrant labour for the rise in lawlessness but police statistics show that only 1 to 3 percent of crimes are committed by foreigners" (The Straits Times August 1, 2009).

In 2007, newsprint reports of armed robbery, rape, burglaries, and other criminal activities perpetrated by migrants in KL led to a controversial Home Affairs Ministry proposal:

> Under the plan, the workers, mostly employed in the construction, manufacturing, and plantation sectors, will be confined to their ramshackle quarters— known locally as *kongsi*—which usually consist of zinc roofing sheets and plywood and are located inside or near their workplaces. The proposed rule will apply even on their days of rest, when many off-duty workers head for the cinemas, shopping complexes or beer parlors. If the new law is passed, it will see them confined to their quarters unless they have express permission from their employers to leave their workplaces. Employers will also be required to keep a logbook detailing the daily movements of their foreign employees for spot inspections by police.
>
> (Asia Times Online March 3, 2007)

Simply put, the proposal was for state-stipulated, employer-enforced "entrapment zones" to isolate or segregate regular migrants in the world-class city (Turner 2010, 244). Ultimately, Home Affairs retracted the proposal because of vociferous criticisms from employers and NGOs.

In the world-class city, public discourse associating transnational migrants with rising crime rates has fuelled the phenomenon of new gated multiracial housing developments distinguished by physical enclosures and security guards. Communities in relatively older upper-middle-class developments also have organized to hire private security guards and to install street-level closed-circuit surveillance cameras (The Straits Times August 1, 2009).

Thus, state implementation of the migrant diversification strategy, together with migratory pathways established by the liberalization of the tourism and education sectors, have had the effect of compounding public anxieties. The dominant perception is that KL continues to be invaded by unsavory foreigners because of the economy's demands for low-wage migrant workers, international tourists, and students. The large transnational migrant population—particularly the population of irregular migrants—is seen as an economic, cultural, social, and physical threat. In the effort to more effectively and visibly protect the nation, the state has pursued a unique privatization strategy based primarily on enlisting help from the citizenry.

Privatizing Security Operations

From the late twentieth century to the present, public discourse clearly demarcated lines between unwanted and wanted outsiders. During the 1970s, "irregular migrants" was the preferred phrase in reference to the former group. This shifted to "illegal migrants" in the 1980s, and "illegals," "illegal aliens," and "illegal foreigners" since the 1990s (Spaan, van Naerssen, and Kohl 2002). By the first decade of the twenty-first century, the presence of nearly two million irregular transnational migrant workers represented a crisis of immense scope for the country. As discussed, the Ministry of Home Affairs has assumed oversight of the country's internal security relating to transnational migrants, while other ministries and departments are responsible for monitoring and managing migrants in their respective areas.

Similar to receiving countries in the Global North, the Malaysian state is beginning to rely on biometric technology to register and track transnational migrants. State elites have called on the private sector to facilitate this process:

> Companies, associations, and the bodies keen to become agents can apply online on the Ministry of Home Affairs website. The companies should not act as outsourcing companies as their role is "to help the government reach out to the illegal immigrants. We wish to avoid similar problems faced in the past when we outsourced these tasks."
>
> (New Straits Times June 9, 2011)

In this way, for-profit and nonprofit organizations can assist in helping protect the nation against transnational migrants.

A more significant mode of privatizing security operations involves the state's expansion of the idea and practice of citizen volunteerism as embodied in the People's Volunteer Corps or RELA (Ikatan Relawan Rakyat Malaysia), run under the Ministry of Home Affairs. RELA's membership is open to any "healthy" Malaysian citizen above the age of sixteen (with the exception, for example, of those who already serve in the security forces or who are diagnosed with mental health problems): members come from "all walks of life, including the unemployed, traders, and farmers" (New Straits Times March 13, 2007).

At the end of 2010, the monthly electronic RELA newsletter announced that it had about 1.15 million members in the country: 72% men and 28% women (with another 1.4 million members who were not yet registered in RELA's electronic database). Within the FT of KL, there were 39,017 members: 30,119 men and 8,898 women. If the KL metropolitan area that spills into Selangor is taken into consideration, the total increases to 203,209 members: 141,454 men and 61,755 women (Ministry of Home Affairs 2010, 20). With a gender ratio of roughly three men for every woman, RELA is a masculinized civilian volunteer corps. There are no available data on breakdown of membership according to race-ethnicity. State elites' exhortations for RELA to be more inclusive (and their denial that one of RELA's brigades is linked to a Malay supremacy group) as it strives to meet the target of 2.6 million members, imply that the Malaysian civilian volunteer corps is comprised mostly of Malays (The Star February 3, 2011).[7]

RELA was established initially in 1972, following the May 13, 1969, conflict between Malays and Chinese, the two largest Malaysian communities. The Emergency (Essential Powers) Act 1964 and the Essential Regulations 1966 (implemented earlier to combat the spread of communism) provided the legal foundation for its existence. At that point, RELA's core objective was "to help maintain security in the country and the well-being of its people" (Hedman 2008, 375) by assisting security forces in maintaining public order via serving as the "eyes and ears of the government" (*"berfungsi sebagai mata dan telinga kerajaan"*) (Ministry of Home Affairs 2011). In other words, citizen-civilian volunteers were asked to help protect their nation against selected "insiders" whose actions threatened relations among the three major communities.

In 2005, the state revived RELA by specifically clarifying and broadening its original assist-and-monitor functions: this time, its core mission centered on "outsiders": transnational migrants. RELA's director-general confirmed that "the government had, from early 2005, directed Rela to address the problem of illegal immigrants. This task is now Rela's 'core business,' aside from other activities" (New Straits Times May 11, 2007).

Heightened public discourse on the crisis of irregular migrants in Malaysia provided the requisite justification for state expansion of RELA's functions and power. An amendment to the Essential Regulations 1966 accorded RELA members the right to enter any premises in the public and private domains; to request individuals for proof of eligibility to be in the country; and to stop and search any car, bus, van, train, boat, and plane suspected of transporting irregular migrants. The state authorized RELA members of officer ranks to carry weapons during their missions. Bluntly put, RELA was given the right to conduct armed warrantless searches for irregular migrants (who are known as "*pendatang tanpa izin*" or PATI). Between 2005 and early 2011, RELA could do so without police or immigration supervision: this volunteer corps enjoyed greater immunity than police and immigration officers, since its members were protected against any legal recriminations arising from their mission to search for and arrest irregular migrants.

In the earlier phases, the state paid RELA members RM80 for the arrest of every irregular migrant. In the midst of domestic and international criticisms, this reward scheme eventually was replaced by an allowance given to every member. The official explanation was that in most security operations, the total number of RELA members tended to outnumber the total number of irregular migrants who were arrested. According to an unnamed "government" source:

> Thus the final payment [RM80 multiplied by the total number of arrests], when equally shared among those involved in each operation, works out to be very little. As such, the Government feels that it is fairer to pay Rela officers an allowance [RM4 per hour for ordinary members and RM5.80 for officers] each time they are involved in an operation, as acknowledgement of their service and contribution.
>
> (The Star June 6, 2007)

RELA members also received minimal training in their security operations against irregular migrants. As its membership began to grow over time, the director-general of RELA admitted that it was impossible to train approximately two million members: only 8000 members would receive year-long full training while the rest participated in a one-day orientation course (The Nation [Thailand] August 20, 2010).

By privatizing key security operations in this way, the state transformed its citizen-civilian volunteer corps into an officially sanctioned, minimally trained vigilante "strike force deputized to hunt down illegal immigrants" (International Herald Tribune December 10, 2007). During a major security operation in 2005, state authorities "requested [the media] to provide coverage on the official crackdown on illegal immigrants" (Kaur 2005, 77). Publicity on raids, together with the state's other repressive measures, were expected to "put fear in [irregular migrants]" (Bernama February 13, 2007). RELA's migrant arrest records expose the world-class city's centrality to the state's project of removing irregular migrants from the nation: "Since March 1, 2005, until December 31, 2009, RELA have arrested 111,852 PATI throughout Malaysia. Selangor recorded the highest number by arresting 43,052 PATI, followed by Perak by the sum of 24,361 and Kuala Lumpur [Federal Territory only] for 24,361 PATI" (Ministry of Home Affairs 2011).

For approximately seven years after state expansion of RELA's powers, the citizen-civilian volunteer corps conducted raids of apartments, homes, workplaces, and even refugee camps and settlements in jungles:

> Terrorized by Rela, many of the migrants have left their apartment in the city and built shacks of leaves and branches in the surrounding jungle. But Rela pursues them here as well, the migrants say. [According to Doctors Without Borders,] "Some jungle sites are periodically cleared by local authorities, the inhabitants are displaced, valuables taken away and at times shelters are burned to the ground."
>
> (International Herald Tribune December 10, 2007)

Refugees have not been exempt from RELA raids. Despite the fact that some refugees possess UN identity cards (issued while they await resettlement to third countries), they nonetheless have been treated as "illegal aliens" by RELA. The state has refused steadfastly to ratify the 1951 United Nations Convention Relating to the Status of Refugees.[8] Malaysia's foreign minister offered the official rationale: since many refugees are economic migrants, they represent "a burden to our society" (New Straits Times March 9, 2007).[9]

RELA members have thus adopted a blanket approach toward protecting their nation against irregular migrants: detaining and arresting those who entered to work without authorization; those whose passports were kept by their employers and who therefore could not provide documentation upon request; and those who sought refuge from abusive employers, traffickers, conflict, or persecution in their home countries. During RELA raids, members have been reported to have indiscriminately physically and verbally assaulted migrant men, women, and children. RELA members also have arrested trafficked Myanmarese migrant women and men, sent them to the Malaysian-Thai border, and handed them over to traffickers who then either made the migrants pay more for transport to their home country or trafficked them back into Malaysia (New York Times December 10, 2007).

Publicity of RELA raids amplified how irregular migrants had infiltrated the nation: no places and spaces seemed free of them. The state, in turn, was portrayed as justified in the deployment of all means necessary, including and especially its citizen-civilian volunteer corps, to protect the nation. In their zeal to identify and arrest irregular migrants, RELA and other security forces arrested individuals who fit their profiles of irregular migrants from different countries. Two of the most embarrassing cases involved RELA's arrest of an Indonesian diplomat's spouse whose proof of identification was ignored, and an unannounced raid of an Indonesian student's home. His proof of identification also was ignored by RELA members (New York Times December 10, 2007).

State privatization of security operations in the form of a minimally trained paramilitary force could not but encourage the misuse and abuse of power. Suara Rakyat Malaysia, or SUARAM, a Malaysian NGO, wrote a memorandum in 2006 to the Human Rights Commission of Malaysia that documented cases of RELA members' assaults on migrants and theft of migrant possessions in the course of their security operations (SUARAM 2006). The director-general of RELA responded to overall public criticisms by stating, "We have stopped such volunteers from participating in raids," but he also indirectly challenged negative reports of RELA members' conduct by blaming the victims of the raids: "If there is cooperation between the illegal immigrants and Rela members during raids, then no problems will arise" (New Straits Times May 10, 2007). As if to further defend RELA members' conduct, he also insisted that irregular migrants have surpassed communists in becoming "enemy No. 2"—second only to drugs. (International Herald Tribune December 10, 2007).

In time, the state charged RELA with the responsibility of guarding migrant detention centers as well. These centers are full-fledged "zones of exemption" in which "illegal aliens" are physically and symbolically removed from the everyday life of the nation (Rajaram and Grundy-Warr 2004, 38). Despite newsprint and NGO reports of substandard food and living conditions (especially the spread of diseases) in these centers, the state reaffirms its volunteer corps' integral role in safeguarding their nation against unwanted transnational migrants. Further, RELA has been assigned the responsibility to help combat urban crime (for example, patrolling streets and assisting police) especially in the country's four major hot spots for crime, with KL at the top of the list (The Nation [Thailand] August 20, 2010; New Straits Times May 26, 2011).

By early 2011, the state began rebranding RELA to give its 2.6 million members greater cohesion and responsibilities in the "seven aspects of volunteer service, comprising its image, role, membership, program, physical presence, members' welfare, and organizational structure" (The Star February 3, 2011; see also Ministry of Home Affairs 2011). In March of that year, the state halted RELA's independent operations against irregular migrants (although the official announcement occurred a few months later): "The decision was made following complaints received, including allegations, that Rela members accepted bribes from illegal immigrants and their employers" (New Straits Times June 24, 2011). In the words of RELA's director-general, "The decision was made after considering the good and bad effects of the operations conducted since 2005" (The Star June 24, 2011). Persistent NGO and international criticisms of RELA members' conduct ultimately prompted the official announcement that the citizen-civilian volunteer corps no longer would be allowed to conduct raids against irregular migrants on its own.

Ostensibly, this decision signals the state's retreat from its unique strategy of privatizing some security operations by delegating key functions to citizen-civilian volunteers. Yet, RELA's relegation to an assistance role in security operations against irregular migrants (that is, only upon request of police and immigration), while guarding migrant detention centers and helping the police to stem urban crime, cannot but retain the state's ethos and practice of co-opting the citizenry in its effort to protect the nation against transnational migrants.

CONCLUSION

In lieu of a comprehensive and coherent policy on transnational migrant labor, the state's strategies of diversifying migrant nationalities and privatizing security operations reinforce a vicious cycle by magnifying the crisis of transnational migrants in KL and the country. The first strategy prevents dominance of one or a few migrant nationalities by officially expanding the number of labor-sending countries, as well as corresponding sectors and industries approved to employ low-wage migrants. Occurring alongside the two additional migratory pathways established by liberalization of the tourism and education sectors, the state's migrant diversification strategy directly and indirectly opened the immigration doors for many more migrant men and women for many more types of work. In KL, Malaysians' ambivalence and anxiety toward migrants are captured by the text message predicting specific types of migrant conduct according to ascribed racialized-ethnicized and gendered national cultural traits.

Malaysians who wish to actively protect their nation against transnational migrants are able to realize this via the state's second strategy of privatizing security operations, using citizen-civilians. The state initially empowered RELA to act independently in security operations against migrants, and then restricted RELA to act only in concert with trained security forces. Despite this change, RELA remains involved in guarding detention centers and patrolling urban streets. The message to irregular migrants remains unequivocally clear: there is no safe public or private place or space. RELA's existence symbolizes the postcolonial era of a culture of surveillance and control within and beyond the global city.

Notably, border control no longer is limited to security forces' patrols of territorial-maritime borders and surveillance-clearance at ports of entry. The state's dual strategies of diversifying migrant nationalities and privatizing security operations extend the ideas of "borders" and "border control" inward, to the everyday life, places, and spaces of the nation. While more and more expatriates and upper- and middle-class Malaysians live in gated communities, able to come and go as they please, it is neither a right nor a privilege for irregular migrant workers—and even some international tourists and students—to do so. Work sites, eateries, airports, shopping malls, homes, factories, construction sites, and so forth are considered internal borders of the nation and are monitored by citizens and security forces. Transnational migrants' experiences of these borders are shaped by intersections of their nationality, gender, race-ethnicity, class, and occupation. A person need only appear to be an "illegal"—in ways framed by negative public discourse associating migrants' physiognomies, nationalities, cultures, and genders with different expressions of illegality—for them to be questioned and detained by the authorities. Such actions exemplify racialized-ethnicized and gendered petit apartheid practices.

From this perspective, KL's thriving contact zones are characterized by sharply unequal power relations as the world-class city remains under surveillance by the state, its agents, and citizens. It is in this larger context that transnational migrant women enter to perform sex work.

CHAPTER 4

"What Is Wrong with Being a 'Miss'?"

Transnational Migrant Women and Sex Work in the Twenty-First Century

Essentially, treating women as victims of oppression once again places them in a male-defined framework: oppressed, victimized by standards and values established by men. The true history of women is the history of their ongoing functioning in this male-defined world, on their own terms.
—Gerda Lerner (1979, 148)

Transnational migrant women sex workers' presence in KL has its historical roots in the colonial era, wherein the British encouraged and regulated women's in-migration to address demands from the low-wage migrant male population, international traders, seafarers, colonial officers, and soldiers. From end of the nineteenth century to independence in 1957, however, the colonial state gradually moved to legislate prostitution as an illegal and immoral activity. Subsequent closure of the immigration gates meant that Malaysian women dominated sex work. Toward the end of the twentieth century, newsprint reports of transnational migrant women arrested for prostitution broadcasted their presence in the city once again: women's in-migration occurred in tandem with KL's ascendance as a global city.

Unlike Bangkok's Patpong, Singapore's Geylang or Tokyo's Shinjuku, an explicitly vibrant and thriving red-light district, with sex shows, go-go bars, and so forth, is not a signifier of KL's formal or informal identity. Nevertheless, this became a point of contention in 2006, when a member of Parliament likened Bukit Bintang to Patpong: he "was quoted as saying that the Middle Eastern friends he met recently told him that the sex activities made Malaysia 'better than Thailand'." The tourism minister, however, insisted that Bukit Bintang's massage parlors, nightclubs, spas, and foot reflexology centers were "clean and legal" (The Star November 26, 2006). One week later, another member of Parliament's comment that Bukit Bintang was ruled by pimps who "blatantly offered prostitutes to passers-by," prompted a reply from the deputy home minister that authorities conducted frequent vice raids in the area (New Straits Times December 5, 2006). RELA, police, and immigration officers periodically "cleaned up" Bukit Bintang and other parts of the city.

A major difference between the past and present is that women from a wider range of nationalities perform sex work in more places and spaces. As a networked global city, KL has become a destination and a transit site for migrant women within and beyond the region.

TRANSNATIONAL MIGRANT WOMEN, SEX WORK, AND THE COLONIAL STATE

In the precolonial period, Malay women sex workers were "slaves, servants, mistresses, and female followers of kings and Malay royalty": according to one account, they were expected to give their earnings to the ruler. When rural poverty increased as a result of the economy's monetization under British rule, more Malay women turned to prostitution as a chief means of caring for their families. A Malay writer in his travels to Kelantan on the east coast of the peninsula observed "'wild' women who visited commercial ships in the harbour in the evening" (Hasan 2005, 98).

During the colonial era, women from within and beyond Southeast Asia migrated to the peninsula for sex work. Historical records from the late 1800s show that Japanese women (*karayuki-san*) worked in Kuala Lumpur and Singapore brothels. Women's families and the state encouraged their out-migration as sex workers to offset the negative effects of an economic downturn. However, when the Japanese state banned migration prostitution in 1921, women who returned home were treated as outcasts, despite having provided financial assistance to sustain their families and the national economy (Warren 1990, 174).

Chinese women and girls composed the majority of migrant sex workers in British Malaya. Secret societies in China organized their recruitment, entry, and placement to address an overall ratio of two Chinese migrant men to one woman. In Singapore, the ratio had reached an alarming six men to one woman (Manderson 1997, 51). The women, as well as girls between the ages of thirteen and sixteen, were sent mostly to Penang, Malacca, and

Singapore (collectively administered under the British Straits Settlements), and eventually to bustling trading settlements such as Kuala Lumpur.

There were three types of Chinese migrant sex workers: those who were indentured for a period of time, those who willingly migrated for sex work, and those who were sold for sex work (Lai 1986, 29–30). Elderly women helped recruit many of them via deception, trickery, and abduction. The women and girls then "were auctioned to Southeast Asian traders in Hong Kong, who determined from which port they were sold on to local brothel owners, or secret societies from towns in the Straits Settlements and towns and mining camps in the Federated Malay States" (Manderson 1997, 55).

As an entrepôt, Singapore was the designated destination and transit site for women and girls en route to the peninsula, Thailand, India, Burma, and Indonesia. In the Straits Settlements, no restrictions were placed on the entry of so-called self-declared prostitutes so long as they did so of their "own free will" (Lai 1986, 28). Many migrant women and girls were sent to work in brothels controlled by Chinese secret societies; the remainder were bought as wives, concubines, or servants. Secret societies competed with one another to control the three interrelated economic activities of prostitution, gambling, and opium dens.

Brothels were ranked according to class, with high-class brothels serving wealthy men and lower-class brothels serving low-wage migrant men. Given their specializations in sex workers and corresponding clientele, brothels also were racialized-ethnicized spaces:

> Hutchinson's account notes that Chinese prostitutes were patronized by Chinese miners and planters, while women from other nationalities—Thai, Malay, European (often Jewish women from Eastern Europe) and Japanese women—provided entertainment and sex mainly for Europeans. There were also some Tamil women, who may have primarily worked with Indian plantation laborers or merchants; and some Japanese women who were patronized by Chinese men.
>
> (Manderson 1997, 52)

Specifically, KL's High Street and Petaling Street (located in what is now known as Chinatown) had Chinese brothels with a Malay "kip" shop or brothel nearby (Manderson 1997, 51).

Chinese secret societies' stranglehold on the business of selling sex prompted the colonial state to implement key legislation designed to increase its revenue base and, at the same time, protect military personnel from the emerging public health threat of sexually transmitted diseases (STDs). The Contagious Diseases Act 1870 stipulated licensing of brothels and routine medical examinations for sex workers "with the intention of protecting British soldiers and sailors from infection" (Manderson 1997, 56; Lai 1986). The colonial state required every brothel to maintain a registry of sex workers by name, age, and nationality.

The office of the Protector of the Chinese issued sex workers so-called protection tickets that gave them the right to file complaints against brothel owners: upon arrival in British Malaya and prior to brothel placement, women and girls were given the tickets that had to be in their possession at all times.[1] In 1890, there were thirty-nine registered KL brothels with a total of 533 Chinese, twenty-four Japanese and four Tamil women. Two years later, "the number of brothels had risen to 45, with 798 Chinese, 26 Japanese, 3 Malay, and 2 Tamil women, and in 1893, the number of brothels increased further to 50" (Gullick 2000, 91).

At the end of the nineteenth century, the colonial state repealed the Contagious Diseases Act in favor of the Women and Girls Protection Ordinance of 1888, because of pressure from public discourse on white slave traffic and prostitution back in Victorian Britain. This ordinance criminalized sex trafficking of women and girls, prohibited the participation of girls under the age of sixteen, and eliminated medical examinations for sex workers. Brothels could still operate, but they had to be registered with the authorities. Rescued girls were sent to homes such as the Po Leung Kuk (initially known as Office for the Preservation of Virtue) with "rehabilitation" programs that trained them in domestic tasks. Many of the young women eventually were married off while others were placed as domestic workers (Tan 2003, 21). Not all of the women consented to "rehabilitation", for example, there were reports of women running away and if captured, they were sent back to the home and "if they failed to settle in, they were then sent to the lunatic asylum" (Crinis 2004, 142).[2] Three years later, the ordinance was expanded to prohibit women with STDs from working in brothels.[3]

The combination of rising STD cases in British Malaya and trans-Atlantic discourses on "white slave traffic" in the 1920s prompted the colonial state to adopt an even stricter stance by banning the entry of self-declared prostitutes and by selectively licensing brothels.[4] The practice of selective brothel licensing reflected an explicit class bias; that is, licenses were issued for high-class brothels and denied for all others (Lai 1986, 36). By the early 1930s, the colonial state bowed to international pressure by banning all brothels and prohibiting the entry of migrant women for sex work.

This legislation marked the beginning of an explicit state-initiated "domestication" strategy or "a strategy of expulsion [of sex workers] . . . an attempt to banish an assertedly sexualized 'vulgar' Other from the public space" (Ruhne and Löw 2009, 233). Yet, the colonial state's outright ban on brothels as clearly delimited, classed, and racialized-ethnicized spaces for sex work did not eliminate prostitution so much as encourage hybrid spaces, comingling prostitution with other services. While some sex workers still walked the streets in search of clients, others participated in the "sly prostitution" of clandestine brothels, coffee shops, lodging houses, restaurants, and nightclubs (Lai 1986; Manderson 1997; Crinis 2004).

MALAYSIAN WOMEN, SEX WORK, AND THE POSTCOLONIAL STATE

From Independence to end of the twentieth century, Malaysian women of Malay, Chinese, and Indian descent dominated sex work. KL's racialized areas of Chow Kit, Little India, Brickfields, Chinatown, and Bukit Bintang catered mainly to their respective working classes, while wealthier Malaysian men patronized luxury hotels. By carrying forward colonial legislation that banned brothels and the in-migration of women for sex work, the postcolonial state ensured Malaysian women's dominance of sex work until transnational migrant women's growing presence was reported in the world-class city.[5] Although the Penal Code continues to criminalize solicitation for prostitution, it does not explicitly criminalize prostitution per se (Malaysia 2006b).[6] The Immigration Act 1959/1963 (amended 1997 and 2002) bars the entry and employment of "prohibited classes" of individuals, including "any prostitute, or any person, who is living on or receiving, or who, prior to entering Malaysia, lived on or received, the proceeds of prostitution" (Malaysia 2006a, 13).

During the NEP era, Malaysian women's participation in on- and off-street sex work increased in tandem with rapid urbanization and industrialization policies that encouraged urban in-migration, expansion of the middle classes, military personnel in bases near urban centers, and exponential growth of the population of low-wage transnational migrant men (Nagaraj and Yahya 1998, 72). When young women (in particular, Malay women) began migrating from rural to urban areas, their exposure to city life combined with their dislike of low-wage and low-status factory work and housework led some to enter the sex industry or what has been called the "sex sector" (see especially Lim 1998). They joined other Malaysian women already in the urban areas.

According to the few studies of sex workers in KL, Malaysian women were found in all categories of sex work: they could be found on the streets, at open-air markets working freelance as well as for businesses (massage parlors and nightclubs) and escort services. Upmarket sex workers were freelancers or independent prostitutes (*pelacur bebas*), hotel prostitutes (*pelacur hotel*), and special prostitutes for corporate clients (*pelacur khas*).

An example of a former sex worker who straddled the freelance-hotel-corporate categories is Amy, a Malaysian Chinese woman in her late 50s, who now owns and operates a successful small business in KL. During the 1980s, she specialized in wealthy Malaysian Chinese businessmen ("leaders of our community"), whose assistants booked hotel rooms in the city for their bosses' afternoon trysts. Sometimes, at her clients' request, she also performed sex work for local politicians and executives from Japan and England. Amy knew of Malaysian Malay and Indian women who similarly worked by appointment in hotel rooms: their ability to command higher rates had as much to do with their physical beauty as their sexual skills. These upmarket sex workers' experiences were quite different from those in Chow Kit, Brickfields, and so forth.

Amy became a sex worker because, without the wherewithal to pursue higher education, her career options were limited. She refused to be a domestic worker despite some employers' willingness to pay higher wages for local women: "I did not want to be somebody's slave in the house." Even though she was proficient in the English language, she nonetheless chose not to pursue secretarial work because, "You and I know what many of them turn out to be . . . playthings, mistresses anyway . . . [We] can't blame them [the women], if the boss wants, are they going to say no?" Over the years and with financial advice from some of her wealthy clients, Amy wisely invested her earnings in real estate: "I don't have to work if I don't want to; I can live very comfortably from my rental income."

Zakaria's study of sex workers in KL during the late 1980s revealed that not all of the women came from working-class families; some of them were daughters of middle-class families. Many of them had entered sex work with the help of friends or other sex workers. They did so not because there were no other options, but because sex work was a relatively easy way to achieve a higher standard of living.[7] His study of women sex workers in KL sharply contrasts with a study based in the rural northern state of Kelantan, in which younger and older Malaysian Malay women pursued sex work as a result of the lack of education and employment opportunities. Between 1950s and 1970s, Malaysian Chinese syndicates in Kelantan already were bringing in women from other parts of the country as well as women from Thailand and Singapore (Hasan 2005, 104).

Nagaraj and Yahya's 1998 study is to date the most comprehensive publication on sex workers in the country. The general profile of a Malaysian woman sex worker was one who came from a large family but lived away from home; she tended to be a high school dropout and, in some cases, a single parent. The majority of women participated willingly and knowingly in sex work, with the help of friends and acquaintances (Nagaraj and Yahya 1998, 83).

The women chose sex work because their earnings were consistently far greater than they would earn at factory and domestic work or other types of low-wage work. And, "that the [earnings] differentials have widened over time may explain the sustained growth in the supply of workers to the sex sector." During the 1960s, sex work paid three times that of a factory worker's monthly wage. By 1989, the difference was six times greater (Nagaraj and Yahya 1998, 90).

Now, as then, the illicit status of sex work makes it extremely difficult to proffer even rough estimates of the total number of sex workers in the global city and country. During the late 1990s and depending on the formulas used, estimates ranged from tens of thousands to more than a hundred thousand women sex workers (excluding ancillary persons, such as pimps and "mamees" or older women recruiter-supervisors) in Malaysia. Within the FT of KL, very conservative estimates ranged anywhere between 3,000 and 16,000 women (Nagaraj and Yahya 1998, 86).

As a world class-city today, KL continues to attract young Malaysian women from more rural areas throughout the federation. Nur, for example, is a twenty-year-old on-street sex worker, who migrated against her parents' wishes three years ago from Kelantan to KL because she had heard so much about the city and she wanted to experience it. Nur completed some secondary school education but chose not to continue, as she did not like to study. Shortly after her arrival in the city, Nur stayed with a friend of a friend who introduced her to a young Malaysian man. He persuaded her to try sex work so that she could earn enough income to stay in the city. She agreed to do so: both of them rented a room in a makeshift house and he became the boyfriend-pimp who lived off her earnings.

Nur works only in the evenings near a major bus depot: she walks around while he makes arrangements with potential clients at the depot. The clients mostly are working-class Malaysian (mainly Malays) and low-wage transnational migrant men. Sometimes she uses condoms, but often she does not, in order to please the clients. She rarely ventures to work in Bukit Bintang because the area is known more for *pelacur asing* ("foreign prostitutes") and she does not see herself as having the level of sophistication to compete successfully.

The share of income Nur's boyfriend-pimp gives to her averages RM30–50 per night. Sex work allows her to experience life in the world-class city away from her family in rural Kelantan. During the day, she and her friends visit shopping malls to look at new clothes on display and to taste different types of food (*suka lepak*). Nur lives in the moment: she neither questions the nature of her relationship with the boyfriend-pimp nor thinks about what she will do in the future.

Her experiences differ markedly from that of Usha, a Malaysian Indian woman in her late thirties who originally came from the state of Johor on the peninsula's southern tip (connected by two causeways to Singapore). Usha's parents arranged for her to be married at the age of seventeen. By the time she was in her early twenties and after three children, her husband came home one day and announced that he had initiated divorce proceedings. With the help of some friends, Usha secured factory work in Singapore that paid S$700 a month. She was fired not long after, when her employer discovered that she had not completed secondary school. Usha then returned to Johor for factory work that paid only RM500 per month: her monthly wages were insufficient to pay for rent and feed her family. One day, a friend at the factory asked if she was interested and willing to move to KL for sex work. After Usha made arrangements with extended family members to take care of the children, she left for KL with her friend.

Usha and her friend rented a room in the Chow Kit area and worked the streets without a pimp or syndicate. Her friend's friend, who already was working there, advised them on how to evade the authorities, which group controlled what space, and so forth. Usha has never been detained or arrested for sex work because some of her regular clients are policemen.

Even though she finds sex work to be difficult, especially when she is tired or does not feel well, Usha never entertains any second thoughts about the decision to be a sex worker because of the imperative to provide shelter, food, and education for her children. Her plan is to retire to Johor at the completion of her eldest daughter's program of study in nursing.

During the mid-1990s, Usha's earnings averaged RM800 per week (with about six to seven clients per night). By the end of that decade, however, her income dropped precipitously because "the Chinese started to come in and [they] took customers away." Today, she remains in Chow Kit and her weekly income averages RM300–400, largely because she has a regular clientele of Malaysian Indian and Malay men, and occasionally Indonesian and Myanmarese migrant workers.

From Usha's perspective, the presence of *pelacur asing* in KL is negatively affecting Malaysian women sex workers' earning potentials. She uses the phrase *pelacur asing* not in reference to Indonesian migrant women who work in Chow Kit but rather, Chinese migrant women who work in other areas of the city and who charge substantially higher rates. Over the years, she has seen how Malaysian men, who generally could not afford to pay Chinese migrant women's rates, would save up just to experience a foreign woman with a lighter skin tone. In sharp contrast, "We [sex workers in Chow Kit] are like used clothes . . . cheap and dirty." Now as then, Chow Kit, Little India, and Brickfields have well-known sly prostitution spaces catering mainly to working-class Malaysian Malays and Indians, together with low-wage migrant men from Southeast and South Asia.

Usha pointedly draws a distinction between Indonesian women sex workers such as Siti, her friend, and *pelacur asing* by insisting that the former should not be placed in the same category as the latter: "Malaysian, Indonesian, what is the difference? She [Siti] is one of us." In one sentence, Usha tried to redraw the boundaries of "us versus them" in KL via a complex move intertwining nationality, race-ethnicity, and class. Given Chinese migrant women sex workers' growing prominence in the global city, Usha thus deliberately collapses the distinction between Malaysians and Indonesians by juxtaposing an expanded category of local darker-skinned women against the more exotic lighter-skinned foreign women from beyond the archipelago.

Usha's friend, Siti, is in her mid-twenties. She was raped at the age of fourteen by her father's friend. Shunned in her village, she had no option but to follow the man to Jakarta, where he sold her to a brothel. The brothel keeper beat her whenever she refused to have sex with a client. Within a year or so, Siti ran away with the help of a labor broker (a former client at the brothel), who smuggled her by boat to the west coast of Malaysia. She was introduced to another man who paid her passage and told her that she could work in a KL brothel until she paid off her debt. She succeeded in doing so by the age of twenty. Siti had never considered going to a shelter or rehabilitation center or to accept employment as a domestic worker because she had no interest in exchanging one type of confinement for another.

With the help of a Malaysian client, Siti somehow succeeded in obtaining a Malaysian passport and continued working in Chow Kit, albeit as an independent sex worker. Since then, she contracts with a local syndicate to arrange for her release (RM100 per occurrence) every time she is caught in a vice raid. Her weekly earnings range between RM300 and RM500 depending on the number of clients.

Sex work offers Siti a higher income and more control over her work conditions than her compatriots who earn RM400–700 monthly in domestic work. Siti's dream is to get married one day (to her live-in Indonesian boyfriend, who works as a messenger-driver for a small business) and raise children in a life unlike the one that she has led. Despite her strained relationship with family and villagers, Siti travels back to Indonesia every three months or so to give money to her younger siblings.

In the same way as Usha, Siti does not venture to work in other areas of the global city. Their work locations and experiences are reinforced by, and reinforce the association of, on-street sex work with a specific nexus of place, space, class, and race-ethnicity. The women know that they cannot compete with independent and syndicate transnational migrant sex workers in more affluent parts of the city. Their opportunities to work in other areas also are limited by the operations of larger, more powerful syndicates with their spheres of influence.

The experiences of these three on-street sex workers in KL illustrate pertinent points. Whereas sex work for Nur is the means through which she can afford to stay in KL and experience city life, Usha's objective is to be able to take care of her children. Siti, on the other hand, was a rape and sex-trafficked victim in her teens. Despite having paid for her freedom in KL, she continues sex work because of relatively higher earnings and the ability to control her time and work conditions. Usha and Siti explicitly view prostitution as work in which they exchange sexual services for money. Hence, they assert that prostitution in KL ought to be fully recognized as legitimate work in which women need not fear harassment by, or have to pay bribes to, the authorities. Aside from on-street sex workers, those in sly prostitution sites (such as massage parlors and restaurants) also are vulnerable to harassment and payment of bribes because of constant vice raids. On the other hand, spas in luxury hotels tend not to be targets of vice and immigration raids, primarily because of their locations.

Grace, a divorced Malaysian Chinese woman in her late thirties, is a masseuse in one of the Golden Triangle's luxury hotel spas. She began supplementing her monthly income with sex work after a bitter divorce prompted by her former husband's extramarital affairs. Grace was left with a broken heart, mounting debt from liens on their house (incurred by his spending), and a small child.

At the spa, Grace's male clients are hotel guests from Europe, East Asia, and the Middle East. To a lesser extent, she also accepts European female clients. Grace had no clue as to what a spa guest meant the very first time that she was asked to provide "extra" service to the woman. Grace excused herself to consult with the manager: "I had the shock of my life when [my manager] laughed and explained to me what the woman wanted . . . you believe or not, ah? I was shaking." Still in shock, she politely declined the guest's request. She revisited her decision as she continued to receive requests from women hotel guests for additional services. Depending on Grace's sense of the man or woman client (for example, personality, hygiene, and so forth), she may or may not provide additional services. If she does so, she first negotiates the fees upfront. She earns anywhere from an additional few hundred to thousands of ringgit per month within the protected enclosed space of the luxury hotel spa. Even so, as Grace has observed, Malaysian women like her increasingly are being displaced by transnational migrant women.

FIVE-STAR WOMEN FOR FIVE-STAR HOTELS: THE TRANSITION TO TRANSNATIONAL SEX WORKERS

As early as the late 1980s, the presence of "international prostitutes" (*pelacur antarabangsa*) already was noted in some hotels in the city (Zakaria 1987, 48–9). Early in the first decade of the twenty-first century, newsprint media began reporting the arrests of hundreds and eventually thousands of women sex workers from neighboring Southeast, East and South Asia, to as far away as Russia and the former Soviet bloc countries (see Chapter Three). Completion of KLIA, PTT, and KLCC, together with ongoing urban development projects and an increasingly neoliberal development path, elicited more demands and opportunities for all categories of sex workers from within and beyond the region. Their in-migration intersected with KL's transformation into a world-class city, and the state's visceral response was to "clean up" the city. For example, authorities frequently arrested on-street sex workers and raided known sly prostitution sites with the aim of sending an explicit message that neither sex work nor "foreign prostitutes" were acceptable in the city. The state's plan of creating five-star hotels with five-star shopping malls in the Golden Triangle provided an urgent rationale for doing so.

Syndicates based on sex work, some of which can be traced to colonial-era Chinese secret societies, answered by innovating new practices and spaces:

> Instead of reducing the size of the sector, the official crackdown appears to have served to make the sector more innovative, especially in using modern technology (such as mobile phones), managing the operations and making locations more mobile. Raids have considerably reduced the visibility of the sector in most towns.
>
> (Nagaraj and Yahya 1998, 77)

Some syndicates specifically upscaled their operations, while diversifying nationalities of their female sex workers. A syndicate member explained that "*Malaysia Boleh-lah* [the official slogan *Malaysia Boleh*, variously translated as 'Malaysia Can' or 'Malaysia Can Do It', encapsulates state encouragement of a can-do attitude for Malaysians]. They give us five-star hotels, we must give them five-star women. Right or not?" (see Chapter Five).

State efforts to visibly "cleanse" the city of sex workers brought about a similar outcome confronted by its colonial predecessor: sex work was driven further underground and indoors, not just to restaurants, standalone health-beauty spas and foot reflexology centers, but to all categories of hotels, apartment-condominium complexes, offices and shoplots, and housing developments in the suburbs (Bernama August 18, 2004). Neither on-street sex work nor sly prostitution sites catering to working-class Malaysians and migrant workers have disappeared in the city. Rather, they now compete with budget hotels and inns. More upmarket sex work is offered out of what normally are considered nonsexualized retail and office spaces of shopping malls and suburban shophouses, in addition to luxury residences. Luxury hotels, indeed, remain important spaces for upmarket sex work. Simply put, the state's domestication strategy of taming open and enclosed sexualized spaces has had the effect of sexualizing even more commercial and residential spaces and places.

Interviews of transnational migrant women sex workers for this study affirm KL's status as a world-class city in which opportunities abound for them to earn good income. Some women migrate on their own, while other women are recruited by foreign syndicates aligned with KL syndicates, or directly by KL syndicates via their connections to the women's friends or acquaintances. Migrant women enter singly (never in pairs or groups) on tourist or student visas; on work visas for authorized employment; and on rare occasions as "models." With the exception of one transnational migrant woman who, by all accounts, was trafficked at the age of fifteen, the women either knowingly migrated for sex work (and had prior sex work experience in their home countries or other global cities), or began sex work while employed in KL.

Women from the Region

During the colonial era, Singapore was the unofficial transit point for migrant women sex workers travelling to the colonial town and other urban areas in the region. By the late twentieth century, KL had become a transit city as well: "Thai and Filipino sex workers destined for foreign destinations are moved through Malaysia on to Singapore (although it is unclear whether Singapore is the final destination) and to Japan, sometimes after receiving training" (Nagaraj and Yahya 1998, 80). Indeed, some migrant women in this study travel from another global city to KL first, before moving on to Singapore, or vice versa (see also Lim 2004).

Arrest records indicate that for the past decade, women from the PRC have become the dominant nationality of sex workers in the residential and commercial spaces of KL. They enter and work independently (with the help of compatriots and Malaysian friends) or they do so under syndicate contracts. Of the twenty-eight Chinese women interviewed in this study, only four are freelancers. Linkages between Malaysian Chinese syndicates and their Chinese counterparts parallel strong bilateral political, economic, and cultural ties between Malaysia and the PRC. Some syndicate routes for women first involve nonstop flights directly from major cities in the PRC to KL, followed by global cities in the region, while others are less direct, for example Shanghai-Bangkok-Singapore-Kuala Lumpur-Sydney-Auckland-Taipei, and Hong Kong-Singapore-Kuala Lumpur-Taipei-Sydney. Syndicates refer to itineraries that involve more than one Asian global city as "Asian circuits." Figure 4.1 illustrates sample routes taken by Chinese and other migrant women sex workers within and beyond the region.

In recent years, it has become more difficult for Chinese women to enter Singapore directly or via Kuala Lumpur because of Singapore's stricter vetting of visa applications. Consequently, some syndicate itineraries bypass Singapore altogether, or Chinese women agree to circular migratory itineraries instead, for example, Shanghai-KL-Shanghai-KL or Guangzhou-KL-Guangzhou-KL.

If Chinese women are recruited via a KL syndicate's connections to individuals in the sending city, the KL syndicate handles all documentation on the women's behalf. If Chinese women are recruited via transnational connections between sending and receiving city syndicates, both syndicates coordinate their activities to provide the women with travel and entry documents. Chinese women either pay the fees prior to arriving in KL or they reimburse the KL syndicate upon arrival. Depending on the KL syndicate, the women also are responsible for paying monthly board and lodging fees (RM1,200–1700 or about USD400–566 at an exchange rate of RM3 to USD1) and syndicate "taxes," which run between 40 and 50% on their monthly income (see Chapter Five for more details on one syndicate's operations). Assuming that a Chinese woman has between four and five clients a day (any act beyond oral sex and sexual intercourse is subject to the woman's consent and attendant fee negotiations) at a post-tax rate of RM100–150 per client, she will earn a net income of RM400–750 per night and RM2,800–5,250 (USD933–1750) per week. The Chinese women claim that their syndicates permit them to decline requests if they wish to do so (but they still are responsible for monthly

Sample Routes Taken by Transnational Migrant Women Sex Workers

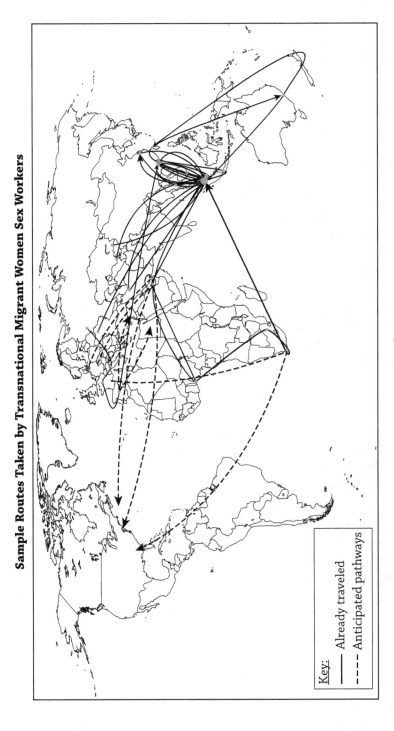

Figure 4.1: "Sample Routes Taken by Transnational Migrant Women Sex Workers"

board and lodging fees), and that they are free to come and go as they please outside of scheduled client times.

After syndicates pay for the women's initial health exams upon arrival, the women then are expected to pay and undergo weekly tests for STDs at syndicate-recommended clinics. The highest tier of women sex workers (that is, those specializing in VIPs) are tested every other day. Although some syndicates provide women with condoms, others do not.

Chinese women sex workers refer to themselves as "Misses" and sex work as work performed by a "Miss."[8] In this study, all of them took great umbrage at the respective Mandarin and Cantonese nouns of "chicken" and "goods" in reference to sex workers as crude and demeaning of their persons and work.[9]

During the course of fieldwork, a group of four Chinese women consented to speak with me as they ate a late lunch at a restaurant in the Golden Triangle.[10] They met each other when the syndicate assigned them to stay in one of its condominiums. All four had completed secondary school education and they decided to pursue sex work for different reasons.

Xiaofan needed to help take care of her parents but her first job (clerical work) in Shanghai did not pay her enough to do so. For Meizhen and Ning, sex work offered higher incomes than what they considered paltry wages of office and factory work. They emphasize that it is not just about the income per se, but that the income permits them to be financially independent and free from anyone else's control. One of their goals is to be able to travel and experience as many global cities as possible in Asia, Australia, and New Zealand, before venturing to the United States and Europe.

Although Jinghua shares this goal, she is known in their social network as being very thrifty with her earnings. Ning teases her by saying that, "If there is no driver to take her to the hotel, she [Jinghua] will walk instead of taking a taxi so that she can save money. Imagine how 'fragrant' she'll be when she sees the client!" Jinghua's main objective for engaging in sex work is to save money for her future; one that eventually includes pursuing a degree in marketing.

The tone of our conversation changes dramatically as the women discuss whether prostitution is degrading work. Each of them insists—augmented by head turning and banging of chopsticks on the table—that not only is it work, but that if women are smart, they need not labor in someone else's home, office, or restaurant for minimal wages. Assuming the final role of spokeswoman, Jinghua elaborates:

> What is wrong with being a "Miss"? We work hard and do not cheat people. We earn our money with dignity. Look around you, look at that [Myanmarese cook at

a hawker stand across the street]. Look at the Indonesian servants. Should they be more respected than us? We earn in a month what they cannot dream of even in a year. Of course, if we don't save money, then the game is over [as she looked at Xiaofan, who apparently has a penchant for expensive designer handbags].

Meizhen then adds, "Everyone here [in the area] knows who we are. Yes, some give us their faces [signifying disapproval] and curse us but others leave us alone because we do not bother them . . . It is the police who bother us." Although the women are afraid of being harassed and caught in a raid, they also know that they are less vulnerable than those who work on the streets or in shophouse health spas and foot reflexology centers, primarily because they are protected by the syndicate. Syndicate protection means that their luxury condominium and clients' hotel rooms are less vulnerable to raids by police, immigration, and RELA. In the event that they are detained by the authorities, the syndicate will arrange for their release from detention and subsequent erasure of any records. Still, the women insist that the authorities frequently target Chinese women, in order to earn extra income from the women or from the syndicates (this is because Chinese women are more visible in public spaces, and many work under syndicate protection).

The women's clients are middle- and upper-class Malaysian men, and international executives and tourists. Once a woman accepts the client, a syndicate driver will take her to a designated hotel, condominium, or town-house. Upon completion of the session, she will call for pickup. According to Meizhen, on rare occasions, cash-rich middle-aged Malaysian Chinese hawker stall owners will request her services. She mostly turns them down because she considers the men to be crude and without proper education. Such hawkers lack the sophistication of her executive clients: "They are rough; they just grope me as if they have not touched a woman in a very long time." Meizhen's comment elicits a sharp rebuke from Jinghua, "Are you here to work or play? So long as they do not beat you and they tip well, why do you care?" The women always take condoms with them when they work, but whether or not condoms are used depends on how much extra a client is willing to pay for a condom-less experience. Ning is the only one who refuses to proceed even if a client offers more money because, "My health is more important than a few hundred dollars more."

In addition to Chinese women with only secondary-school education, there also are women such as Ruolan and her compatriot friends, who already have earned undergraduate degrees. They became sex workers first in the PRC because they were not able to pursue their careers after graduation (for example, with degrees in communication, political science, English), and they were very frustrated by their failure to do so. Ruolan came to know of KL from Tourism Malaysia's campaigns and by listening to Malaysian expatriates who shared information on their country's cultures, sites, food, and people. She then decided on a "change of scenery" path. For the past two years, she and her friends traveled in and out of KL with the help of a syndicate: "It is too much trouble to do it alone. They bring me the clients. I do my work and share the money." She works exclusively in luxury corporate apartments for a multinational clientele.

Similar to all of the migrant workers in this study, Ruolan did not tell her family what she did in KL or other global cities in the region (Singapore, Sydney, Hong Kong, Auckland), only that she has an executive-level job that requires constant regional travel. If her parents ever find out the nature of her work, Ruolan says, "They will commit suicide out of shame. Their university-educated daughter is a whore. . . . This is what they will say to themselves; it is what others will think and say, too. But for me, this is just another type of work. It is my body, not my heart or my soul." She explains further:

> Some women already have families with money, with connections. Others are fortunate to find good positions with companies. I worked very hard but couldn't get a good job with decent pay. . . . Shanghai, Shenzhen, Guangzhou, Hong Kong are very good places to do business, yes, but for those of us who come from the rural areas . . . even with university degrees but without connections, how many will succeed to have good careers, large bank accounts, live in brand new houses, buy whatever car they want and designer clothes? I am not ashamed [of sex work], but I need to protect my parents.

Ruolan plans to save enough money so that she can pay for graduate school overseas, eventually launch a career in the media industry, and purchase an apartment.

The Chinese women above participate in syndicates' Asian circuits. Asian global cities are chosen for these circuits depending on specific demands, opportunities in each city, syndicates' alliances, and women's ability and willingness to meet the demands. Other examples of Chinese women on these circuits are Chunying and Huifen, whose respective journeys began with migration from homes in the western and southern PRC to Hong Kong. From there, Chunying traveled to Ho Chi Minh City, and Huifen traveled to Macau and then to Bangkok for a very brief stay before arriving in KL. Despite local syndicate protection in those cities, the women have more positive experiences living and working in KL, because Malaysian Chinese syndicates assigned them to work only in luxury hotels, apartments, and condominiums. The women consider such spaces to be "cleaner" and "safer" than what they had experienced in the other cities.

Both women admit that their families would disapprove vehemently of their sex work. Nevertheless for Chunying, sex work mitigates what she believes to be her very weak intellectual aptitude that only promises a life of want (she had failed to secure a university seat—"I was not smart enough to go to university"). Huifen, on the other hand, had grown up observing how her parents struggled constantly to make ends meet while begging local authorities to assist them with their land during periods of drought: she made a promise to herself that she would be financially independent and not have to beg for assistance from another person. To maximize their time in KL, Chunying asked her syndicate mamee (women employed by syndicates to address migrant women's needs, and who may also be recruiters) to identify an intensive English language course so that she could perfect her command of the language before going to another global city. Huifen, who did not complete her university studies, wants to enroll in a computer science program so that she can gain a set of marketable skills: "All of us will grow old . . . so I must have insurance. I cannot do [sex work] forever."

In addition to luxury residential spaces, Chinese women also are in the more commercialized spaces of standalone health-beauty spas, foot reflexology centers, and nightclubs. At some of these spas and centers, syndicate men will stand outside to "catch" clients (international and domestic tourists, in addition to locals) and invite them inside to review booklets with pictures of women, which is followed by fee negotiations. Depending on the syndicate, Chinese women may also stand outside holding testimonial photographs as evidence of health benefits from various treatments.

The women net RM150–500 per day in addition to massage or reflexology fees. However, they serve more clients than their counterparts specializing in residential spaces. The women's accommodations are also less luxurious: they live in syndicate-owned flats located in lower-middle class neighborhoods, and they pay lower monthly board and lodging fees. Syndicate taxes, however, remain the same.

Syndicates' assignments of Chinese women either to residential or commercial spaces are based on evaluations of women's physical beauty, comportment, and command of the English language. Women specializing in residential spaces, more often than not, are those considered by syndicates and clients as "beautiful" (read: men's criteria that include unblemished, lighter or paler skin tone) and "classy" (read: exuding the confidence, sophistication, and consumption preferences of elite women). Migrant women in commercialized retail spaces, such as Quiyue and Qing, are of a lower tier or class of sex workers: less beautiful, less proficient in the English language, and hence less exclusive than the top tier.[11]

Quiyue worked in a Shenzhen factory before she discovered that some of her co-workers dressed up to go out at night and they returned flush with cash early in the mornings. When she finally figured out what they did in the night and asked to join them, some said that it never occurred to them to ask her because she was not particularly pretty, and she had not previously expressed any interest. In time, they were all recruited by men acquaintances for sex work overseas. As part of their "training," the women underwent quick courses on foot reflexology, massages, and facials. The sending and receiving syndicates then collaborated to arrange for their transportation and entry to the first Asian global city destination. Quiyue paid for the airfare and visa fees directly from her savings as did her friends, although she was aware of instances in which receiving syndicates paid upfront when their recruits could not afford to do so. The syndicates only charged for the exact amount because, "They are desperate for women. They even trained us [in spa services] for free."

In KL, Quiyue is assigned on a rotating basis among the syndicate's health spas and centers. Although she has to work harder and in less luxurious environments than top tier sex workers, Quiyue's income of thousands of ringgit per month is, nevertheless, far more than what she used to earn in factory work. Her goal is to purchase land on which to build her own house.

Quiyue is aware that although sex work is the road that leads to financial security for her, it still is stigmatized work that not all women can or should want to do. She has seen some compatriots turn to "little white pills" that make them feel good, even though the underlying purpose is to "deaden their hearts." For Quiyue, sex work may be bad work from society's perspective, but it does not mean that the women are immoral. However, those who do not succeed in separating their self-worth from what they do will be constantly "haunted by voices."

The case of Qing, to some extent, reflects this internal struggle. Qing had a very different reason for pursuing sex work. She needed money specifically to pay for her ailing mother's chemotherapy treatments (without disclosing the sex work to her mother). She first entered and worked in Hong Kong without authorization, but she did not like the environment because the Chinese there explicitly discriminated against less sophisticated or unworldly mainlanders. Often she lost clients to other women who were more experienced in attracting them. When a bartender acquaintance saw her crying one night, he asked if she wanted to work in KL instead, because he knew someone who could help her. Once she agreed, arrangements were made first for her to acquire foot reflexology training.

Although Qing's client schedule in KL is filled always, and she is able to pay her mother's medical bills, she intends to leave the profession once her mother passes on. Qing has experienced much "headache" and "heartbreak" as an irregular migrant sex worker in the global city. She finds her life to be "lonely" and of little meaning. Qing acknowledges that she desperately wants to build social relationships with other migrants and Malaysians, but she does not allow herself to do so because she is fearful of being exposed as a "prostitute" in general, and as a "foreign prostitute" in particular. Thus, she keeps to herself as much as possible despite the fact that her syndicate roommates are compatriot sex workers.

As syndicates' lower-tier migrant sex workers, Quiyue and Qing participate only in circular migration, as do the following four freelance Chinese women in this study. These women are able to migrate and work independently of syndicates primarily because they have developed social relationships over time with Malaysians or other transnational migrant workers. Meilin rents a bedroom in an apartment owned by a working-class Malaysian Chinese woman; Xuilan rents a luxury corporate apartment; Zhenzhen lives in her Malaysian boyfriend's apartment; and Baoyan stays in a budget hotel that rents by the day, week, and month. The women's freelance sex work substantially cuts down costs, because they do not have to pay monthly fees and taxes to syndicates. Their incomes, however, depend on the extent of social networks in KL, and whether they are able to evade vice and immigration raids.

Meilin and Zhenzhen initially contracted with syndicates, and branched out only after they had developed the necessary contacts, such as those of taxi drivers and hotel concierges. Xuilan, on the other hand, had traveled frequently as a tourist to Asian global cities before she decided to be an independent sex worker in KL. Of the four women, Baoyan, at the age of forty-two, is the oldest and most experienced freelancer, and has worked on and off in KL since 2004.

In the late 1990s, Baoyan's husband left her and their two young children to fend for themselves in one of the western provinces. She was too proud to ask her parents for financial help (her father was the general manager of a state-owned factory and her mother was a school teacher), so she found work in a factory. There, she met a man who told her to train as a beautician so that she could work for him in Singapore. He offered her three times the monthly salary of her factory work. The overseas job, however, never materialized because the Singapore state rejected her visa application. She then independently researched employment opportunities in

Malaysia, and with the help of a labor broker she was approved to work in one of KL's restaurants. Her parents agreed to take care of the children.

After a few months as a server, Baoyan quit the job because her pay (RM600) was too low and she had to work very long hours: "I was always exhausted and I did not earn enough even to survive." Her coworkers told her about a karaoke bar near the restaurant where, in addition to her monthly salary, she could earn tips for selling expensive drinks to customers. She did earn more but her income plummeted every time the bar was raided by authorities in search of "foreign prostitutes." Again, she said that the heavens had been looking out for her when one day, she met up with younger compatriots at a nearby hotel: "They told me that I could work as a Miss," and she would earn much more than one thousand ringgit a month. They taught her how to dress appropriately, comport herself, make eye contact with potential clients, and so forth.

From the mid- to late-2000s, Baoyan earned a very good income stream of tens of thousands of ringgit during each stint as a tourist in KL (she relinquished her work permit and went home before returning on a tourist visa). In recent years, however, it has become more difficult to do so because of raids by police, RELA, and immigration officers. Initially Baoyan contracted with a syndicate to arrange for her release from detention, which cost RM2,000 per incident. She discovered later that the market rate of security officers was only RM500 so she began paying for her own protection. In early 2011, Baoyan paid a total of RM7,000 to be released from detention.

She stays in a KL budget hotel for one month or so at a time after which she returns to the PRC for a two- to three-month stay before going back to KL. Her parents and children are not aware of what she actually does for a living: they only know that she travels frequently to KL for her work as a contract beautician. Income from sex work has allowed Baoyan to pay for both children's education while investing in real estate: "Think about it, after what I've been able to earn, how can I go back to 3000 renminbi a month [my wages at the factory]?"

Over the years of working in KL, Baoyan has come to know of "regular" syndicate and freelance Asian and African women: just like her, they are sex workers of their own free will. According to Baoyan, some women claim to be sex-trafficked when they are arrested because "they do not want to be treated by the police as 'bad' women who sell their bodies for money. . . . The police will pity them [as sex-trafficked women] and not abuse them." Such cases pose a tremendous challenge in distinguishing between trafficked and nontrafficked women sex workers. A high-ranking police official was described as emphasizing the challenge of ascertaining this difference:

Some, he added, made up stories of being trafficked into Malaysia by syndicates when they were picked up in police raids. . . . "Many of the women were able to service their debts in one or two months but trouble started when the syndicates kept on demanding money from them. Feeling played out and cheated, the women would seek the assistance of non-governmental organisations and the embassies of their respective countries. They never told the truth and would report that they were trafficked into Malaysia."

(New Straits Times, September 27, 2009a)

By claiming the status of sex-trafficked victim to prevent being abused and deported by the authorities or to break syndicate contracts, migrant women reveal the use of a unique avoidance strategy as the means to a specific end (see also Agustín 2007).

From Baoyan's perspective, there are two types of "coercion" with regard to women and sex work. If women are "coerced" into sex work by their need to feed children and take care of family, then "washing dishes by the roadside, picking up people's trash, taking care of their children, or working in a factory for little pay must be the same." In other words, she differentiates between women's exercise of agentic power in response to structural constraints, with that of women who are coerced or forced into sex work by another person's threats of physical harm to them or their family: "Women who are threatened, beaten, and forced by men to work as a 'Miss' are the people who should be saved. This is wrong but we are not those women. . . . It was wrong also to pay people like me RM600 for restaurant work. After deducting rent, what is there left?"

In her freelance work, Baoyan obtains clients via her social network that includes taxi drivers and hotel concierges, who will call or text her mobile phone for appointments on behalf of clients. She acknowledges that, on occasion, she has made eye contact with potential clients while strolling in luxury shopping malls.[12] She claims success because "I am skilled at catching them." She first will make eye contact with a potential client who is accompanied by his family. Once there is an implicit understanding, and if the man is interested in moving forward, he will return to the same place by himself shortly thereafter and take her to a nearby hotel.

Baoyan is able to work freely without syndicate harassment because syndicates in the area know that she neither works for a competing syndicate nor solicits clients in syndicate-controlled entertainment and health establishments. The cordial relationship that she established over time with some lower-level syndicate members also provides a degree of protection because they alert her (via text messaging) to ongoing or pending raids. This does not mean that all syndicates allow freelancers or women from competing syndicates to work in their spheres of influence. Baoyan has witnessed that some syndicates in KL deal with their competitors' sex workers by reporting the women's presence to the authorities.

In less than a decade, Chinese women appear to have displaced Southeast Asian migrant women (such as Vietnamese, Cambodian, Filipino, and Indonesian women) as the most in-demand nationality of sex workers in the city. During the early 2000s, Vietnamese and Cambodian women sex workers were reported to command double and even quadruple the rates of women from other nationalities: "It was learnt that the foreign women, especially the Cambodians and Vietnamese, charged between RM500 and RM1,000, depending on the services. Other nationals were believed to be worth between RM200 and RM600" (New Straits Times June 15, 2002). Since then, the novelty has worn off and the rates of Southeast Asian women have waned because of Chinese women as well as women from other nationalities.

Southeast Asian women, thus, are relegated mainly to lower tiers of sex workers who operate out of shoplots, working-class karaoke bars and nightclubs in the city, and suburban housing developments. Positioned at the bottom of the migrant women sex worker hierarchy are Indonesian and Nepalese women, whose clientele base mostly consists of male compatriots in the construction, agriplantation, and service sectors (see, for example, New Straits Times September 20, 2004).

An exception to the norm is Huong, a Vietnamese woman in her late 20s. When her supervisor (with whom she has never had any sexual relations) in Hanoi was transferred to KL, he asked her to accompany him as his executive assistant. She was flattered because women with training from secretarial colleges rarely, if ever, have the opportunity to accompany their supervisors for overseas assignments. While in KL, she got to know an older Malaysian woman who, one day, gently asked if she was interested in earning much more money as a "high-class" sex worker. Huong took some time to consider the ramifications, especially since she already had a boyfriend back in Hanoi. She consulted with friends in KL, who helped her work through the material benefits and social costs. Huong ultimately agreed to do so, because she saw another way to earn income for investments in real estate and publicly listed shares (potentially as retirement income) for herself and her family. Neither her parents nor boyfriend are aware of what she does in addition to the position of executive assistant.

Huong works by appointment, only on weekends. Her nightly income ranges between RM1,000 and RM3,000. The woman recruiter eventually asked Huong if she was interested in going to Sydney to work: given her pale skin tone, distinctive facial features and command of the English language, she could earn even more in Australian currency. All travel and entry arrangements would be handled on her behalf, and she could return to KL whenever she wanted to do so. Huong decided against it because "You cannot tempt fate so many times. I am not greedy; I just want to make enough to achieve my goals. I don't want to leave my position or KL."

Some transnational migrant women in the hospitality industry also participate in part-time sex work to supplement their income. Lia, a Filipina, is in her fourth year as a concierge for a luxury hotel. Prior to that, she had been a domestic worker in Singapore before she quit her job and returned home as the monthly wages simply were not commensurate with inordinately long work hours and constant verbal abuse by her employers. They treated her as if she was stupid and ignorant even though "I have a university degree [in journalism]." Lia first left the Philippines because she failed to secure full-time employment on which she could be financially independent, let alone contribute to her family of two parents, four siblings, nephews, and nieces in Manila.

Shortly after she quit the job of domestic worker and returned to Manila, a recruitment agency succeeded in placing her with a KL hotel because of her command of English, university degree, and "strong customer service" orientation. Initially, Lia earned RM1,100 a month as a concierge. She quickly discovered that some hotel guests gave generous tips for helping them with a host of requests, such as arranging dinner reservations, private tour guides, and so forth. Her entry into part-time sex work began when a European hotel guest asked her for restaurant suggestions and then wondered if she would join him for dinner. Lia said that she had never contemplated sex work and was shocked at the end of the evening when he gave her RM500 and asked her to buy something nice for herself. She recounted how she kept thinking about what had happened: "I did not feel dirty because it was not my intent. I liked him."

Lia has no desire to pursue full-time sex work because she wants to build a career in the hospitality industry: she places her career first, followed by her small but growing investments in mutual funds, and then, possibly, a long-term relationship. In the meantime, she only engages in part-time sex work if conditions are right, that is, if she likes the hotel guest and if he treats her "like a lady." Lia does not see herself as "a hooker, a whore, a prostitute, or a call girl" because "You are not what you do. Your character matters more." From her perspective, migrant women sex workers should never be denigrated by others because they are trying to make a living for themselves in the best way that they know how:

Why these women are looked down, I do not agree. Is it worse than being a maid? You read the newspapers . . . some are slapped, punched, and beaten by employers? For a few hundred ringgit, only if employers pay them? Why should this be more acceptable [than sex work] to society? Until we walk in another woman's shoes, we cannot say that we know her life and we cannot judge her.

Based on her knowledge of migrant women sex workers specializing in luxury and deluxe hotels, Lia asserts that "we must be careful not to generalize. Many of these women are not forced [to perform sex work] here. . . . Those [sex-trafficked women] are in *gelap* [dark] places only some know." She vehemently objects to the practice of forcing women into sex work. "If she wants to, then okay. If she doesn't, then she must be able to walk away . . . no harm to her or family."

In the position of concierge, Lia connects hotel guests, at their request, with transnational migrant sex workers. She and her male colleagues are paid on a commission basis by syndicates. The women are driven by private luxury cars to the hotel for encounters in rooms booked under pseudonyms and paid for either by the client or syndicate. Lia confirms the claims of some syndicate members that any physical violence on the part of clients will be dealt with swiftly by syndicate drivers who double as security for the mobile-phone equipped women.

Women from Very Distant Shores

The Malaysian state's policies on liberalizing tourism and education services to sustain KL's competitive identity as a global city have established additional migratory pathways not only for sex workers throughout the region including South Asia, but also for women from Africa, Eastern Europe, Central Asia, and the Middle East. At the time of field research, recruitment of full-time black African women sex workers appeared to be the near-exclusive right of one syndicate, based in a housing development outside of the FT but that operates throughout the KL metropolitan area. Women from Nigeria are the dominant nationality, although there are Kenyan, Gambian, and Ghanaian sex workers as well in the global city.

Three separate interviews of Nigerian women in their mid-twenties revealed that each woman contracted with the same syndicate and that they entered KL on six-month tourist visas. Upon arrival, they were taken to a local college, where they registered for a program of study. The syndicate paid their tuition and additional fees. The college then applied for student visas on their behalf. This is known as the "6 [months] + 1 [year]" system that allows women eighteen months of uninterrupted stay in KL.

Some women are based in suburban townhouses, whereas others are accommodated in condominiums and hotels.

The Nigerian women's migratory routes are similar to some of the Chinese women; that is, they work in other global cities prior to arriving in KL. From Lagos, Margaret migrated to Johannesburg and then to Cape Town; Ndidi migrated from Lagos to Dubai, followed by Doha; and Adeola migrated from Lagos to Dubai. Each of them paid approximately USD1,500 to the Malaysian syndicate for their transportation and visas to KL, with an additional RM1,700 in monthly board and lodging fees, and 45% in syndicate taxes on their incomes.

KL is a transit city or Asian hub for many of the women on their way to other Asian global cities before turning westward to London or a Western European city, or eastward to North American cities. Bangkok is not on their itineraries. This is unusual, given the city's history of sex tourism and the existence of several established African communities there (see especially Lehtinen 2004). Margaret offers an explanation that is supported by syndicate members. Although Bangkok is known as the sex capital of Southeast Asia, KL's larger syndicates generally prefer slightly older and experienced women—that is, upmarket migrant women are marketed to clients as offering the best in sexual encounters.[13] To be sure, larger syndicates also want to avoid harsh punishments for harboring underage sex workers (see Chapter Five).

Prior to arriving in KL, Margaret, Ndidi, and Adeola already had prior experience as sex workers. Margaret supplemented her income from petty trading with sex work in Lagos because she needed to help take care of her extended family. Since the emphasis was on educating boys with the family's limited resources, she and her sisters had to find work. Some of them cleaned and cooked in employers' households: It was a man's world, in that the women and girls had to make do with whatever life circumstances threw at them. Margaret refused to perform domestic work for what she considered very low wages and very restrictive work environments. Against her parents' wishes, she eventually left with friends (one of whom had a brother who worked in Johannesburg) in similar situations for South Africa.

When they first arrived in Johannesburg, the young women found work in a brothel servicing traders from all over Africa. Margaret and one of her friends left for Cape Town not long after, because the men had refused to use condoms and some treated them roughly. In Cape Town, they earned more working for a woman who brought them international clientele. Margaret quickly realized that she could not earn as much as some of her friends. Frequently, she was passed over by wealthy international clients because of her skin color: "Hey, I am too black for them [stretching out both arms to make the point] but I am proud of who I am." Once a Malaysian client asked if she wanted to work in KL, Margaret agreed, since she could travel, earn income, and experience the city's multicultural lifestyle, all while under syndicate protection. Ultimately, she plans to return to Nigeria in order to address a social injustice: her objective is to save and invest the income from sex work to build a school for girls.

Ndidi and Adeola, on the other hand, got involved in sex work while struggling to pursue their secondary school education. When Ndidi's family no longer could afford to keep her in school, she had to let go of her dream to be a "career woman." Compounding a bleak future were her family's expectations that she help care for younger siblings, very dim job prospects, and continued sectarian and political strife in her country. She came to the conclusion that "Life is all about money. Malaysians say, 'No money, no talk.'" In her home city, Ndidi was subjected to physical and verbal abuse by her boyfriend-pimp and some men clients, until an older client offered her the opportunity to work in Dubai. He arranged for her travel and accommodations. From there, she eventually left to work in Doha, before deciding to travel to KL. Ndidi planned to earn enough to pay for her university studies and an apartment somewhere in the west: "Near [a] university. This is my dream, to pay for everything myself."

Unlike Ndidi, who wants an education, Adeola quit school because she did not see the value of studying hard only to be jobless in her country. Given that her cousin, an irregular migrant worker in England, had failed to keep his promise to help her obtain an overseas education, she then decided to do the same as some of the young women in her class. When her mother arranged for her to marry a young man she barely knew, Adeola left home because she was afraid that her activities would be exposed, hence cause much turmoil for the family. A male friend introduced her to another man who operated a syndicate that arranged for women to work in the Middle East. She spent nine months working in Dubai's luxury hotels before accepting another syndicate's offer to work in KL.

The Nigerian women are acutely aware that they have to earn as much as possible before they are considered old and hence less desirable to clients. Ndidi explicitly makes the point that "Prostitutes are workers. We work with our bodies. Some work with their minds [pointing at me] but not us. This is our asset [hands running down her body]. We have to use what we are given before it goes away." None of the women's families are aware of their work: as Ndidi says, "I lie to them" in order to protect them from shame. Despite and because of how "girls [in her family] do not matter," Adeola remits money to her sisters and brothers whenever they send her emails recounting financial difficulties.[14]

Each of the women averages between RM150 and RM200 per client, after deductions of monthly expenses and syndicate taxes. Assuming that the women work six days a week with four clients a night, a conservative estimate of their monthly income is about RM14, 400 (USD4,800). In KL, the women's clients are not as broad-based as those of their Asian counterparts. Nigerian and other women from African countries occupy a niche market, with local and international clients (including male compatriots), who specifically request and are able to pay the rates for black women. Notably, none of the women has ever had a Malaysian Chinese client, largely because of the men's racial-cultural preferences or—bluntly put—their prejudices against black women. At the same time, some large Malaysian Chinese syndicates do not allow the women, who are protected by a competitor Malaysian Malay syndicate, to solicit in their business establishments or other spaces in their spheres of influence (see Chapters Five and Six).

Malaysian Chinese syndicate members and even Chinese women sex workers throughout the global city are known to call the authorities and report "black prostitutes," as if to remove an unwanted presence. Consequently, African women sex workers in KL are not as invisible as their Chinese counterparts, nor can they move as freely in public spaces. Inter-syndicate competition and the women's fears of detection and harassment by local residents and the authorities tend to keep many of them indoors. In this way, they practice a modified version of self-and externally-imposed "geographical sequestration" that minimizes contact among migrant women, and with specific residents and the public-at-large (Jeffreys 2009, 180).

Even so, the Nigerian women's working conditions far surpass those of a twenty-five-year-old on-street sex worker. Awiti has lived on the streets since the age of fifteen when her adopted father (*bapa angkat*) passed away. She either cannot recall her country of origin or refuses to name it; nor can she recall her birth family. Awiti does not possess any legal documents with her birth name and country of origin, nor does she possess a Malaysian identity card. For the past few years, she has been arrested and jailed two to three months at a time for solicitation. She was even hospitalized in a mental health ward for a few months ("I was mental-lah") before running away from the hospital. She denied my request and that of others to take her to a women's shelter by protesting vehemently that "I am like a snake-head fish," ("*Saya sebagai ikan haruan*") implying that she is strong, hardy, and able to survive anywhere.

Awiti lives in an abandoned house with a local transvestite. At night, they walk the streets in search of clients. Although Awiti says that she charges RM120 per session, often the men clients refuse to pay her after the fact. Sometimes, residents in the neighborhood buy meals for her, and restaurant owners permit her to use their water taps in the back alleys to wash herself. Policemen who patrol the area also tend to leave her alone, as do syndicates and migrant sex workers. The unspoken agreement is that Awiti can walk the streets so long as she does so quietly and without the aid of methamphetamines (on several occasions, residents had to call the police when, under the influence, she screamed and cursed at everyone). Whether or not she ever can or will recall her past, the only life she knows is the one in which local residents tolerate her, clients abuse her at will, and a transvestite does her best to protect Awiti. She appears consigned to a life on the streets in the world-class city.

In KL, there also are migrant women sex workers who come from countries farther away than West and East Africa. The Malaysian state's ongoing efforts to develop bilateral trade relations with Russia, Eastern Europe, and the Commonwealth of Independent States in Central Asia have established new air routes for the movement of trade and services, hence migratory pathways for sex work as well. For example, new ASAs connect Moscow and KL, Almaty and KL, and Tashkent and KL.

The women's presence in KL already was reported as early as the 1990s. Some allegedly entered as international students:

> "If it is found that many of the foreign students registered at a certain college are engaged in vice activities, then we will take action against that college. This includes barring the college from taking in any more foreign students," [Deputy Home Minister] Tajol Rosli said when asked to comment on a Berita Harian report today which stated that foreign prostitutes from Russia, Ukraine, Uzbekistan and Kazakhstan in particular, were becoming popular with locals. The report, based on statistics of prostitutes detained by the police, stated that although Indonesian women still made up the highest number of prostitutes detained, women from Russia and Uzbekistan were increasingly in demand while prostitutes from Ukraine and Kazakhstan had surfaced only this year.
>
> (New Straits Times August 15, 1997)

The women also entered on tourist visas:

> Girls from Uzbekistan are the most elusive among foreign women who enter the country to work as prostitutes, according to Malaysian police. The Harian Metro yesterday reported that the girls, who entered the country on a tourist visa, were able to evade arrest because they operated independently. They were also able to avoid attention as they operated in small groups and from different

hotels. The head of the gambling and vice branch, Superintendent Mohamed Fawzi Arshad, said that the Uzbeki girls offered sexual services through a fellow Uzbek who acted as their agent in making all the contacts with the clients.

(The Straits Times July 17, 2001)

According to syndicate members, there always have been fewer Russian, Central Asian, and Eastern European sex workers than those of other nationalities in KL because of the geographic distance and transnational connections of syndicates and individuals. Moreover, in recent years, frequent vice raids and KL syndicates' decisions have reduced substantially the women's visibility and numbers (see Chapter Five).

Ekaterina, a Russian woman in her late twenties, claims that she is a "model-consultant." Although she does appear on the catwalk at fashion shows now and again, Ekaterina also engages in what she calls "consulting" work for "very powerful VIPs." Her consultant fees reach upwards of RM10,000 (USD3333) per session. She had worked in Europe (including Bologna, Paris, Madrid) prior to Hong Kong and then KL. From KL, she is scheduled to travel to Singapore and then westward to a global city in the Middle East.

To her divorced parents' dismay, Ekaterina began modeling in her late teens because "there was nothing else to do" (she was not interested in attending university or working in an office). What she never told them was that she had fallen in love. Much as she knew that she would miss her younger brother (whom she protected), she left home to live with her French-Chinese boyfriend ("my first love"), whose connections landed her a job in a modeling agency. Their relationship did not last because of his jealousy and her temper. After one of their heated arguments, he threw away all her belongings and kicked her out of the apartment.

She would have been homeless if not for a friend at the agency. The woman introduced her to an opportunity that provided international travel and much more income than she could earn from modeling. Ekaterina pursued it partly to "forget" her boyfriend and partly for the promise of being able to pay for her brother's education and "keep him out of trouble" in Moscow. She did not disclose whether or not she works for a "firm." Rather, her international network is composed of VIPs: some older, wealthy clients pay steep consulting fees and give her gifts of jewelry, clothes, and on several occasions, private jet travel.

This type of consultancy sets Ekaterina apart from the rest of transnational migrant women sex workers, because she moves in social circles not known by the majority of people in KL and the other global cities. Although she claims that "I don't know any poor people [in these global cities]," she also cautions against the belief "that rich people are happy. No one is happy." Her highly paid sex work (which includes bondage, if she consents to a client's request) makes clients "temporarily forget" their unhappiness ("I am a professional"). Sex work for Ekaterina is the means to an end of retiring comfortably in an apartment that she had already purchased in Paris, and eventually, to establish or take over a haute couture boutique in the city.

Ekaterina distinguishes between her consulting work and the women who are "chained," that is, who neither hold their own passports nor enjoy unrestricted mobility in global cities (see, for example, Hughes 2000). The women cannot, under any circumstances, report their activities to the authorities because doing so risks physical harm to themselves as well as family members back home. However, Ekaterina warns against conflating these cases with those in which nontrafficked women and their families blackmail syndicates or individuals by threatening to report them to Interpol or local authorities for sex trafficking if they do not increase the women's income: "Sometimes [blackmail] works. Sometimes not . . . [the women] will be blacklisted." Ekaterina's point underscores complex criminal perpetrator-victim relationships.

Women such as Ekaterina are at the apex of KL's transnational migrant sex worker hierarchy: they are able to command the highest rates per session, largely because they are perceived and treated as "white." Also at the apex are Iranian women, whose physiognomic features and skin tones approximate that of Caucasian women. They enter on tourist and student visas with assistance from male compatriots or local syndicates, they stay in luxury apartments, and they cater only to very specific clientele networks.

Soraya, a twenty-six-year-old Iranian woman, was brought to KL by her boyfriend. She first migrated during her late teens to a neighboring country in the Middle East. There, she worked as a server in a restaurant before she met her boyfriend. After some months into their relationship, they were given the opportunity to travel and earn money as couriers delivering "packages" overseas.[15] This meant that Soraya could be with her boyfriend, fulfill her responsibility to her family (via remittances), and see the world at the same time. Upon request, she and her boyfriend will travel from KL to other global cities in the region such as Bangkok, Hong Kong, Sydney, Tokyo, Jakarta, and Singapore before returning to KL or directly to the Middle East.

When some of their business associates in KL noted Soraya's physical features and asked if she was interested in "escorting" VIPs, she agreed to do so. Her rates range from RM3,000 to RM5,000 (USD1,000–1,666) per evening depending on the total number of overnight hours. If she really likes her client, she even will refuse to accept payment. As she explains,

> My family is well taken care of. They received a lump sum payment of USD500,000. They live in a mansion and they drive Mercedes Benzes. Everything is in their name . . . I am satisfied. I have everything I need . . . I do this [sex work] because I want to. [My contacts in KL] treat me better here than over there [in Tehran]. Here, I have freedom. I have my boyfriend. No one makes trouble for us. We travel anywhere we want.

Soraya's boyfriend handles all the travel arrangements: visas, plane tickets, and lodging. She accentuates the point that her boyfriend is not a pimp, that is, she accepts clients only if she wants to, and she keeps whatever she earns from sex work. According to her, he does not take issue with such an arrangement, because he knows that she loves him. Her curt response to my question makes clear that not all of her clients are his business associates: "Not all the time. I know what you are thinking. Courier and escort are not the same."

Freedom for Soraya means freedom from what she considers religious and cultural constraints of living as a young woman in Tehran. In KL and other Asian global cities, she is free to be herself, especially to be with a man whose religious background never will be acceptable to her family or society.

Afsar, another Iranian woman, arrived in KL a few years ago to perform full-time sex work, but eventually moved to part-time in order to pursue another type of work. She first began sex work in Tehran and was encouraged to consider working in KL by a Malaysian client with syndicate connections. In KL, her clients similarly are considered VIPs: appointments are made via text messages on her mobile phone, after which she is driven to and from the designated sites. Her rate includes "a few hundred dollars" to accept a client's appointment, and at least RM5,000 for a four-hour evening. Unlike the majority of migrant women who pay 40–50% syndicate taxation rates, Afsar's syndicate charges 20–30% depending on the client.

Her family only knows that she is an executive in an international company, hence her frequent travel between Tehran and KL. She did not complete her university studies and has no intention to do so in either city: "I don't need a university degree to make money."

Over time, Afsar took on another job to which she refers only as "logistics": she earns even more from it than from sex work. Yet, she continues sex work, albeit on a part-time basis, because it is a reprieve from the mundane daily routine of shopping and dining in upscale establishments: "I enjoy meeting powerful men . . . their decisions affect many people."[16]

Several times during our conversation, Afsar would start discussing family members or childhood experiences in Tehran before catching herself only to say, "I don't want to talk about this." There seemed to be very painful memories associated with familial relations. For Afsar, life is to be lived "in the present" and she is circumspect, if not cynical, about future plans: "I don't know. Maybe I will travel somewhere else. Maybe I will have my own company. Who knows? Maybe I will meet and fall in love and live happily ever after. What do you think?"

Although Afsar and Soraya engage in part-time sex work as do Lia and Huong, the Iranian women's reticence in discussing their respective "courier" and "logistics" jobs imply that they are involved in the movement of illicit goods. In any case, whether migrant women pursue circular or serial migration exclusively for sex work or in combination with other activities, such practices cannot but highlight the world-class city of KL as one of the many regional and global "turnstiles" not only for credentialed professionals and low-wage migrants, but also for migrant women sex workers (Price and Benton-Short 2007, 104).

CONCLUSION

Over the course of a century or so, KL has transformed from a colonial trading settlement with primarily regional migrant women sex workers into a global city with migrant women sex workers from within and beyond the region. The colonial state's policies and regulations helped naturalize the racialized-ethnicized and classed nature of sex work, with different brothels for different classes of clients and racial-ethnic preferences, as migrant women arrived voluntarily and involuntarily to meet demands emanating from the bustling town.

In time, the postcolonial state's repressive legislation and closure of the immigration gates ensured that Malaysian women dominated sex work in even more spaces of sly prostitution. As seen in the examples of Usha and Nur, the state's domestication strategy did not succeed in eliminating on-street sex work. Malaysian women were joined by sex-trafficked migrant women such as Siti, who originally came from Indonesia. Meanwhile, Malaysian women such as Amy and Grace perform upmarket sex work in the more protected environments of luxury hotels.

Toward the end of the twentieth century, transnational migrant women sex workers in all tiers of sex work returned to meet growing demands as KL emerged onto the global arena as a world-class city. Despite immigration regulations designating the "prostitute" as a prohibited category of migrant, the state indirectly facilitates their entry via migratory pathways established by liberalization of the tourism and education sectors. Thus, a back-door policy parallels the state's front-door policy, allowing entry to migrant women and men for a range of jobs in the formal and informal economies (Piper and Yamanaka 2008, 168).

Whether transnational migrant women sex workers arrive under authorized employment categories or on tourist and student visas, the "women have found a way to navigate networks of migration for their own benefit" (Berman 2003, 46). Even as some women and girls are sex-trafficked to KL (such as Siti and Awiti) and other global cities that have become destination and transit sites, it has to be acknowledged that other women can and do migrate of their own volition for sex work. This point does not and is not meant to "valorize prostitution as a liberating profession" (Platt 2001, 12). Rather, it is to say that in the contemporary era, sex work has become another form of transnationalized work performed by migrant women.

Therefore, given countervailing forces in migrant women's lives, "[their] freedom to make autonomous, rational decisions about sex and sexuality as a money making mechanism must be acknowledged" (Sanders 2008, 709). Whether women migrate for sex work with the assistance of syndicates, boyfriends, friends, or acquaintances, their "mobile livelihoods" are shaped by their ability to identify opportunities and resources, and the strategies they use to ensure constant access to those resources (Briones 2008, 62). Transnational migration for sex work neither is the outcome of women's unconstrained agency, nor that of overly deterministic structural forces in which they are left helpless but to participate in sex work as a last resort. Rather, it is the result of mutually constitutive interactions between structural forces and human agency.

Despite differences in countries of origin and socialization, migrant women's narratives in this study reveal one common denominator that fueled their entry into sex work, that is, women's sense of family responsibility. Many of the women chose to migrate internally and transnationally for sex work to help provide financial assistance to their families and, in some cases, despite how they were treated by their families. At the same time, this familial imperative intersects with personal goals, such as the desire to own and operate their own businesses (Ekaterina and Margaret); a life free from religious or cultural proscriptions (Soraya and Ning); the potential to pursue education (Ndidi and Ruolan); unprecedented opportunities to travel and see the world (Meizhen and Adeola); and the ability to purchase land or homes (Quiyue and Huong). Migrant women's backgrounds and decisions reveal that "it is not abject poverty, brute force, or sheer deceit that propel them to migrate for sex work, but rather the desire for economic, affective, and geographic mobility" (Andrijasevic 2010, 28).

The migrant women rejected low-wage jobs, such as domestic and factory work, in their home countries. Even those with university degrees refused to settle for clerical jobs that were not commensurate with their academic training. For the women, transnational sex work offers a viable means by which they can imagine and realize dreams and hopes for their own future, amid the sense of duty or responsibility to kin. Whether they pursue the independent or syndicate route, migrant women's decisions are grounded in and arise from socioeconomic strategies crafted in the larger context of intersecting personal, household, national, regional, and global forces.

That the idea and pursuit of transnational migration for sex work increasingly has become an integral part of women's "imagination or mind work" today is revealing of the extent to which they are expected to—and do—assume individual responsibility for the betterment of their lives via participation in free markets (Mahler and Pessar 2006, 44). Global cities' sex industries offer another type of labor market in which migrant women can do so. Yet, the nature of this type of labor, together with migrant women's sense of family responsibility, expose a key paradox of global patriarchy in this neoliberal era. Migrant women's "freedom" to exchange sexual labor for income, and their "freedom" to lead independent lives, challenge and at the same time affirm gendered ascriptions, roles, relationships, and identities.

If the women accept low-wage gendered work in homes, restaurants, and offices instead of upmarket sex work, they could be valorized as hardworking migrant women despite very low wages in work environments largely beyond their control. On the other hand, if they disclose their sex work, this inevitably invites familial and societal denigration (as shameful daughters or illegal-immoral aliens who should be caught and deported immediately). From Jinghua and Lia to Ndidi and Ekaterina, nonetheless, the migrant women argue that sex work should be socially and legally considered work. Their assertions are informed by a critical awareness of the structural constraints on them, and opportunities delimited for them, in the twenty-first century, as aptly captured by Baoyan's discussion of "coercion."

Related to this are the migrant women's understandings of what Spindler and Spindler in another context call the "enduring" and "situated" self (Geoffroy 2007; Spindler and Spindler 1989, 1992). For many of the women, the "situated self" in sex work does not define the "enduring self" or who they are and their self-worth. While Ruolan articulates the distinction in terms of a separation between her physical body and her soul or heart ("It is my body, not my heart or my soul"), Ndidi references some women's comparative advantage by working with their physical assets in a limited duration of time ("We have to use what we are given before it goes away"). Lia's words, "You are not what you do, your character matters more," exemplifies migrant women's conscious distinction between the enduring and situated self in sex work.

Maintenance of this distinction, however, requires the women to constantly reaffirm the goodness of their character and sense of self in the midst of actual and anticipated hostile responses from society and family. Of the migrant women, Qing is the one who most visibly struggles with the fact that she performs sex work in a foreign city. Her response is to shut down emotionally and socially. According to Quiyue, some migrant women take illicit drugs to cope with a disconnect between the sex work that they perform and how they want to see themselves (that is, to silence the voices that haunt them). At the other extreme is Afsar, who embraces part-time sex work as a reprieve from the boredom of a materially privileged life in the global city.

In the world-class city of KL, migrant women sex workers' earning potential and related experiences are affected by their positioning in the hierarchy of transnational migrant sex workers. Women such as Ekaterina, Soraya, and Afsar, who exhibit Caucasian-like features, are placed at the apex of a racialized-ethnicized hierarchy premised on intersections of nationality, physiognomy, and tier of sex work. Next are Chinese women sex workers in residential spaces, followed by those in commercial spaces. Placed successively lower are Southeast Asian women with darker skin tones and, whose clients mainly are working-class Malaysians and migrants. Nigerian women's specialization in a niche market segment mitigates somewhat their positioning at the lowest levels. Still, they are not able to escape explicitly racist responses from Malaysian Chinese syndicates and Chinese migrant sex workers.

As transnational migrant women move from one global city to another, they are forced to navigate between who they think they are, and all that is ascribed to and expected of them as variously tiered "foreign prostitutes." As will be discussed in the next chapter, syndicates play an important part in constructing and maintaining these expectations.

CHAPTER 5

"We Sell Services; We Do Not Sell People"

Case Study of "Syndicate X" in KL

[I]n a system containing perfect internal order, such as a crystal, there can be no further change. At the opposite extreme, in a chaotic system such as boiling liquid, there is very little order to change. The system that will evolve the most rapidly must fall between, and more precisely on the edge of chaos, possessing order but with the parts connected loosely enough to be easily altered either singly or in small groups.

—Edward O. Wilson (1998, 97)

The previous chapter discusses two main modes of women's transnational migration for sex work: independent and syndicate-arranged routes and services. In the former mode, women's social networks help them obtain clients, avoid syndicate spheres of influence, and arrange for their release from detention if necessary. These women are able to keep more of their income than those who rely on syndicates. The dominant mode, nonetheless, is that of syndicate-facilitated entry from global cities in the Middle East, Europe, or Asia to KL and vice versa because, as one migrant woman explains, "It is too much trouble to do it alone. [The syndicate brings] me the clients. I do my work and share the money."

With the explicit and complicit assistance of a range of individuals (consular, immigration and police officers; taxi drivers; hotel employees), syndicates have been able to adapt to and thrive in KL's changing business and regulatory environment. As we shall see below, syndicates do not merely respond to clients' demands; they help shape demands for migrant women sex workers. "Syndicate X" is one among many KL syndicates that facilitate the in-migration and employment of women sex workers.

"DEMAND" AND MIGRATION-ANCILLARY INDUSTRIES FOR TRANSNATIONALIZED SEX WORK

At first glance, the phenomenon of transnational migrant women sex workers in global cities seems to attest to unceasing demands from men clients: "Male demand is a primary factor in the expansion of the sex industry worldwide and sustains commercial sexual exploitation" (Raymond 2004, 1157). Clients come from all types of occupations, racial-ethnic groups, nationalities, classes, religions, and education levels. Likewise, their motives for buying sex are just as diverse: sexual ineptitude, loneliness, desire for the exotic, a need to express sexual prowess, and so on (see, for example, Atchison, Fraser, and Lowman 1998). The fact that men can and do purchase sex is indicative of sexualized patriarchal power, exercised in diverse political-cultural contexts. Given prostitution's persistently socially stigmatized and illegal status in the majority of global cities and countries, men's exercise of sexualized patriarchal power in this way then can be likened to "entitlement in secrecy."[1]

A newsprint report of the major reasons underlying married and single Malaysian men's purchase of sex affirms this entitlement in secrecy. While some men pay for sex out of physical-sexual loneliness ("I am not married and do not have a girlfriend, so it gets lonely at times"), others purchase sexual convenience without the obligations and expectations that come with girlfriends or wives ("It is far easier to visit a sex worker as both parties know the deal"). Male clients also are made to feel like "kings" by sex workers. A Malaysian government employee who frequently paid for sex elaborates: "I am married with two kids. But yes, I visit sex workers several times a month. . . . They are mainly from Thailand, China, Indonesia, and Vietnam. . . . The girls know how to treat a man and make him feel like a king." A stockbroker more explicitly states,

> I have no qualms spending several thousand ringgit a month on service girls. . . . Whenever my girlfriend is outstation or abroad for work, I will visit my regular brothel and select a girl or two. I earn a lucrative salary as a stockbroker and this allows me to pretty much do what I want to do. I do not see anything wrong with what I am doing because it is entirely physical. There is no emotion involved. . . . The

place I frequent seems to be "protected" as it has never been raided by the authorities. And anyway, it is the sex workers who get arrested and not the patrons.

(New Straits Times February 7, 2010)

Neither girlfriends nor wives are aware of their partners' activities.

Malaysian men's exercise of sexualized patriarchal power was explained to me when I shared a meal with an informant's three male acquaintances at a restaurant. The three married men insisted that they had never paid for sex (for example, "I got a wife so no need for prostitutes lah"). Still, they seemed overly knowledgeable of who did what, when, where, for how long, and how much. One man invoked a phrase in Malay that encapsulates succinctly what, he argued, was the overall attitude: "*Saya harimau*" (literal translation: "I am a tiger"). I understood it to mean the sexual prowess of a tiger. His friend elaborated when I failed to ascertain the other meaning of this double entendre, "You don't understand ah? *Saya hari-hari pun mahu lah*" ("I want it every day"). His explanation identified two sets of forces at work: the men's self-perceived sexual prowess as a defining dimension of their masculinity, and the ease with which they can exercise it given the flows of transnational migrant women sex workers in KL.

The restaurant owner, a woman, eventually told me that the three men lied about their "innocence." Apparently, they had had many trysts with "foreign girls" because they treated the women to meals and drinks in her restaurant either before or after the fact: "Who doesn't know ah? They prefer the smooth white skin of Chinese chicks. Different one each time. Tell their wives, 'Business dinner, entertain clients.' You tell me, how many clients will rub your thigh underneath the table? Men are like dogs in heat."

At the level of the individual, men's purchases of women's sexual services may be said to be personal or shaped by their specific preferences and circumstances in life. At the structural level, however, it is not just the contextualized exercise of patriarchal power in which they can desire and purchase sex, but increasingly, their demands are shaped and met by groups that facilitate women's transnational migration for sex work. While much has been written about different organizational structures of transnational criminal groups that control some or all phases of sex trafficking, little is known of groups that organize the migration and employment of nontrafficked women.

"Migration industries" have arisen since the late twentieth century to handle different aspects of transnational migration for employment (Chin 1998; Massey et al. 2005; Castles and Miller 2009). These groups are composed of labor brokers, rental housing owners, NGOs, airlines, employment agencies, lawyers and so forth. In Kyle and Goldstein's conceptualization of weak and more robust models of migration industries, individuals and firms in the weak model profit from providing migration services without shaping migratory flows. In the more robust model, however,

> the combination of punitive and restrictive immigration policies, while giving economic markets more power to organize nearly all aspects of social and political life, lead to novel forms of migration industries that increasingly act as gatekeepers and exert much sway over the evolution of migration flows.
>
> (Kyle and Goldstein 2011, 2)

Similarly, there exist migration industries specializing in sex work: they shape, sustain, reinforce, or transform men's demands for women sex workers. These industries intersect with what Sanders identifies as "ancillary industries":

> These ancillary industries are similar to those that support any business, as the sex industry has similar needs to a legitimate business. The differences are that those who work and earn a living are unregistered labourers. The type of work can be legal (such as taxi driving, or supplying legitimate goods), or it can be illegal (such as protection rackets and drug dealing). Sometimes the activities are criminal and involve harm, exploitation and violence. Within these different labour relationships there are some common characteristics. The sole objectives are for all parties to make money and to receive cash profits that are unregistered. For instance, taxi drivers receive "kickbacks" from brothel owners if they bring customers to their establishment. . . . The nature and characteristics of the hidden sex markets demonstrates an entrepreneurialism borne out of opportunism and necessity as options for making money in the "normal" mainstream economy are not options for all.
>
> (2008, 712)

Taken together, these migration industries and ancillary industries for sex work are composed of participants in the formal and informal economies, ranging from travel agents, employment agencies, state agencies, airlines and consulates, to direct and indirect "profiteers," such as acquaintances, friends, pimps, drivers, syndicates, hotel concierges, and some agents of the state (Samarasinghe 2009, 40–1).

Despite legislation in many receiving countries that criminalizes prostitution and prohibits the entry of sex workers, the flows of and demands for transnational migrant women sex workers have increased rather than abated because of "the sustained capacity of the industry to adapt and rejuvenate" (Sanders 2008, 708). As industries in the formal economy adapt and rejuvenate within changing national, regional, and global contexts, so too do the migration and ancillary sex industries. Hence, it is not just clients' demands that fuel the persistence of prostitution; industry transformation attracts and financially sustains many more direct and indirect participants.

In this regard, global cities are prime sites for transnationalized sex work because they are nodes for flows of women and men. Within cities, migrant women's entry and positioning in hierarchies of sex workers are informative of contextualized ways in which existing and new demands are organized and institutionalized accordingly. The migration and ancillary industries for transnationalized sex work "may exploit existing demand within an established community, as well as exploit intersecting racial and gender stereotypes to meet, reproduce, or indeed, create a demand for their human commodities" (Turner and Kelly 2009, 195).

Even though some women migrate on their own or with the help of friends or acquaintances, extralegal or illicit groups are major anchors in the migration and ancillary industries because of the scope or scale of their operations. In anti–sex trafficking discourse, such groups are akin to "organized crime" (see, for example, Chu 2000; Block and Chambliss 1981; McIllwain 1999): they are large, hierarchically structured, sufficiently disciplined, and they have the necessary resources to conduct their activities transnationally. Even so, constantly changing business and regulatory environments encourage the development of different organizational structures.

An example is the business or enterprise model, in which groups are horizontally arranged and networked with looser ties to facilitate adaptive flexibility by expanding or contracting when necessary. It is argued that these groups' transitory or temporary alliances evince "transit crime" more than "organized" crime (Kleemans 2007, 163; see also Duyne 1996). Other researchers posit a continuum: "What we know about both smuggling and trafficking suggests that it would be more accurate to view them as a continuum, shading into and out of one another across a number of dimensions" (Kelly 2005, 238).

Importantly, Shelley's identification of six business-enterprise models illustrates the need to account for different cultural-political contexts, for example, the natural-resource model of Russians and Ukrainians, in which women are sold in ways similar to commodities; and the trade and development model of the Chinese, in which women's debt bondage is the main mode of control (2003). In some cases, there are open temporary alliances between groups of different nationalities-cultures, and in other cases, some groups may elect only to do business with members of their own diaspora. The diversity of groups and alliances expose a "global trade under local management," in which women are smuggled and trafficked for sex work (Turner and Kelly 2009, 193; United Nations Office on Drugs and Crime 2010b).

Regardless of groups' organizational structures and nature of their alliances, they are controlled and managed by men. Research has begun to problematize the gender dimension by questioning gender-neutral analyses or by highlighting women's participation in the groups, such as female recruiters' participation in the trafficking of women and girls from West Africa (Shelley 2003, 126) or women's participation "in running 'recruitment' agencies, organizing transportation and controlling respondents' work in street prostitution" (Andrijasevic 2010, 68). Even if some women occupy higher ranks in groups, their participation is shaped by gendered ideologies in highly masculinized operations.

The world of trafficking and smuggling migrant women for sex work then remains mainly a man's world, so to speak. Women are relegated to perform the kind of feminized responsibilities based on their presumed gender traits: for example, their perceived strength in communication-persuasion, attention to detail, and nurturing nature, as opposed to strategic thinking or financial management (see especially Agustín 2006, 2007; Turner and Kelly 2009; Zhang, Chin, and Miller 2007).

While research on sex trafficking groups in different regions of the world recognizes cultural specificities as well as changing organizational structures and operations, not much is known about who or what facilitates nontrafficked women's migration for sex work. This gap in knowledge cannot but encourage the automatic conflation of groups specializing in nontrafficked migrant women with those specializing in trafficking. The key question, then, is under what conditions have the former emerged, and how do they operate within contexts of changing national regulatory environments and the global economy?

The next section on Chinese secret societies provides the larger historical context from which emerged "Syndicate X," a contemporary KL syndicate specializing in nontrafficked migrant women. Its historical roots in a Chinese secret society, which controlled women sex workers via debt bondage, easily lead to miscategorization of Syndicate X as a sex trafficking group. The syndicate's business model at the outset also bears similarities to some of those groups. Nevertheless, it is markedly different because Syndicate X does not accept or control sex-trafficked women. Instead, it has a contractual relationship with migrant women: they provide specific services to the women in return for agreed-upon fees.

CHINESE SECRET SOCIETIES

In KL, groups that facilitate women's in-migration and employment for sex work are known as "syndicates" or "vice syndicates" in public discourse. Occasionally, they are referred to as "triads" or "secret societies." The latter two nouns invoke specific Chinese groups that existed during the colonial era. Depending on the colonial administrator-scholar, secret societies also were called *kongsi* or *hui*: "Kongsi is a generic Chinese term for a range of social and economic configurations that includes everything from business partnerships to clan and regional associations to secret triad societies" (Trocki quoted in Ownby 1993, 18).

Secret societies in British Malaya initially were thought to be "transplanted" versions of the original Triad, or Heaven and Earth Society, in China. During the late 1700s, a group of "militant monks" belonging to a Shaolin Monastery in Fukien Province helped protect the Chinese emperor against an invasion. After the fact, however, and at the behest of his ministers, the emperor set fire to the monastery. Only five monks survived and they made an alliance with one minister who had been sacked by the emperor for protecting them. The group quickly dispersed to evade the emperor's army. Wherever they went, the monks separately swore in new members via secret and elaborate initiation rituals. They swore to come together eventually and overthrow the Ch'ing dynasty (ruled by Manchus), in order to restore the Ming dynasty that was ruled by the majority Han people (Wong and Wong 1960, 99). This founding myth naturalized a revolutionary origin for the triad.[2]

When the Chinese emigrated to North America and Southeast Asia, they were assumed to have established secret societies in accordance with cultural practices back home. While one school of thought retained the conceptualization of secret societies as political opposition or revolutionary groups-in-waiting that emerged only during times of conflict (for example, at the fall of the Ch'ing dynasty and the rise of Sun Yat Sen, who called on Chinese secret societies' support from North America and Southeast Asia), others drew an analogy between secret societies' religious rituals and European freemasonry (Ward and Stirling 1925; ter Haar 1998; Wynne 1941).

Secret societies were "secret" primarily because of their rituals and rules. A book of rules discovered in an abandoned British Columbia lodge owned by Chinese miners revealed detailed rules governing rituals as well as miners' participation in the commercial enterprise (Lyman, Willmott, and Ho 1964). This secret society was integral to the establishment and maintenance of social order for single Chinese migrant men. In general, secret societies' rituals and rules evinced an "incipient democracy" or egalitarian social order with principles of equity and fairness (Trocki 1993, 91). This order, notably, applied only to men and not women.

In British Malaya, there existed a complex relationship among Chinese secret societies, the *kapitan* system, and the colonial administration. During the initial phases of colonial rule, the British relied on Chinese leaders, or *kapitans*, in the community to keep order, since they neither had sufficient resources nor personnel to govern effectively: "In Malayan towns, Chinese systems of authority developed under the veneer of British control" (Lees 2011, 51). The British modeled its *kapitan* system after the Spanish version; that is, a Chinese leader was "officially vested with certain executive, administrative, and, to some extent, judicial powers over his own people, and invariably acted as 'the channel between the Government and the community'" (Mak 1981, 26).[3] There emerged "a subsystem of indirect rule within the indirect rule system," in which Chinese secret societies organized around speech-group (for example, Hakka, Hokkien, and Teochew) and occupation, to govern their own members (Mak 1981, 27).

What the secret societies had in common was an established structure in which to integrate new male arrivals: "They provided immigrants with an organized group in which they could find a place for themselves in the absence of traditional territorial and kinship systems" (Freedman 1960, 35). Secret initiation rituals for newcomers were designed to instill loyalty and brotherhood. These groups functioned as part mutual aid and part enterprise:

> The kongsi was one of those social and economic institutions that can be considered a "carrier" of Chinese culture and history. The kongsis made it possible for the Chinese to leave their homes; to occupy territory in foreign lands; to set up functioning communities; to establish viable economic systems; and to maintain an organized social structure.
>
> (Trocki 1993, 94)

Secret societies gradually transformed during British colonial rule: membership became more diverse as the groups fought over control of economic interests and territories (Mak 1981, Chapters Four and Six, passim). Secret societies in British Malaya differed from those in China because of requirements for working and living in a foreign land. In China, triads rejected social outcasts, such as brothel operators, graveyard diggers, and coffin carriers. In British Malaya, however, men from all walks of life were eligible to be secret society members: "The contrast between the China Triad and local secret societies . . . is not surprising since both types of secret society emerged from different rationales and evolved into very different organizations" (Mak 1981, 58).

Before the British passed legislation that criminalized human and sex trafficking, brothels, and so forth, secret societies' businesses were not considered illicit or illegal activities.[4] Nonetheless, the groups engaged in turf wars to protect their revenue streams:

> Complex corporate activity in frontier environments frequently required armed might to protect the profits and the assets of the corporation. In addition, much "corporate" activity in these frontier environments was at least predacious if not criminal in many cases—for example, secret society involvement in drugs, smuggling, prostitution, and gambling in both South China and Southeast Asia—which made violence a frequent part of "corporate strategy" even if not all of these activities were technically illegal.
>
> (Ownby 1993, 16–7)

As one of KL's *kapitans*, Yap Ah Loy was a wealthy Chinese leader of the community and a secret society member who aligned his group with a Malay ruler against another secret society and their Malay ruler ally (in the so-called Selangor wars). He had his own security force, established rules of business engagements for the Chinese, and mediated intracommunity disputes as well as those between the British and the Chinese:

> Yap Ah Loy's most important roles during this period were economic and philanthropic. The kapitan personally held title to approximately two-thirds of the urban property in Kuala Lumpur east of the Klang River, including the main market, the gambling sheds, and the brothels . . . As a philanthropist, he built a refuge that offered food and shelter for the sick and he played a leading role in building Kuala Lumpur's first Chinese school.
>
> (Carstens 1993, 131)

Conflicts between secret societies escalated with British rule and commercial activities. Trocki's analysis of the Ngee Heng society in Singapore, which predated the British, ascertained that the society initially had coexisted autonomously and peacefully with the colonial administration, and even became an "unofficial partner of the *laissez-faire* state" in governing the Chinese (1993, 90). Ngee Heng did not compete against the British because their plantation exports were geared toward the Chinese market as opposed to European markets or commercial networks. Gradually, however, when successful Chinese merchants took over leadership of the group, they began to identify less with community members:

Wealth and economic dependency replaced loyalty and solidarity as the founda-
tions of Chinese life. The ties of brotherhood and mutual support that had originally reinforced economic relations within the society became the foundation
for a complex debt structure, and the secret society itself became a coercive
agency in the service of moneylenders and tax farmers, the wealthiest of the
Chinese *taukeh* or bosses.

(Trocki 1993, 90)

As a result, Ngee Heng split into factions. Competition between the factions
often led to bloodshed that ultimately warranted British intervention.

The British tried to exert direct control over secret societies with the
Dangerous Societies Ordinance of 1869, which required registration of
every group. When the groups refused to do so, the Dangerous Societies
Suppression Ordinance of 1882 stipulated selective registration, that is,
registration only of the most dangerous groups: those that refused to do
so would lose their role in indirect rule. Not only was this ordinance
ignored, but some members of a secret society brazenly attacked the
Chinese Protector, a colonial administrator assigned specifically to work
with the Chinese community. By then, the British feared that secret societies
collectively had become "an empire within an empire" challenging their
colonial power:

The powerful Chinese secret societies, which were sworn brotherhoods, had
enrolled a very large part of [migrant men] and took upon themselves many of
the normal functions of government in what amounted to an unmistakable
though not necessarily unfriendly disregard of the official administration.

(Jackson quoted in DeBernardi 1993, 227)

A few years later, the ordinance stipulated registration of those that had
"legitimate objectives" and that "all unregistered societies were considered
dangerous, and were subject to suppression by force" (Mak 1981, 56). It also
forced a transfer of all deregistered and unregistered secret societies' properties (except for religious temples) to the state (DeBernardi 1993, 214).

However, the ordinance did not succeed in eliminating secret societies.
Having given up their meeting halls and other material possessions signifying their identity, the groups went underground. One important change
was that members no longer could expect secret societies to afford the
same benefits and protection they once did:

Protection is available to members when they are victimized by others, but it does
not include finding employment for a member or protecting him on the job. If a

member is dismissed by his employer, the society does not interfere in the matter. However, if a member's family experiences a crisis, e.g., a death, the society makes a small contribution to the member concerned. The size of the contribution depends on the member's rank and on the quality of his service to the society.

(Mak 1981, 85)

In the decades that followed, some secret societies specialized in protection services that generated revenue "within their own operational territories." Besides operating their covert gambling dens and brothels, they also were known to "create a situation in which protection is called for, and then . . . provide the needed protection" to small business owners (Mak 1981, 82–6).

Secret societies obtained their operational territories via direct and indirect approaches. The direct approach required consultations among secret society leaders who controlled adjacent areas. The other approach entailed indirect challenges to another secret society (generally one that was smaller in size and weaker in control of its territory), such as demanding protection money from a business already under another group's protection. The business owner would be told to convey the message of change (Mak 1981, 88–9).

Members in secret societies mostly were young men in their twenties and many had only a primary school education. With slight variations, each secret society had the following structure: at the apex was the headman or a "big brother" responsible for negotiating with other big brothers; the treasurer kept accounts; "fighters" collected "subscription" monies from individuals and businesses while enforcing territorial boundaries; and ordinary members ranked according to length of time in and loyalty to the organization (Mak 1981, 63–4). This rigid hierarchy was sustained by and sustained discipline and order in the midst of a hostile environment.

By the late twentieth century in KL, the combination of rapid industrialization, which created more education and employment opportunities, and the postcolonial state's urban development and redevelopment projects, which reconfigured use of space and place, led to the demise of some secret societies, while fundamentally altering the structure and operations of others.

SYNDICATE X: ORGANIZATIONAL STRUCTURE AND OPERATIONS

KL has many syndicates specializing in trafficked and nontrafficked migrant women sex workers. According to syndicate members, there are syndicates that control all phases of sex trafficking; that is, they collaborate with transnational counterparts to control the recruitment, transportation, and control of migrant women in sex work. There are smaller local syndicates that "buy" trafficked women (Southeast Asian and especially Indonesian women) for their operations. Syndicate members travel to a remote site (often jungle areas) outside of the KL metropolitan area or even another state to view, select, and purchase the women, after which they are transported to urban centers for sex work or domestic work.[5]

In addition to syndicates that control sex trafficked women, there are small and large syndicates that offer the sexual services of nontrafficked migrant women. The smaller ones are less organized (some comprising only a few individuals) and more opportunistic: their operations depend on interpersonal connections and luck rather than systematic planning. These groups may be composed entirely of Malaysians, foreigners, or a mix of both. Large syndicates call them small fry or *ikan bilis* ("anchovy") operators. Some try to persuade migrant women already employed in the city to be sex workers or encourage competitor syndicates' women to join them.

Large syndicates specializing in nontrafficked migrant women are led by Malaysians of Chinese, Malay, and Indian descent, with more diversity at lower-level positions. Within the FT limits, some syndicates are headquartered in well-known areas of racialized sly prostitution. Beyond the limits, syndicates are located in newer housing developments. Depending on resources, networks, and negotiations among syndicates, operational territories extend to the entire KL metropolitan area or they are limited to the immediate environs.

Syndicate members claim that Greater KL has eight large syndicates. The majority of them are controlled by Malaysian Chinese men. They have the organizational structure, transnational ties, longer-term business plans, and strategies for accruing profits, mainly from nontrafficked transnational migrant women sex workers. These syndicates have their respective operational territories or spheres of influence. Phrased differently, although migrant women in all syndicates can work in luxury hotels and condominiums, they are not allowed to work in business establishments such as karaoke bars, massage parlors, health-beauty spas, or foot reflexology centers, which are directly owned by another syndicate or are under that syndicate's sphere of influence.

Inter-syndicate competition with regard to territories and the provision of upmarket transnational migrant women sex workers is tempered by inter-syndicate cooperation, especially in the subcontracting of migrant women during times of shortage. In the event that one syndicate is not able to meet a particular client's request, it will contact another syndicate and pay a one-time fee between a few hundred to one thousand ringgit, depending on the request. The receiving syndicate is expected to reciprocate when it is deemed necessary to do so. Migrant women's rates remain the same as determined by their respective syndicates.

Syndicate X is one of the eight major syndicates in the global city. It originated from a Malaysian Chinese secret society that had a tightly controlled hierarchical structure. It was led by a "big brother," and its members were working-class Malaysian Chinese men, many of whom barely had completed a primary school education.

From the 1950s to the mid 1990s, the secret society's revenue streams were based on protection or subscription monies from local businesses, and on on-street prostitution. Some "fighters" were responsible for collecting monthly "taxes" from restaurants, bars, and small retail shops, while others worked as pimps. Young women sex workers were recruited from Malaysian Chinese communities within the city and rural areas of the country. Many women worked under a debt bondage system (for example, they were "pawned off" by their families) that was exacerbated by very high interest rates in addition to board and lodging fees. Pimps guarded them on the streets, while mamees—retired sex workers paid by the secret society to keep the women from running away—kept an eye on them in the apartments. Mamees neither had much influence nor voting power within the group. As a retired syndicate member confirmed, "It was our [men's] world. Women were goods."

The secret society initiated members via elaborate rituals that required offering incense and food at an altar, praying for protection from harm, while swearing allegiance to the group. Similar to its colonial predecessors, the secret society had an extensive list of rules (oral as opposed to written), including those governing the conduct of business and punishments for transgressions. The big brother mediated internal conflicts. External conflicts were addressed first via meetings of all big brothers. In lieu of a satisfactory resolution, opposing groups would settle on controlled violence, that is, a day and time of retribution via wooden bats and knives. Besides its for-profit operations, this group also carried forward some of the mutual aid practices of colonial-era predecessors, such as feeding the poor and donating money to help cover funeral and medical expenses for its members as well as the community.

Toward the end of the twentieth century, however, a confluence of external and internal forces led to its transformation, as the secret society's two main revenue streams came under persistent attack. The state's ongoing reconfiguration of urban spaces and places to attract transnational capital involved the rezoning of land and the demolition of small, older business establishments in favor of large-scale mixed-used development projects that created hotels, offices, and shopping malls. The state's domestication strategy, characterized by frequent raids and detention of on-street sex workers, also put pressure on the group. As the physical and economic landscapes changed and as some older members of the secret society passed away, the remaining ones retired in favor of the next generation.

The younger men who took over leadership positions were not interested in what they considered backward rituals and rules that constrained innovative ideas and practices. Of the four known principals or leaders in this group, only one had prior ties to the secret society: he joined earlier as a result of his father's membership. Beginning in the mid-1990s, the secret society morphed from a tightly held, hierarchical organization with one leader into an organization with a relatively decentralized structure. The position of big brother or supreme leader was abolished in favor of four putative principals, responsible for their respective divisions or groups.

Since then, protection services have been replaced with legitimate income from the purchase of real estate and businesses. Instead of protecting businesses owned by others, the syndicate has invested in commercial and residential property, and it owns and operates businesses via an elaborate labyrinth of indirect ownership. Women recruited from different parts of the world have replaced local women. Within a short period of time, transnational migrant women in upmarket sex work took over from on-street Malaysian women sex workers. The traditional debt-bondage system gave way to month-to-month verbal contracts discussed prior to and reconfirmed upon migrant women's arrival in the global city.

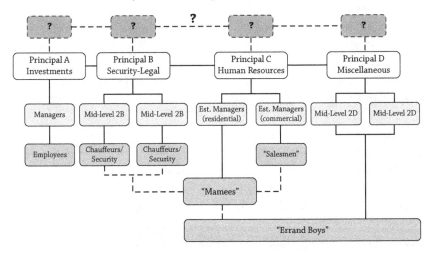

"Syndicate X" Organizational Chart

Figure 5.1: "Syndicate X" Organizational Chart

As depicted in the organizational chart (Figure 5.1), Syndicate X has a business or corporate-like organizational structure. The four male principals are in charge of investment, security-legal, human resources, and miscellaneous divisions. Principal A is responsible for sourcing new investments in real estate and other businesses. Principal B is responsible for security and legal matters relating to transnational migrant women sex workers. Principal C is responsible for employees in residential and commercial operations, including mamees and salesmen. Principal D is in charge of all miscellaneous matters. Simply put, A is the syndicate's equivalent of a chief investment officer; B is the equivalent of a chief counsel and security officer; C is the equivalent of a chief human resources officer; and D is the equivalent of a chief operations officer. This division of labor, based on specific specializations, encourages mutual dependency among the four principals. There may be even higher and more powerful leaders beyond these four, and if so, they remain in the shadows: lower-level members suspect their existence, but no one knows their names or has met them.[6]

Principal A and his group are focused solely on investment and recruitment opportunities. Principal B's group provides security for migrant women, including arranging their release from detention. Principal C's group is in charge of employees and operations in the syndicate's residential and commercial establishments. Principal D's group has responsibility for all miscellaneous matters, from arranging air transportation and visa applications, to managing the syndicate's internal correspondence and delivery of food to women in syndicate housing. The principals directly supervise middle managers in their groups who in turn supervise lower-ranked personnel, such as drivers, who double as security personnel; salesmen for sex work in commercialized retail spaces (men who advertise the benefits of services offered by their establishments); mamees; "errand boys"; and other employees. None of the four principals interacts directly with transnational migrant women or lower-level personnel. Although the majority of the lower-level personnel are young and older working-class Malaysian Chinese men, Malaysian Indian and Malay men also work for Syndicate X.

Of the four major principals, only Principal A is responsible for overseas recruitment of transnational migrant women. His extensive travels on behalf of legitimate businesses subsequently assist in the identification of overseas syndicates and the cultivation of possible alliances. Alliances with counterparts throughout Asia, Europe, the Middle East and, to a lesser extent, North America are not permanent: they shift in accordance with the quality of the relationships, the syndicate's needs in KL, as well as the syndicate's ability to provide migrant women for overseas partners.

Principal A, in consultation with his colleagues, assesses opportunities and emerging trends, after which he arranges with overseas counterparts to recruit migrant women. Conversely, he terminates existing alliances in favor of new ones or drops a labor-sending market entirely. Women's ability to migrate from a global city to KL, or to migrate from KL to another global city of their choice, depends on alliances established by Principal A, as well as the work of Principal D in arranging travel documents.

In Syndicate X's organizational structure, the four distinct yet interdependent units are connected by principals at the highest level. At the lowest levels, there are interactions, although less frequent, between Principal B's chauffeur-security personnel, Principal C's salesmen and mamees, and Principal D's "errand boys." While the principals are in charge of developing and managing high-level local contacts with individuals, businesses, and agents of the state in the migration and ancillary industries, middle management work with their level of counterparts in the city. This structure is designed to ensure that if and when migrant women or the lower-level personnel are detained in sting operations, vice raids, and immigration crackdowns, they are unable to disclose much detailed information regarding the entire business operations or identify upper-level personnel.

This organizational structure came about in direct response to forces described previously. As the state grew more intolerant of sex workers visibly walking the streets in the world-class city, new younger leaders radically revamped the former secret society's business operations. At the same time, the growing mass of international and domestic elite male clients with disposable income—from corporate executives to tourists—affirmed their decision to upscale and transnationalize Syndicate X's business operations (as in, "They give us five-star hotels; we must give them five-star women").

Similar to its predecessor, Syndicate X has mamees. Instead of guarding migrant women, the mamees are charged with taking care of their needs. Mamees tend to be former local sex workers who have had international experience, and they are paid to help ensure that migrant women have the appropriate apparel, demeanor, and skills to entertain elite clients. Mamees are encouraged to earn extra income by drawing upon their overseas networks to help recruit women for the syndicate. Recruitment fees range from RM250 to RM500 per migrant woman.

Mamees are ranked formally at the second lowest level, and they consider chauffeur-security personnel as occupying the base, or lowest level, alongside errand boys. The women are well-known in this syndicate for refusing to interact with or take instructions from these two groups of men. Mamees do not view the men as occupying the same social status, because the men are less worldly or sophisticated than they are, and they believe the men's work is less important compared to their own responsibilities (see Chapter Six).

Syndicate X does not buy or accept trafficked women because it requires "extreme control" of women and the penalty is "deadly" if syndicate members are caught by the authorities. According to a member in Group B:

> We are a business. We sell services [such as transportation, security, housing]; we do not sell people. We are brokers: women pay us for our services and clients pay us for "chickens" [colloquial Cantonese for sex workers]. . . . This is win-win, everyone wins. There is no need for force, no need to keep the women's passports, no need to guard them 24 hours a day. No need for headaches.

Moreover, whether or not some migrant women had been trafficked in the early phases of sex work did not concern the syndicate: "We have no control over what happened in the past. We can only control now by making sure that they are free to work, come and go as they please. . . . When they are happy, clients are happy, we are happy."

One preventive measure taken by Syndicate X is to ensure that transnational migrant women understand contract terms during the recruitment phase, and upon arrival in KL. Syndicate X recruits migrant women via overseas counterparts (and on occasion, via mamees' overseas networks). The syndicate pays finder's fees (ranging from several hundred to several thousand ringgit) to overseas groups, while migrant women pay for their syndicate-arranged air transportation and visa application fees. Once they arrive at KLIA, they are picked up by a driver and sent to one of the syndicate-owned apartments or condominiums. Mamees are charged with meeting the women and reconfirming contract terms.

If transnational migrant women do not pay associated fees prior to arrival in KL, they reimburse Syndicate X upon arrival for their air transportation and visa, as well as for the first month's board and lodging of RM1,700 (RM1,000 for housing and RM700 for local transportation, personal security, and food). Payment is expected upon arrival, because the leadership is intent on not continuing the debt-bondage practice of its predecessor. Once the women start working, Syndicate X deducts a 40% "tax" from their daily income. According to one member, "Why charge the women so much upfront [prior to arrival] when we can make at the back end? She walks away with lots of money, we walk away with lots of money." On average, the women will have anywhere between four and six clients per night (unless they are booked by one client for an entire night, which ranges between four to six hours).

Syndicate X's top tier of migrant women command the pre-tax rate of anywhere between RM500 and RM1000+ per session, whereas third-tier migrant women earn the pre-tax rate of RM200–250 per session. Assuming that a woman in the latter category has five clients a day at RM200 per session, her gross income for the day is RM1,000. If she works seven days a week, the total is RM7,000, giving her a monthly pre-tax income of approximately RM30,000. After deduction of her monthly board and lodging and 40% taxes, her income is approximately RM16,300 (or USD5,433 at an exchange rate of RM3 to USD1). If the same conditions apply to a top-tier sex worker at a conservative rate of RM500 per session and four clients per day, then her pre-tax monthly income will be approximately RM60,000 and the post-tax income is RM34,300 (or USD11,433). Syndicate X's monthly gross revenue (from women's board and lodging fees, in addition to 40% taxation rate) amounts to millions of ringgit (excluding overhead costs and income from legitimate investments, such as rental and sales income related to commercial businesses). Monthly revenues are augmented further by fees charged to freelance migrant women for arranging their release from detention. A key outcome of Syndicate X's contractual relations with migrant women is the reputation of treating them well: some migrant women have assisted in recruiting their friends and acquaintances in home countries. They are compensated at the same rate as mamees.

Syndicate X does not guarantee constant work or a certain income, and it permits a migrant sex worker to turn down any clients (although, as mentioned previously, she still will be responsible for her monthly board and lodging). During times of high demand, women are able to generate a very good income. During times of low demand, however, women potentially can experience income deficits and owe the syndicate monthly board and lodging fees. Even so, according to one member, "There is no low demand. Stock market collapse in 1998: high demand. [Global financial crisis]: still high demand. We have to borrow [women] from [other syndicates]." At any given time, the group has approximately 250–300 transnational migrant women on its payroll and averages about ten to twenty-five new entrants per month. The numbers fluctuate because some women may decide to migrate to another global city; some may have to leave so as not to overstay their visas (those on tourist visas will cycle in and out, depending on the length of their visas); and some may be on "temporary loan" to or from other syndicates. Although Syndicate X's target age range for sex workers is from eighteen to thirty years ("eighteen years old because the law says no young girls"), the majority of migrant women are in their mid-twenties: the syndicate's aim is to provide "experienced" women for their clients.

The syndicate offers three tiers, or classes, of transnational migrant women sex workers. Women at the highest tier cater only to local and foreign VIP clients, and for what are called "corporate parties." They are fluent in English and are considered some of the most beautiful migrant women, with a light or pale skin tone. The main nationalities are women from the PRC and Central Asian countries. Below this tier are women whose command of English may not be as good, and they may not be as polished, but they still are considered beautiful. Third-tier women are those with walk-in clients at health-beauty spas, nightclubs, and so forth.

Syndicate X eschews print advertisements and Internet websites, unlike other syndicates, in order to prevent running afoul of even more laws in the Penal Code. Rather, their extensive contacts as well as walk-in establishments generate a constant stream of clientele. The syndicate's list of the most elite clients is guarded so closely that even mid-level members are kept in the dark: chauffeur-security personnel drop off migrant women at prearranged sites and then drive away to await the women's phone calls for pickup.

The first and second tiers of migrant women sex workers are chauffeured to their clients. Syndicate X pays drivers RM80 a day if they use company cars (imported luxury models) or RM120 if they use their own cars (which must convey luxury). Upon conclusion of her session, the migrant woman dials a dedicated toll-free number on her syndicate-supplied mobile phone to request a pickup. Third-tier sex workers have "salesmen," who stand outside of the commercial establishment to attract clients. The syndicate prohibits chauffeur-security and salesmen from engaging in sexual relations with the women.

Syndicate X accepts only heterosexual male clients. It does not cultivate women clientele because "this is unnatural." In the same way, Syndicate X does not offer the services of men sex workers because this, too, is considered unnatural. According to one member: "What [other syndicates] do is their business, but we don't. . . . What man would allow his woman to go with a 'male chick'? Better get rid of her if she is so horny." Demands from elite women and gay men for male sex workers are met by syndicates and individuals specializing in transnational "modeling" and "body building" circuits.

Syndicate X specializes in migrant women on the Asian circuit of Hong Kong, KL, Singapore, Sydney, Auckland, and Taipei. The syndicate also offers sexual services of migrant women en route from the Middle East to Asia or from Asia to Europe. Some members confirm that more and more Chinese women prefer to participate in circular migration between major Chinese cities and KL, partly because of the Singapore state's denial of visa applications and partly because they enjoy the KL lifestyle.

The syndicate initially brought in Southeast Asian women, especially those from Vietnam and the Philippines, as well as women from Kazakhstan and Uzbekistan. At the time of field research, there were no women from the two Southeast Asian countries and only a handful of women from Central Asia. Syndicate X considers Vietnamese women and Filipinas to be "too low-class" for their operations. Over the years, they have become "cold dishes," deemed unappetizing to elite clients. Bluntly put, their novelty has worn off. The women no longer are considered beautiful or sufficiently sophisticated to command high rates per session. Although the syndicate still receives requests from its Philippine counterparts, it refuses to accept Filipinas because the women's reputation for being "fussy" (for example, making demands for additional amenities) does not warrant syndicate efforts in facilitating their entry. One member said that he was not surprised in the least by reports of Filipina women running away from their day jobs to be sex workers: "What they earn in one week, they cannot even dream of earning in one month as a maid. But the big bosses say 'Don't want anymore.' They are too difficult to manage." Thus, not only must migrant women conform to Syndicate X's norm of the upmarket sex worker, but they also have to be compliant or more demure than the allegedly assertive Filipinas.

With regard to Central Asian women, Syndicate X demonstrably prefers women whose physiognomic features resemble those of "white" women. According to some members, women from Central Asia must "look like white women" (as opposed to those of Chinese, Turkish, Mongol and other descents) in order to work at the syndicate's highest tiers. Syndicate X used to bring in Kazakh women, until their counterpart overseas asked for more money. According to the Kazakh group, some of the women and their families threatened to report the group to the police for sex trafficking if it did not pay them more money. The Kazakh group then asked Syndicate X to increase payment for recruiting women. Syndicate X refused to do so and ended their agreement. Syndicate X's experiences with Kazakh women supports Ekaterina's point on the challenges of ascertaining women's sex-trafficked status (see Chapter Four).

Syndicate X's numbers of Uzbek women have also dwindled dramatically in recent years. This is neither due to threats by women and their families nor vice raids. Rather, mamees, drivers, and even mid-level syndicate members' inability to quell verbal and physical altercations between Uzbek and Chinese women first led to the decision to house the women separately, and ultimately, Uzbek women's removal from the payroll (see Chapter Six for more details).[7] In place of "white" Uzbek women, Syndicate X's leadership has begun cultivating alliances with South African and Brazilian groups to explore the possibility of bringing in "white" South African women and light-skinned Brazilian women to promote interest in men VIP clientele and increase profit margins at the same time.[8]

These two countries are of specific interest to Syndicate X because of established and growing economic ties between Malaysian firms and their counterparts. The ties encourage overseas travel and assignments for corporate executives as well as tourists. In this way, transnationalization of the sex industry can and does follow paths forged by states and firms in the regional and global economy. Large syndicates such as Syndicate X then serve as trend-setting anchor groups for the migration and ancillary industries in sex work.

Significantly, Syndicate X places inordinate value on transnational migrant women who are fair, pale, or light-skinned, and those whose features approximate the physiognomy of Caucasian women. This is affirmed not only by the selection of "white" Uzbek women, but also by syndicate members' potent stereotypes of and discriminatory practices toward dark-skinned women from African countries. One afternoon, as I purchased a drink from a hawker stall in the Golden Triangle, a lower-level member who was driving by stopped and said, "Hey, Professor, do you know that respect and boundaries are very important in our business?" He parked the car and motioned for me to sit with him. Then he related what had happened the night before at a nightclub (presumably owned and managed by Syndicate X). Two pimps from another syndicate (one with which there was no cooperation) brought three black women sex workers with the aim of procuring clients. When the nightclub's security officers asked them to leave, the women started shouting at the men, and the entire group took the verbal altercation out on to the street. The syndicate member then said to me in a very angry tone, "They did not ask for permission. This is not their area. They do not have the right to bring black women into the place. It 'darkened' the entire place. They blocked out our *feng shui* [the flow of good, positive energy]. No good for business. The women are big, ugly, and rude. No good for business." When I asked him what countries the women came from, he said, "Gambia, Kenya, eh, who cares! . . . No welcome here."

On the other hand, his syndicate took no issue with a small building within their large sphere of influence that was known to house women sex workers from several African countries. According to him, the women there kept to themselves and did not come out to make noise or trouble; that is, they were not visible and they were not intent on stealing his clients. They worked for another major syndicate, and there was an agreement between the two syndicates to coexist harmoniously. Harmonious coexistence basically means that black women sex workers neither are seen nor heard from much within Syndicate X's sphere of influence. As a syndicate with profits derived mainly from the provision of sexual services by transnational migrant women, Syndicate X's operations with regard to the recruitment of migrant women and their placements with clients are informed explicitly by the intersection of racial and heterosexual ideologies.

Money Changers and Back Channel Remittances

Of all its partners in the migration and ancillary industries, Syndicate X's relationship to "money changers" is vital for the mobility of its operating capital (for example, to reimburse overseas counterparts) and investments, as well as for its promise of assisting transnational migrant women in their remittances. At the end of the women's stay in KL, Syndicate X arranges for their forward journey to another global city and helps them establish connections to the syndicate there, or arranges for the women to return to their home countries. Prior to that, Syndicate X assists women in remitting their earnings to personal bank accounts overseas or to designated recipients. Even though migrant women have the option of remitting their earnings via Western Union or direct bank transfers, they often do not do so because of the fear of detection by state authorities. While independent sex workers tend to carry their cash earnings when they leave the country, migrant women in large syndicates often draw on syndicate alliances with select money changers to do so.

The Asian Development Bank's study on migrant remittances describes this phenomenon:

> In Southeast Asia, particularly among those countries studied, informal money transfer markets are less prevalent than in other regions. Most clients use regulated institutions to send and/or receive remittances. The presence of informal networks for money transfers continues to be puzzling. As mentioned previously, some immigrants rely on informal transfers because the technological infrastructure is costly, prohibiting companies from providing affordable services to the customer, or because strict government regulations on how to send money lead immigrants to use less traceable mechanisms.
>
> (Asian Development Bank 2006, 41)

Remittance via money changers is considered informal at best and illegal at worst, because this practice draws on the modern banking system but at the same time bypasses regulations and fees governing electronic transfer operations.

Money changers have their historical origins in culturally specific *hawala* (South Asian) and *fei ch'ien* (Chinese) systems. Both systems date back hundreds of years and are based on trust between parties. The British colonial state relied on *hawala* until the late eighteenth century with the establishment of the first Western-style bank in Calcutta. Since 9/11 however, these systems have been one of the targets of anti–money laundering laws at the national and international levels. Despite these efforts to eliminate them, culturally specific remittance systems persist because of lower costs and the ease with which monies can be transferred: "Thus, calling hawala an 'underground system' of banking, as it is commonly mentioned in Western literature is not correct, as the system has been operating in the open with complete legitimacy for centuries" (Shanmugam 2004, 37). As a culturally specific mode of remittance, *hawala*

> allows money to be transferred around the globe without actual money movement or wire transfers, offers financial services to many remote parts of the world, unusually unreachable by conventional banking services. Hawala is quick, efficient, reliable and inexpensive and has a much wider scope and is more effective than conventional money transfer systems, as it can get money to even the remotest village. It provides anonymous services, operating out of nondescript little shops and bazaars.
>
> (Shanmugam 2004, 38)

Syndicate alliances with *hawala*-style money changers in KL provide a viable, alternative, informal remittance channel that is quicker, less expensive, and less bureaucratic than conventional banking channels. It does not require formal identification or legal status—which would be required to open a bank account in the city—but merely trust and the promise of secrecy between parties. Not all money changers provide this kind of remittance service: only some do, and since they do not conduct remittance business out of their regular money changer storefronts, it is extremely difficult for the state to identify them.

Syndicate X advises transnational migrant women to select among its preferred money changers, describing it as the most efficient and cost-effective way to remit earnings. A migrant woman who elects to do so will deposit her earnings into an account specified by the money changer at a local bank and subsequently hands over the endorsed deposit slip to a syndicate member who, in turn, will give it to the money changer.[9] Following receipt of the deposit slip, the money changer will text or fax his counterpart in the receiving city-country to deposit the corresponding amount (based on a predetermined currency exchange rate) into an account specified by the woman. The deposit slip is given to the woman's designated representative in the receiving city-country or faxed back to the syndicate so that the woman has proof of remitted funds. The entire process only takes anywhere from four to twenty-four hours, compared to the seven to ten business days required by a foreign bank to receive and process the transfer. The money changer's commission is in the range of 1–5%, depending on the total volume of transactions involving the designated country of receipt: the higher the volume, the lower the fees. Money changers' currency exchange rates tend to be better as well than those offered to the public by commercial banks. The total fees charged by money changers are significantly less than bank fees that involve fluctuating foreign exchange rates, commissions, and a host of bank-related fees for electronic transfers.[10] For syndicates as well, these lower fees substantially reduce the cost of transnational transactions.

Syndicates' relationship with money changers, therefore, is an indispensable dimension of the migration and ancillary industries. Money changers provide informal transnational banking services to syndicates and by extension, to migrant women.

CONCLUSION

The postcolonial state's strategies of reconfiguring urban spaces and places while trying to remove sex workers from the streets in KL have affected indelibly the operations of Chinese secret societies. As discussed, these strategies encouraged the transformation of Syndicate X's predecessor from a hierarchically and tightly organized secret society to a more horizontally structured business group.

On the surface, Syndicate X evinces a business model similar to that of some sex trafficking groups, and both have transnational alliances established for the recruitment and migration of women sex workers. Yet, Syndicate X is dissimilar in the nature of its operations. Instead of owning and controlling trafficked migrant women, the syndicate offers fee-based services related to migrant women's entry, employment, and forward journeys. In return for monthly board and lodging fees and taxes, the syndicate's connections to a range of firms, agencies, and individuals offer migrant women a one-stop shop for services: clients, personal security, housing, transportation, and banking. Syndicate X and its seven counterparts are the informal economy's version of the formal economy's conglomerates in the world-class city of KL.

Despite the professionalization of Syndicate X's operational structure and attendant positions, the group nevertheless is akin to its predecessor in terms of its masculinized and racialized upper-level management. While

Malaysian Chinese men occupy higher and mid-level positions in the four areas of investment, security-finance, human resources, and miscellaneous matters, lower-level positions are occupied mainly by Malaysian men from all three major communities. Malaysian Chinese women also are members of this syndicate, but they participate in the feminized roles of caring for transnational migrant women sex workers, and to a lesser degree, recruitment via their existing overseas networks. The entire operation and ensuing profits rest on the sexual labor of migrant women. For this particular syndicate, its focus on the upscale sex market and taxation system means that revenue derived from migrant women's sex work financially sustains not just the women and syndicate members but also agents of the state, who take bribes; money changers; taxi drivers; restaurant and hawker stall owners; airlines; hotels; condominium associations; nightclubs; car dealers; spas; and other businesses.

Syndicate X's short- and long-term alliances with counterparts in the Global North and South illustrate a major way in which migration and ancillary industries organize, manage, and benefit from the flows of transnational migrant women sex workers. Significantly, Syndicate X's alliances draw from and mirror changing flows of capital and global talent in the world class city. That is, alliances follow global highways and migratory pathways linking KL to other global cities. These alliances shift according to such factors as client demands, relationships with counterparts overseas, and conflict among migrant women from different nationalities. The most popular nationalities of migrant women sex workers today, therefore, may or may not be the most popular in the future.

Large syndicates' existence and operations reveal their gatekeeping function in women's transnational migration for sex work. Although some women migrate independently, many more women are recruited by syndicates specifically to meet and, at the same time, shape demands emanating from the world-class city. As discussed, Syndicate X mediates demands at the nexus of race-ethnicity, gender, nationality, sexuality, and culture. If Syndicate X were concerned purely about profits, it would facilitate the in-migration and employment of male sex workers and black women from various African countries, and it would allow migrant women to cater to women clients. Instead, the syndicate chooses not to do so. It operates from a distinctly racist-culturalist-homophobic basis. There are no women VIP or homosexual clients. There also are no black women sex workers, because they can never fit the norm of a fair, pale or light-skinned woman who is sufficiently "sophisticated" in her conduct and speech for the syndicate and its clients. Syndicate X's resolution to conflicts between Chinese and Uzbek women sex workers attests to the leadership's privileging of racial-cultural proximity by gradually removing Uzbek women from its operations. The plan to recruit white South African and light-skinned Brazilian women only affirms the syndicate's racialized schema.

In their gatekeeping functions, Syndicate X and others similar to it explicitly and implicitly stipulate uses of spaces and places in which access is given or denied to migrant women based on their nationalities, race-ethnicity, cultural practices, and so forth. This raises the question of whether migrant women, and syndicate members who work with the women, can even exhibit cosmopolitan practices and worldviews in the global city. The next chapter examines this in greater detail.

CHAPTER 6

Knowing and Living in KL's Contact Zones

Gendered, Racialized, and Classed Cosmopolites

Let me try to speak of mutable referents. People take life as their root and knowledge as their teacher, consequently they become attached to right and wrong. As a result, there are names and realities, consequently they take themselves as subjective substance and cause others to take them as their own paragon.

—Chuang Tzu (1994, 233–4)

Ostensibly, it is irrelevant to consider whether transnational migrant women's and syndicate members' views of and encounters with the Other in KL encourage mutual openness to and acceptance of difference. The imperative of earning income undoubtedly upholds rather than dislodges them from parochial identities and loyalties. Taken to its logical conclusion, the future of intercultural communication and relations in this era of neoliberal globalization assuredly rests with global talent, who move around the world dispensing much-in-demand knowledge and skills.

Yet the question is germane for its potential to illuminate individuals' humanity beyond those one-dimensional representations, epithets, and caricatures associated with one or another aspect of transnational migration for sex work. Subsequently, it challenges the dominant conceptualization of a "cosmopolitan" as the hypermobile professional, who has transcended the particularities or narrow-mindedness circumscribed by her or his community of birth or place of origin.

COSMOPOLITANS: EMPIRICAL REALITIES

Global cities offer immense opportunities for encounters between individuals from all over the world. As major nodes through which ideas, goods, services, and people constantly flow, global cities have the potential to attract, nurture, and affirm what Kurasawa calls an "ethos of cultural openness" (2004, 240). The world-class city of KL is not an exception to this. On any given day, tourists mingle with residents in restaurants, shopping malls, and heritage sites; international students sit beside Malaysian students in classes taught by faculty trained overseas or from overseas institutions; and international executives collaborate with citizens in corporate offices. The city and its residents are connected by KLIA and MSC to the rest of the world.

More often than not, categories of the expatriate, tourist, international student, and scholar are considered emblematic of cosmopolitans who possess and exhibit a "cultural or aesthetic disposition toward difference" (Molz 2006, 2). They have the resources to travel, and in their resultant encounters with difference, they are able to transcend loyalty to any particular place, culture, or even politics.[1] In brief, cosmopolitans are rootless elites who reject parochial associations, worldviews, and identities that seem to plague their poorer counterparts.

According to this schema, nonelite transnational migrants, namely temporary workers, guest workers, and refugees, cannot possibly be considered cosmopolitans. The circumstances in which they migrate, stay, and work in receiving contexts are not typically associated with key attributes of cosmpolitans, such as the willingness to engage with and learn from the Other for its own sake (see especially Hannerz 1990, 2004). Their "struggle for survival and communication barriers" prevent them from being so (Hiebert 2002, 215). In fact, they are expected to favor practices that recreate "home" in receiving contexts.

Thus, the dominant schema is problematic not only for disqualifying transnational migrant workers and refugees, but for doing so at the expense of minimizing, while affirming, unequal relations between groups. In the past and to some extent today, the cosmopolitan remains "a *class* figure *and* a White person, capable of appreciating and consuming 'high quality' commodities and cultures, including 'ethnic' culture" (Hage 1998, 201).

Indeed, this often-unacknowledged nexus of class and race-ethnicity informs the norm of the cosmopolitan. Roudometof criticizes what is a selective labeling of elite white expatriates and travelers as cosmopolitans, and nonwhite migrants as transnationals: "Acting as labels, these terms are employed selectively with regard to people of different classes as well as different racial and ethnic backgrounds" (2005, 115).[2] Notably as well, this norm betrays a gendered, as in masculinized, dimension: cosmopolitans, by and large, still are elite men (see, for example, Pratt 2008; Kofman and Raghuram 2006; Yeoh and Willis 2005).

In the past decade or so, scholarship on cosmopolitanism has begun responding to the complexities elicited by transnational migration amidst economic restructuring processes. Empirical studies of contemporary hypermobile elites, such as corporate executives, question the assumption of a coherent and stable cosmopolitan subjectivity; that is, elites' attitudes, practices, and worldviews are not as rootless or open to the Other as was theorized in the past:

> Too much of the celebratory writing on cosmopolitanism is not substantiated by empirical evidence and is more concerned with generating a new orthodoxy of theorizing social life based on the entitled and privileged subject, who enjoys unfettered movement, effortlessly consumes different cultures and places and is free to proclaim multiple identities.
>
> (Kofman 2005, 94; see also Calcutt, Woodward, and Skrbis 2009)

Whether they come from Asia (Chan and Chan 2010; Yeoh and Huang 2011; Ong 1999) or Europe (Gustafson 2002, 2009), elites are attached to and remain involved in the culture and politics of their homelands. Since hypermobile elites do not exhibit stable and rootless cosmopolitan subjectivities, conceptual spaces then are opened wide for examining other categories of mobile and nonmobile people.

The ever-growing contact zones of global cities render unavoidable people's encounters with difference. This is the case especially for migrant and citizen workers in the service sector, who are exposed to and learn new "tools of functional communication." In the process, they are said to become

> more and more cosmopolitan, not in the sense of a *louche* playboy, a *rentier*, or a debonair, rootless, stateless member of the elite, but in a more prosaic sense. Cosmopolites can also be of working class origin. They acquire an international language (often English, or a passable version of it). They are "streetwise" in knowing who is likely to exploit them or turn them away from a border. They learn the cultural "manners" of their hosts—their gestures, greetings, and preferred sports and leisure activities.
>
> (Cohen 2004, 145–7)

Arguably, these practices are more utilitarian than cosmopolitan because they are learned and adopted mainly to assist workers in carrying out job responsibilities: their goal, after all, is to continue earning wages. Moreover, migrants and even some citizen workers contend with unequal power environments that cannot but shape the nature and extent of openness toward and acceptance of difference (Werbner 1999; Kofman 2005).

Nevertheless, in culturally diverse and stratified contexts of global cities, transnational migrant and citizen workers' encounters and resultant worldviews need not always be governed by, nor adhere exclusively to the either-or of functional-nonfunctional, local-global, parochial-universal, and other simple binaries. This is evident from migrant practices of "strategic cosmopolitanism" (Kothari 2008) or "tactical cosmopolitanism" (Landau and Freemantle 2010) that embody cosmopolitan attitudes, practices, and worldviews in repressive or hostile environments. For example, Kothari's empirical research on transnational migrant peddlers in Barcelona reveals that

> even though they may be cosmopolitan at work and more parochial when they leave the street, this *does not mean that the skills and capacities of migrants are acquired and mobilized solely as an economic strategy to get by in a globalising world* [emphasis mine]: rather, these skills and capacities are born out of, and further enable, multiple social and cultural encounters founded upon philosophical and ethical considerations.
>
> (2008, 502)

Similarly, empirical research on nonmobile middle and working classes demonstrates that while some citizens reject the presence of transnational migrants or minorities or reject working with them, others develop understanding and empathy that are shaped by the "expectation of 'learning from each other' and of mutual respect" (Brett and Moran 2011, 201; see also Lamont and Aksartova 2002; Skrbis and Woodward 2007). In the process, they may even integrate alternative ways of living, being, and doing.

Hence, encounters between transnational migrants and citizens in global cities do not and need not always signify or affirm the either-or schema. Rather, they evince a "mix of atomisation and fluid associations" in relation to individuals' respective positionalities; the local/particular/utilitarian/functional coexist and overlap with rather than supplant the global/universal/nonutilitarian/nonfunctional (Landau and Freemantle 2010, 381). Encounters between migrants and citizens that include and result in the sharing and learning of new knowledge are indicative of "cosmopolitan sociability" or "an ability to find aspects of the shared human experience including aspirations for a better world within and despite what would seem to be divides of culture and belief" (Schiller, Darieva, and Gruner-Domic 2011, 403).

Still, it has to be emphasized here that focus on the lived everyday forms of cosmopolitanism largely is delimited to white men in the Global North, and to a lesser extent, migrant men from the Global South. Much empirical research remains to be conducted on women and the ways in which emerging cosmopolitan subjectivities may be gendered and racialized in the process.[3]

SAMENESS AND DIFFERENCE: ENCOUNTERS IN KL'S MULTIPLE CONTACT ZONES

The extent and nature of transnational migrant women's encounters with one another and with residents in KL vary most visibly in accordance with their status as syndicate or independent sex workers, their place of residence, and their backgrounds. For Chinese migrant women in syndicate housing, their accommodations either in or within walking distance of Malaysian Chinese neighborhoods serve as a safe haven or base from which they can explore the city's multicultural-racial-religious ethos. The women live within a cocoon of syndicate protection: their interactions with residents are circumscribed mostly by syndicates' vetted suggestions of places to eat and shop, places to avoid, and so forth.

Nonetheless, the women do recognize and marvel at diverse nationalities of workers in the city (the Indian bellhop, the Myanmarese cook, the Filipina domestic worker, the Vietnamese saleswoman, and the Pakistani security guard): as foreigners, they are not alone in KL. Huifen, who had worked previously in Macau and Bangkok, best summarizes the majority of syndicate-based migrant women's perceptions of KL as a "very warm and welcoming city" with diversity of cuisine, people, architecture, shopping, and entertainment outlets. Despite their fears of the authorities and reactions of some Malaysians toward "foreign prostitutes," the women express an "aestheticisation of taste" that historically has been a major characteristic assigned to elite cosmopolitans (Datta 2009, 364). Meizhen acknowledges, "I know we are different from the Chinese here. Some don't like us, but others don't seem to mind. They know what we do, but they don't make trouble for us."

Syndicate-based Chinese migrant women do not consider intercultural communication with residents as a major challenge or barrier because their interactions are primarily with Malaysian Chinese small business owners and syndicate members who also are proficient in Mandarin and Cantonese. To the migrant women's amazement, some Malays even speak to them in Mandarin. Although command of the Malay language is not a job requirement, some women want to learn it because, as Chunying says,

Why not learn another language? You can never be at a disadvantage from learning [another language]. When we learn their language, we say [to them that] we are grateful, we are appreciative. Malay is nicer to listen to than Vietnamese [she previously worked in Ho Chi Minh City].

Indeed, a number of women in this study endeavor to express their appreciation or to reciprocate by learning Malay words and phrases, and practice them with Malaysians whenever they are able to do so. On a daily basis, Liyu, a syndicate-based Chinese migrant sex worker who has a penchant for *teh tarik* ("pulled" tea), walks to a *mamak* stall (instead of having it delivered) near her syndicate condominium, orders the tea, and drinks it while practicing new words and phrases with the Malaysian Indian-Muslim owner and some of his Malay customers.

Reciprocity is key in Chinese migrant women's ability to acknowledge and be acknowledged by Malaysians, their hosts in the city. Jinghua, for example, makes it a point to buy snacks for an old Malaysian Chinese hawker stall operator who always asks after her. Now and again, he offers her a complimentary plate of noodles. "He touches my heart," because the old man knows what she does for a living but he neither holds it against her nor asks for a free session.

She does not say the same of a shopkeeper, who spits on the ground every time she walks by. His actions clearly send the message that she is not welcome in his shop or the area. Jinghua, however, does not generalize his conduct to all Malaysians: "You have good and bad people everywhere. I don't believe all Malaysians are bad just because some are rude."

Meizhen qualifies Jinghua's statement, "Except for the policemen. It doesn't matter if they are [Malaysian] Chinese, Malay, or Indian. They think all Misses are banks. End of the month, not enough pay, stop a Miss. They are all the same." Xiaofan, in turn, scolds Meizhen for saying so: "We make more money than them anyway. We don't live here, so be quiet, earn your money, and go." Xiaofan's words evince the "rhetoric of self-exclusion" exercised in response to their ascribed status as foreign prostitutes (Landau and Freemantle 2010, 382). This rhetoric at once elevates Chinese migrant women above lowly paid Malaysian policemen and underscores what should be the women's central focus in KL.

The brief exchange above is informative of how each woman makes sense of and legitimizes her presence in the world-class city. Jinghua and Meizhen fold the city's cultural diversity within a common humanity in which they, too, can claim their right to be present. This humanity is replete with "good" and "bad" people, regardless of their nationality, race-ethnicity, and cultural backgrounds. Xiaofan, on the other hand, explicitly articulates another line of reasoning. She knows that she neither belongs to nor is welcome in the city, and she invokes the power of her income as an equalizer to mitigate a negative identity and traits ascribed by her immigration status and nature of work.

On the surface, Qing (who works in a foot reflexology center) holds a similar attitude to that of Xiaofan. Qing's laser-like focus on making money is the way in which she can avoid encounters leading to relationships that potentially can hurt her. Although she likes the young Indonesian and Malay women who work in a Thai-Muslim restaurant near her syndicate apartment, she consistently turns down their invitations to walk the mall and eat "roundabout sushi" (sushi dishes on a revolving conveyor-like belt on top of a large oval table): "They are very nice and funny. Always smiling and laughing. They have a lot of friends whom I don't know. Sometimes I really want to go with them but I am afraid. What if they find out [that I am a sex worker] and call me bad names?" She also turns down invitations from a Malaysian Chinese cook who gives her "special treatment" in the restaurant and who makes her smile with his renditions of Chinese love songs: "Maybe he thinks I will give him free [sessions] . . . I don't know. No time for love, so no need for heartbreak later."

Qing's self-exclusion is not merely at the level of rhetoric; it is an emotional and physical struggle against the inclination to engage others, be they migrant or Malaysian workers. This type of self-exclusion is based on her fear of being exposed, derided, and detained as a sex worker, as well as the potential of developing emotional attachments to a Malaysian man with whom she cannot possibly envision a future. Hence, she constantly reminds herself that she is in the city only to earn income.

By virtue of their status as freelance sex workers, some Chinese migrant women tend to have more sustained (affirmative and negative) interactions with other transnational migrants and Malaysians in KL. Baoyan, who stays in a budget hotel managed by a South Asian man, recounts people of a host of nationalities (from the Middle East, Europe, Africa, and throughout Asia) whom she has encountered. For her, this is one of the major attractions of working in KL—the range of nationalities, cultural practices, and worldviews encountered on any given day, and the knowledge she gains from conversations with people. Although Baoyan admits, "We are all trying to make a living. You help me and I help you. This is the way to survive," she does not develop exclusively utilitarian-based relationships.

Baoyan works alongside and socializes with freelance women from the PRC, Southeast Asia, and Africa. They exhibit strategic or tactical cosmopolitan practices in how they look out for one another; teach new arrivals and less experienced women to identify potentially violent clients; and alert each other via text messages to police, RELA, and immigration presence.

What initially binds Baoyan to other freelance migrant women is the understanding that they are doubly vulnerable, that is, as "foreign prostitutes" who work independently of syndicates in the city. Beyond the explicitly functional aspects of their relationship, the women are not required to care for one another or develop emotional bonds. Yet, they do so and in mutually affirming ways. Given their linguistic differences, the women communicate by stringing together English and Malay words. They even teach one another words and phrases from their respective mother tongues and share stories from home (how families are structured; the challenge of raising children; what constitute problems and how they are discussed, and so forth). In doing so, they come to understand and appreciate the similarities and differences in their lives as women raised in specific cultural and national contexts.

Their relationship, then, is not purely utilitarian. Rather, the centrality of making a living from stigmatized work intersects with a genuine desire to know and learn from one another: the migrant women have "a shared sense of common sensibilities [that] does not reside but coexists with ongoing diversity of perspective and practice." Their intercultural communicative practices symbolize and affirm cosmopolitan sociability that creates "social relations of inclusiveness and openness to the world" (Schiller, Darieva, and Gruner-Domic 2011, 402).

Xuilan, another freelance Chinese migrant sex worker, has a different social network. She rents an apartment in a high-rise luxury complex for her month-long stays. With her proficiency in English, and with assistance from her compatriots as well as Malaysian and other migrant workers, Xuilan successfully navigates the global city. She describes her friends and acquaintances as "international. Not just one country. When I go back to China, I always miss them. We have different skin, eyes, hair, smell, body shapes, but we all have a heart and a liver."

Even though Xuilan remunerates some of her men and women friends based in luxury hotels who help match her with clients, they have developed strong bonds of friendship in the process (for example, they stay in touch via international calling cards whenever one of them leaves the city). Her decision to work in KL "changed my outlook on life. I traveled all over Asia but I still had a narrow worldview . . . saw everything only from Chinese eyes. But after working here, I can say that I am broad-minded. I have learned a lot from everyone." She remarks that even her friends and family members back home have noticed the change, such as her ability to offer multiple perspectives on issues, and to explain alternative and equally legitimate ways of living, being, and doing. Xuilan has absorbed and integrated new cultural knowledge into attitudes, practices, and worldview.

Zhenzhen, on the other hand, does not exhibit the same receptiveness to difference as Baoyan or Xuilan. Whenever she is in KL, she stays with her on-off Malaysian Chinese boyfriend in order to save even more money. Her boyfriend, a secondary school dropout, lives in a low-cost apartment obtained in his parents' name and only works when he feels like it, choosing instead to be financed by his father, who drives a tour bus, and his mother, who sells pastries at an open-air market. Zhenzhen sees him as "lazy" and without "self-love" in that he is not ashamed of living off his parents: "I work for a living. He doesn't . . . acts like a prince. At least I don't have to take care of him. I stay in the apartment and sometimes give his parents money. I will never marry him. No woman should marry him. I stay there to make my purse bigger!" Her boyfriend's usefulness is limited to the extent of Zhenzhen's rent-free accommodations. However, she reciprocates his parents' kindness by occasionally giving them money.

Her social network consists predominantly of women sex workers from different regions in the PRC (some with whom she worked when they were under syndicate protection in earlier years). The fact of having come from the same country accords the women a sense of fellowship and protection in the global city: "We are together because we speak the same language and do things the same way. Working alone [without syndicate protection] we can only rely on each other." Undoubtedly, the migrant women find comfort in being with each other. Trust that is grounded and legitimized only by a specific nexus of nationality and culture, however, has the effect of mitigating the women's desire to know and interact on a deeper level with people who are different from them.

Zhenzhen's utilitarian approach in her relationship with the boyfriend extends to interactions with non-Chinese migrants and Malaysians. Her encounters with them are driven and framed by their facilitation of her ability to earn more income. Even so, her self-exclusion is not based entirely on the same criterion as that of Xiaofan's. Zhenzhen's disparaging remarks on everyday life in the city betray an attitude of "transient superiority" (Landau and Freemantle 2010, 382). She criticizes the way that some Malaysians use their right hands in place of cutlery when eating, how they consume durian (a very pungent fruit with a hard thorny outer shell) at hawker stalls, and so forth. She puts up with what are perceived as the Others' inferior ways of doing things only because she is in the city temporarily for work.

Unlike Zhenzhen, Meilin rents a room in an apartment owned by a Malaysian Chinese woman, whom she got to know when she initially was under a syndicate's protection. After she made the decision to work independently, Meilin was advised to live in a predominantly working-class

Malaysian Chinese neighborhood because life would be more "convenient" for her. In the early phases of freelance sex work, Meilin's Malaysian room-mate (a clerk at a company) went out with her whenever they could, in order to help her learn to identify and steer away from dangerous spaces in the city (for example, police-RELA presence, syndicate controlled establish-ments). Meilin continues to reciprocate by cooking regional Chinese dishes for her roommate, taking care of her when she is ill, describing life at home, and bringing her souvenirs. She even agreed that whenever her roommate saves enough money and vacation time, Meilin will be her host in China.

Despite guidance and support from a local woman, Meilin still bears the brunt of inhospitable acts by residents in the neighborhood. Young and old men harass her by grabbing their crotches whenever she walks by. Women sneer at her on the street, and they make derogatory remarks within ear-shot about Chinese women sex workers. Meilin rationalizes the women's conduct by trying to understand their perspective: "The Chinese here are different from us. The way they talk. What they wear. How they see the world. It is not the same, but it is alright. They are brought up here. We are brought up in China. But we should have respect for each other."

For Meilin, respect is not merely an act of performing deference to the Other. It is a fundamental belief in the need to acknowledge the Other's right to exist despite and because of differences in nationality, culture, nature of work, comportment, accent, and so forth. The fact that she per-forms sex work (although she has not publicly acknowledged this in the neighborhood) should not matter, because she is not a bad person. She does not steal or cheat, unlike one local restaurant owner who is known to water down soup or reduce expensive ingredients in dishes. Whenever cus-tomers drive up in imported luxury cars, he arbitrarily inflates his prices for them. Yet, the same men and women who judge Meilin will greet him warmly, only to gossip behind his back afterward.

Meilin's view of humanity is distinct from Jinghua's and Meizhen's. She acknowledges the existence of not just one humanity, but humanities that emerge from and are embodied in people of different cultures and nation-alities. Thus, respect is a prerequisite for harmonious coexistence. At the same time, Meilin is acutely aware of the hypocrisy and power imbalances in gender relations:

There are so many Misses in KL. The men want us but [the women who sneer at me] should know that many of us are not interested in stealing their husbands. If life is reversed, we'll probably say the same thing. I understand. Women, we are still not equal [to men]: "When the cock crows, no one will notice. If the hen should crow, then they will chop off her head" [Chinese proverb].

Meilin "imagines the other [in this case, Malaysian Chinese women] in a way that generates sympathy or empathy" (Calcutt, Woodward, and Skrbis 2009, 181). She understands how women can share common experiences in a culturally diverse but resiliently patriarchal world.

Not all Malaysian Chinese syndicates or the Chinese migrant women are accepting of women sex workers from other nationalities and cultures. Until 2011, Chinese and Uzbek women—two of the most in-demand nationalities of sex workers—used to live together in housing provided by Syndicate X. Even though demands persist for the Uzbek women, the syndicate gradually is removing them from its payroll. In the past few years, constant disputes between the groups of women (for example, over demeanor, material possessions, ways of speaking and doing things) led to very loud and heated arguments. At times, the arguments descended into physical altercations in which some women assaulted one another. Syndicate X's initial response of placing the women in separate condominiums failed, because some of the Chinese sought retribution by calling the authorities to report Uzbek women (even those from the same syndicate) whenever they saw the latter in public spaces.

From the male-dominated syndicate's perspective, these conflicts emerged because "women are women," so to speak, and they should never have been housed together, since they are prone to fits of jealousy and envy. From Chinese women's perspectives, there are few distinctions among women from Uzbekistan, Russia, Ukraine, Kazakhstan, and so forth. They perceive women from Eastern Europe and Central Asia as having similar styles of communication and attitudes: the women are seen as arrogant, rude, and insensitive to the feelings of others. According to Meizhen, "If you want to borrow something, then ask politely. They speak as if they are instructing you to do something. They are not well brought up." Ning similarly claims, "You must always be mindful of others. This is the proper way to behave."

At the outset, the conflict appears to be a case of cultural misinterpretation arising between individuals with markedly different styles of communication, that is, indirect and direct styles learned from socialization in their respective cultural contexts (Ting-Toomey 2005). While some cultures privilege a more indirect style of communication so as not to upset or insult feelings of others (that is, an "other"-centered style), there also are cultures that privilege a more direct style of communication designed for clarity and efficiency (that is, a "self"-centered style).

However, compounding the women's opposing communicative styles are their differential insertions or positions in the global city's racialized-ethnicized hierarchy of transnational migrant sex workers, with "white" women at the apex. The latter group includes Eastern European and Central Asian women whose physiognomic features approximate that of Caucasian women. Mediated by this hierarchy, a case of cultural misinterpretation cannot but mutate into one of superior-inferior relations, informed by received historical memories.

China's relationship to Central Asia is shaped by a long history of conflict between the dominant Han Chinese state and the non–Han Chinese Xinjiang province that serves as a buffer to the west. Culturally, the Han Chinese see themselves as superior to the "barbarians," who live in Xinjiang and Central Asia (see especially Harris 1993). In the global city of KL, although Chinese migrant women perceive themselves as culturally superior to non-Han women from Central Asia, they are confronted by another layer of complexity. The Chinese migrant women are outranked by "white" Uzbek women in the hierarchy of transnational migrant sex workers. Jinghua's comment explicitly links Uzbek women's communication style to her belief that they are entitled "Westerners" (read: white and arrogant).

Syndicate X's separation of Uzbek and Chinese women may have prevented further physical altercations, but it did nothing to resolve the conflict. Instead, it reinforced Chinese women's negative stereotypes of Uzbek women and encouraged their actions, such as calling the authorities. From the syndicate men's perspective, nonetheless, the conflicts only confirm a self-evident gendered truth: women are petty in their interactions with each other.

Interestingly, the three freelance Chinese migrant sex workers, Baoyan, Xuilan, and Meilin, neither view Uzbek women or women from other nationalities negatively, nor do they speak of them in derogatory ways. They are fully cognizant of the larger context in which transnational migrant women work, that is, as "illegal foreign prostitutes" who always are vulnerable to harassment by the authorities and, at times, by Malaysians. This awareness, together with the migrant women's respect for and openness to learning from the Other, encourage their identification of similarities that bind women, while appreciating and accepting cultural practices and worldviews that set them apart. This is the case with Lia and her social network in KL.

Lia, the Filipina concierge and part-time sex worker, is one of two transnational migrant women who make explicit references to religion. She marvels at how Malaysians are religious, noting the number of mosques, churches, and temples in the city. Specifically, she is curious about her Malaysian Chinese colleagues at the hotel, who buy incense, order special cardboard boxes filled with gold-and silver-leaved papers, and buy an assortment of paper clothes in preparation for the annual Ching Ming observance. During this observance, family members visit their ancestors' grave sites to clear them of weeds, after which they light incense and burn the cardboard boxes as annual offerings. Even though Lia believes it to be a total waste of money ("Is there proof that their ancestors will receive the boxes? Why not donate money to charity?"), she still points out that every culture has its own way of expressing religious piety. She exhibits "cosmopolitan curiosity" in her desire to know of different religious practices (Appiah 2006, 14). This extends to her attempts at juxtaposing religious practices and worldviews different from her own, that is, monotheistic religions' one god versus the many gods in Mahayana Buddhism, Taoism, and Hinduism ("Each god must have a different function").

As a practicing Christian, Lia attends a Catholic church in the city whenever she can on Sundays, alongside many of her compatriots who work in Malaysian households. She sees no contradiction in being religious and doing part-time sex work, although she admits that some of her compatriots would call her a hypocrite if they knew what she did on the side. Her colleague-friends at work, however, neither mind nor care about her side job. Lia's relationship with them affirms practices of cosmopolitan sociability that also characterize Baoyan's and Xuilan's networks:

> They come from so many countries in the world. You know the tall thin guy, the valet? He has an engineering degree from Bangladesh. . . . [The other valet] is from Kashmir. My manager is from Switzerland. Some of the receptionists are from Ho Chi Minh, [Kuala Kubu Baru], Jakarta, Seremban. . . . There is always a get-together because of birthdays, national holidays, festivals . . . When Ashif is the only man [in the group], he wants to pay for all of us because he says he is a man [thus he should pay], but we always say no because his pay is not so good. He says "Don't tell my [compatriot] friends" [that he cannot afford to take women out]. We tease him. . . . Sometimes he does not have enough money to send home. He doesn't say anything but we know he cries because he can't take care of his parents and brothers. So we create a donation pool for him. Ashif says we are his family in KL. Yes, we are all family.

Lia's narrative reveals explicitly that cosmopolitan sociability assumes not only behavioral but emotional and cognitive dimensions. Members in this network value and practice the idea of the "family" that cuts across national, cultural, gender, racial-ethnic, and religious boundaries. The act of creating a donation pool for Ashif highlights the "cosmopolitan generosity and reasoning" of Lia and her colleague-friends (Skrbis and Woodward 2007, 731).

Aside from acts of reciprocity and the sharing of cultural knowledge among migrant women and their coworker friends and acquaintances, some of them also gain knowledge of global cities from clients. The women have differing opinions of their clients. For example, some prefer foreigners to locals, while others draw sharp distinctions between different nationalities and cultures based on their approaches to gratuities, sex, and so forth. Migrant women also learn from clients' descriptions of everyday life, tourist attractions, and cuisine in other global cities. For the most part, whether they practice serial or circular migration, new knowledge gleaned from clients shapes migrant women's desire to visit or work in those cities. Ruolan, for example, wants to visit and work in Rio de Janeiro because of how a client described his city and the preparations for the Olympics. Xiaofan, Huong, and Lia want to travel to Paris and Rome, the city brands for romance and fashion. Chunying, Mingyu, and Ning have their sights set for cities in Western Europe and North America, because of their clients' descriptions of local ways of being, doing, and living.

Nigerian women sex workers' experiences in KL, on the other hand, are quite dissimilar to their Asian counterparts. The women's negative views and experiences center on Malaysian Chinese, the majority of whom they consider to be blatantly racist. As Margaret bluntly says, "They don't like us because we are black. They don't even see us as human beings. . . . They judge us before they even know us." Cosmopolitan sociability thus cannot exist in this context, despite Margaret's desire for it.

Although not all Malaysian Chinese verbally express their disdain toward her, Margaret astutely observes that shop owners are much more relaxed in their body language and outwardly friendly toward Chinese women (such as taking the time to chat with or explain the application of new products). The ostensibly simple acts of shopping for toiletries, clothes, food, and so forth inevitably cause much consternation for Margaret: the shop owners will hastily ring up her purchases or show frustration and impatience whenever she inquires about the cost of products or takes her time to make selections. Often, Margaret responds by refusing to make purchases or by disgustedly throwing money on the counter.

Adeola, who had worked in Dubai, does not see significant differences between Arabs and Malaysian Chinese in their perceived superiority to black Africans in general: "Africa is not one country. But we are the same to them. They don't care if you are from Nigeria, Zambia, Cote D'Ivoire, South Africa. Poor people always asking for help. . . . Garbage of the world." Adeola did not have positive encounters with Arabs in Dubai (for example, she was yelled at and told to go back to Africa). Her experiences in KL seem to be the same: "Do you speak Cantonese? *Wu nga* (black crow)? *Hak tan* (charcoal)? I know *gagak hitam*, black crow in Malay." She pays very close attention to phrases uttered repeatedly either in passing or indirectly about her by some Malaysians: she knows that the phrases do not connote anything positive in relation to her.

In her comparison of Malaysian Malays and Indians to the Chinese, Adeola reasons that

> [Malays and Indians] do not have a problem with us. You know why? They are brown and we are black. So they don't care. They want to know us as people, where we come from, who we are. . . . I tell Mohamad [who drives me to client appointments], "Don't leave me alone with the [Malaysian] Chinese. This is a nice country, beautiful; but some are not so nice."

In general, while Malaysian Chinese tend to deny Adeola her humanity, Malaysian Malays and Indians acknowledge her existence as a fellow human being, albeit one who has been socialized in another country and culture.

Adeola's response to the disparaging phrases and negative stereotypes is to hold her head higher and walk more confidently in public, as if to signify pride in her body, culture, and country: "Let them stare at me. I stare back. I have a right to be here. . . . I do not harm anyone. We are all visitors on this earth." Instead of engaging in the rhetoric and practice of self-exclusion, Adeola stakes her claim in this unique way: since everyone has a limited time on earth, the planet then belongs to all and to no one. As such, everyone has the universal right of mobility and employment, so long as they do no harm to others.

Ndidi, in stark contrast, carries herself in a way designed not to draw attention to her person: whenever she walks in public spaces, she is slightly hunched over as if she needs to be as inconspicuous as possible, and she avoids eye contact with others. Ndidi has never been threatened explicitly, but she is mindful of the racial tensions and the possibility that someone will call the police to report "illegal Africans" in the area. For Ndidi, some residents are to be as feared as the authorities.

The Nigerian women consider foreign and Malaysian owners of small restaurants and bars catering to European clientele as much more accepting of their presence. The women can walk into an establishment and sit down for a meal or a drink without experiencing much unease or discomfort. Margaret explains:

> We can just talk like normal people. We debate which country has the "best" dictator; who knows how to kill people in one thousand ways; we complain about this weather [long stretches of heat and humidity interrupted by brief periods of torrential rain], make a lot of people sick.

The women's desire for and ability to engage in cosmopolitan sociability is restricted to these spaces that offer momentary fellowships. The ease with which Margaret interacts with the owners and their customers confirms for her that people who have international experiences are more open and accepting of the Other. Sameness can coexist with difference: "normal" people, regardless of their origins, always will find common ground if they wish to do so. The migrant women's views and experiences illuminate how cosmopolitan subjectivities neither emerge from a cultural vacuum nor are they merely a function of class or personality traits. Existing hierarchies into which migrant women sex workers are inserted in global cities cannot but affect their experiences, attitudes, practices, and worldviews:

> Openness is therefore most likely to be endorsed as a feature of the global world when it is associated with enjoyable experiences that cultivate one's identity, when they offer fulfilling experiences . . . At the same time, they are negatively coded when it is experienced as an engagement with other cultures that is perceived to be threatening or challenging,
>
> (Skrbis and Woodward 2007, 744–5)

Of the transnational migrant sex workers in this study, women with Caucasian-like features have experiences that contrast remarkably with those of the other migrant women. These women reside in the Golden Triangle's luxury condominiums or in wealthy southwest and northeast suburbs known also for their expatriate communities. Ekaterina deliberately restricts her encounters to what she considers an "elite of the elite" network, hence "there is no need for me to know ordinary people [be they middle- or working-class Malaysians or migrant workers]." Her rhetoric and practice of self-exclusion is explicitly classed: she focuses on doing her work within an exclusively limited cocoon that minimizes encounters with nonelites in global cities. Ekaterina does not see the need to "know" KL nor its people in any way beyond what is set up for her to work: KL is just one global city among many.

Similarly, the social networks of the Iranian women (Soraya and Afsar) are composed primarily of elite Malaysians and expatriates: both women stay in well-known expatriate suburbs of KL; they interact with expatriate-dominant social networks; and they shop and dine only in upscale establishments. Even so, from Soraya's perspective, there is less pretense in KL with regard to how Muslims are required to perform their piety in public, and she notes that relations between Muslims and non-Muslims generally are peaceful: "This city is amazing [especially how easy it is to meet people from so many countries]. . . . Muslims pray on Friday, but for everyone else, it is a normal day. . . . People are more free in this country [compared to Iran]. Women are more free in this country." She is careful to qualify her point, "The women in my country also can do what they want, but not outside." The freedom "to do," then, is dependent on the freedom "to be": for Soraya, this means that differences are accepted as opposed to repressed or erased in KL.

Afsar, on the other hand, celebrates neither the city's visibly multicultural, multiracial, and multireligious population, nor an ever-growing supply of luxury consumer goods (she quickly got bored of this). The main attraction for her is the elite male clientele. Despite their differences in nationalities and cultures, the men have in common their adoration of her physical beauty, as well as their power to "change lives" with business decisions and directives. On one level, Afsar's perception of men as the more powerful gender that makes and implements life-changing decisions recalls Meilin's comment on the cock and the hen. Yet Afsar celebrates elite men's power; she does not critique unequal gender relations.

Transnational migrant women sex workers' emerging cosmopolitan subjectivities, therefore, are not static or homogenous: they vary in accordance with the confluence of structural forces and personal proclivities: "Varieties of cosmopolitanisms are produced in a variety of localized contexts, each of which provide different access to power and capital, and produce different attitudes and behaviours toward others" (Datta 2009, 357). The contact zones of KL experienced by Ekaterina, Soraya, and Afsar are not similar at all to the contact zones experienced by migrant women from Asian and African countries.

WHITHER COSMOPOLITANS AT HOME?

If transnational migrant women sex workers' emerging cosmopolitan subjectivities are shaped by different sets of structure-agency relationships, can the same be said of Syndicate X's members in KL? Of all the syndicate members, mamees have the most frequent interactions with migrant women. While some mamees perform a minimal amount of work (for example, they process client requests from middle management and pass them along to the women), others are involved actively in helping younger and relatively less experienced women acclimate to new work environments.

One of the mamees, Alice, who migrated between the mid-1980s and 1990s to perform sex work in Hong Kong, Singapore, and Sydney, is ambivalent about how "times have changed" in KL. She asserts that sustained economic growth has not brought about greater opportunities for all, because there are sharp distinctions between the nouveau riche and the working classes. For women and men who neither have the political connections nor the requisite education and skills, life in the world-class city increasingly is lived and experienced in materially and symbolically segregated ways: some drive luxury cars, live in high-rise condominiums, dine in upscale restaurants, and shop in Pavilion, whereas others have to "work until they die" just to be able to pay their rent and put food on the table. Class disparity has become even more explicit than the racial divide: "Those people [the rich and politically connected] only take care of each other. They are all the same. Nobody cares about the poor even in their own group." Women and girls in poorer families bear the brunt of inequality.

KL's rise as a global city is accompanied by what Alice considers a deluge of transnational migrant men and women workers. Their presence creates anxieties and complicates growing class disparities among Malaysians. Although low-wage migrants perform the jobs that Malaysians do not want to do, their presence also broadcasts how some Malaysians seem to benefit easily while others struggle despite decades of sustained economic growth.

At the same time, Alice acknowledges that the in-migration of women sex workers provides the women and Malaysians with opportunities to earn income. She explains her support of migrant women sex workers from the class-gender nexus: "Everyone needs to eat and live. . . . Who doesn't want to live in a big house and drive a nice car? [The women] should not be ashamed that they have to use their bodies. No one has the right to say that they don't have good upbringing, right or not? To be a woman is a curse, so everyone has to do for themselves what they can to make it in this world."

When Alice failed the Form 3 exams (national exams administered halfway through secondary school), she had to help her parents operate their hawker stall. Within a few years, her boyfriend, who was a syndicate member with connections throughout Asia, arranged for her to earn foreign currency as a sex worker. Alice's overseas work experiences instilled in her an empathetic orientation toward transnational migrant sex workers:

[The Chinese proverb] "One grain of rice can feed eight different kinds of people" is very appropriate. I am not kidding you ah. In this world, there are so many different people with different outlooks in life. Malaysia is my home and will always be so. [Transnational migrant women sex workers] are the same. Their outlook expands as they work elsewhere. From narrow, [their worldview] becomes broad. You see how people overseas do things differently. Just because we don't do it like that doesn't mean it is wrong. But you know lah, us [Malaysian] Chinese people. We must always be right.

Alice exudes the ethos of a "rooted" cosmopolitan, grounded firmly in the particularities of her place and culture of birth, yet one who is able to ascertain and appreciate similarities and differences between people (Appiah 1997, 618). Most notably, she emphasizes the gendered similarities.

In the initial phases of working overseas, Alice was a greenhorn, who knew next to nothing about life beyond her hometown. Her most jarring experience was in Hong Kong, wherein she expected camaraderie based on similar racial, cultural, and linguistic backgrounds. What she received in return were constant put-downs because her Cantonese accent and demeanor exposed her as an "overseas Chinese" or "less-than-authentic-Chinese." With the help of her mamee, she quickly adapted by learning to speak without the suffixes of "lah" and "ah" at the end of each sentence, and she adopted nonverbal cues that signified her as a legitimate member of the dominant culture in Hong Kong. Alice learned the verbal and non-verbal cues required for functional communication: in time, they legitimized her as a cultural insider in Hong Kong.

According to Alice, it is no longer necessary for Chinese migrant women to confront the same blatant challenges because, once again, "times have changed" and "everyone knows that [the Chinese women] are foreigners." This does not mean, however, that every transnational migrant woman is accepting of the Other. Alice references the issue of physical altercations between Chinese and Uzbek women. Each side believed that it had accurate perceptions of the Other, and each side refused to amend its views when confronted with alternative interpretations, "Nobody gives in. So who is right, you tell me? Both also wrong. . . . Wah, terror lah when they fight. This one say we take side because they are Chinese. That one say we take side because we like white women. How to win?" Syndicate X's ultimate decision ensured that women with racial-cultural-linguistic proximity prevailed.

Alice offers her explanation for why the Malaysian Chinese dislike women sex workers from Africa: "I blame the syndicate [that brings in African women]. They should teach the women how to behave, how to walk, how to talk. They are so rough [in speech and conduct]." Alice's point invokes the well-known phrase, "When in Rome, do as the Romans do." As she had to do in Hong Kong, so too should the migrant women. By criticizing the African women's syndicate, Alice implies that only Malaysian Chinese syndicates provide the "appropriate" migrant women sex workers. Explicitly absent from yet undergirding her explanation is the racial dimension.

Alice upholds the syndicate's norm of a successful transnational migrant sex worker as a pale or light-skinned Asian woman who is refined, graceful, and sophisticated in her comportment. What she fails to admit (despite her acknowledgment of multiple ways of being, as opposed to one universal humanity) is that negative encounters between Malaysian Chinese and migrant women from African countries cannot but nurture mutual perceptions of threats that reinforce each party's schema for perceiving and relating to the Other. As the more powerful party, Malaysian Chinese ultimately control the conditions of encounters and dictate the criteria of evaluation. Alice admits this to some extent, "Yes-lah. [Malaysian] Chinese people, sometimes we can be very bad . . . because many have not been exposed to the world and they think they are the best people on earth. I keep telling the boys [the chauffeur-security personnel] that they should see the world, expand their horizons."

Some of the chauffeur-security men worked overseas when they were younger, as regular and irregular migrants in Australia, New Zealand, and Western Europe. Nevertheless, they worked in and lived among immigrants and migrants of Chinese descent in Chinatowns. An older man explains, "The country doesn't matter. Everywhere I go, I must find a Chinatown . . . There is no other place on earth that has our food." In the same vein as Zhenzhen, the men sought out and found comfort in safe foreign spaces characterized by "familiar strangers" and languages. Being in such spaces limited the opportunities for extensive interactions with dominant and minority groups in those cities. In this context, cosmopolitan sociability can be said to exist only to the extent of the men's interactions with members of the Chinese diaspora.

In Syndicate X, older men with transnational work experiences are elevated to a slightly higher social status (and bragging rights) compared to younger men who have never traveled or worked overseas. As chauffeur-security personnel, they command the respect of their younger counterparts. For example, if and when migrant women want their food to be purchased and delivered by the syndicate or the women ask to be driven somewhere other than client appointments, the older men tend to transfer this task to the younger men. They also regale their younger counterparts with stories of how everyday lives of foreigners in foreign lands are strange at best and incomprehensible at worst.

The fact that younger chauffeur-security men have no international experiences does not imply that they are unwilling to learn, or that they are inflexible or intolerant toward the Other. As Lamont and Aksartova caution, in their study of working-class black and white Americans,

> Their personal lives are often deeply embedded in very stable social networks and they tend to live within somewhat circumscribed communities . . . However, this should not be taken to mean that they are bereft of cosmopolitan

imagination—they engage with difference perhaps just as often as the paradigmatic cosmopolitans, albeit on a local, as opposed to a global, scale.

(2002, 2)

Since one of the syndicate men's main responsibilities is to drive migrant women to their appointments, one might assume that they have ample opportunity to interact with the women. Unfortunately, this is not the case. One afternoon, a syndicate chauffeur-security man invited me to drink beer with him and his four co-worker friends at a makeshift table just outside an auto-mechanic garage. As we chatted, I began to share with them what I had overheard the evening prior. Two men were having dinner next to my table at an open-air restaurant when a third man arrived, sat down, and started cursing vociferously. He told his dinner mates that he had waited quite a while for a migrant woman who "took her time to come downstairs." When she finally emerged from the hotel and got into his car, he tried to start a casual conversation with her. He told his dinner companions how the woman responded, "Do not speak to me and do not look at me. Just drive." She apparently had insulted him despite what he thought was kindness on his part. He then said, "I would not ____ her even if it was free. Who does she think she is, ah? A dirty, stinking stuck up ___. How many men have _____ her ah? Eh, my ____ won't rise looking at her."

While I narrated this to the men, some of them started to laugh and others clapped out of glee. One of them interrupts by saying, "It has to be Dog Head. He is so stupid, he never learns. The 'goods' [women sex workers] are arrogant. I will not waste time trying to talk to them. Dog Head is different. He wants to know about the world. He will never give up [trying to engage migrant women in conversation] so he always gets angry. He has a foul mouth but a very good heart."[4] One of the men explains further:

> These are not "goods" of the past that you can do whatever you want with them. . . . Now it is "See, no touch." The girls don't want to know us and they don't want us to talk to them when they are in the car. Those from China are the worst—they don't even look at you. At least the others will say "hello" and "thank you." You can't tell them what to do. They tell you what to do.

His colleague advises, "Next time tell [Dog Head] to switch [radio] channels. Let them listen to Indian music [in the car]. What can they do? If they don't like it, then tell them to get out of the car. See who wants to walk home."

The men initially had high expectations that, given racial-cultural-linguistic proximity, Chinese migrant women would be friendly or friendlier toward them, and in the process they could learn about the country, the women's lives there, the places to which women have traveled, and so forth. For the men who have not seen any place beyond the peninsula, they admire the women for their courage in leaving their families and countries in search of income. So, they want to know of migrant women's experiences. Men such as Dog Head, however, can and will respond to women's rebukes with derogatory gendered expletives designed to help him recover some sense of rhetorical dignity.

Migrant women's social distance from the men is shaped partly by the syndicate: women are informed on arrival of the need to ensure professional work relations, especially with chauffeur-security personnel. Similarly, Syndicate X supervisors inform the men, when they are first hired, that they are not pimps. As chauffeur-security personnel, they are expected to conduct themselves in a professional manner. Exacerbating the syndicate-constructed and -enforced social distance between migrant women and chauffeur-security men is women's higher earning power that fuels their attitude of superiority in relation to the men. Income and occupational stratification within the syndicate sharply demarcate the men's relationship with upmarket migrant women sex workers.

Black women sex workers from Africa elicit the most ire from the syndicate men. The men's unpleasant and negative comments expose an explicitly racist-culturalist dimension in their attitudes toward the women, despite the fact that (and because) there are no African women in their syndicate. One of the men rationalizes their disdain in the following way: "Every time they open their mouths, it is like they want to fight you. *Samseng* [hooligan] only lah." I proceeded to explain to the group that different cultures imbue different meanings in their verbal and nonverbal cues (tone and volume of speech, coupled with direct or indirect eye contact and body movements). So, when the men employ their own culture's criteria for feminine communication to evaluate the women's conduct and demeanor, then it surely would lead to misinterpretation at best. He pauses for a few moments, shakes his head, and replies, "Too black, not trustworthy." Since my explanation resonated to some degree, he then resorts to what can never be challenged: skin color offers irrefutable proof of African migrant women's character and conduct.

Of interest is that none of the men take issue with Awiti, the homeless on-street sex worker. Some of them (including Dog Head) pay for her drinks and give her cigarettes. They distinguish between Awiti and the other women because "she is crazy and she has no one except for the *pondan* [transvestite] who looks after her." Despite their dislike of African women sex workers, they extend compassionate gestures to Awiti: "She is a pretty girl. Small and delicate. What a shame." In other words, while Awiti's homeless status elicits sympathy, her smaller body frame and lighter skin tone are closer to the men's norm of a transnational migrant sex worker than darker and taller African women.

The men, like many of KL's residents, are ambivalent about the presence of migrant men and women from so many nationalities. On the one hand, they recognize the economy's dependence on low-wage migrants. On the other hand, "the government should do something. Soon we will not recognize our city . . . language, way of life will disappear." On the other hand, one of them notes that migrants would not be in the city if they were gainfully employed back in their own countries and if Malaysians agreed to do many of the low-wage jobs:

> Everyone here is trying to make a living. The men who collect garbage are from Bangladesh. Do you know that they go through the dirty bins to see what they can take and sell so that they can make some money on the side? What kind of leaders do they have? Look at the Indonesian maids. Either they steal your things and run away, or they are beaten and they go crazy.

Their ambivalence, however, has not prevented them from developing friendships with some migrant men from South and Southeast Asia. On a daily basis, the syndicate men encounter migrant workers who collect garbage, clean hotel rooms, park cars, cook food, bus tables, and sell goods. Over time and instead of holding an attitude of superiority toward all migrants, the men have come to acknowledge commonalities (as members of the working classes) and differences (cultural practices and worldviews), especially between them and migrants with whom they have frequent interactions. Similar to migrant women discussed earlier, the syndicate men practice a form of reciprocity. Interactions among syndicate and migrant men can be likened to mutually beneficial sociocultural educational exchanges; syndicate men help solve migrant men's problems related to getting things done in KL (such as obtaining legal documentation, medicine, clothing, housing) in return for wide-ranging vistas of everyday life in Kashmir, Pakistan, Myanmar, Nepal, and Vietnam—and, on occasion, opportunities to taste homemade dishes cooked by migrant men. Akin to Baoyan and her coworker friends, the men communicate in basic Malay interspersed with Urdu, Mandarin, English, and so forth. If they still are unable to convey a specific point, then "we use fingers, point at the sky and earth . . . draw. Eventually we know what is said."

In this context, cosmopolitan sociability is limited to a specific nexus of gender and class as embodied by relationships among the syndicate and migrant men. Their interactions take place in regularly patronized coffee shops and *mamak* and hawker stalls, as opposed to each others' residences. As one of them describes it, "I know the area [where some migrant men live], but I don't know exactly where and which section. It doesn't matter. We meet around here or over there." The men's interactions illustrate Kothari's point about being "cosmopolitan at work and more parochial when they leave the street" (2008, 502).

The syndicate men also have friendships with Malaysian coworkers of Malay and Indian descent. They share meals, visit one another's families during festive seasons, and help each other with a host of issues:

> We are Malaysians. This [job] is our rice bowl [a means of bringing in income]. The problem is not us [working-class Malaysian Chinese, Malays and Indians]. It is the big-tailed snakes [wealthy businessmen and politicians] who stir the pot and make trouble. They steal from companies, rob the people, then hire lawyers, stay out of jail, and still live in big houses. If you don't believe me, then read the newspapers. Everyday there are scandals. How can they say we are bad . . . gangsters . . . we do not have guns, we do not rob, and we do not steal so we break what law, they break what law?

As far as the men are concerned, a central issue confronting Malaysians in the present time is not race or ethnicity, but class. One of the men elaborates:

> My father [who just passed away] used to say that "if you have money, you can even hire ghosts to push your car." We are not bad people. Eh, you [referring to his friends] remember when [a local resident's] son committed suicide? He couldn't see how to repay his gambling debts. His mother didn't even have money for funeral expenses. So [a higher-ranking syndicate member] just gave her money to cover the costs. Do you think any of those big-tailed snakes offered to do so?

Just as he says this, a policeman on a motorcycle whizzes past the group. They nod to him as he returns the gesture. The syndicate man continues, "Small fry. They take money from us because they don't get paid enough. Meanwhile, the big-tailed snakes say they donate money to this and that charity. How much? What they give is the equivalent of a booger compared to what they have. We don't see them helping poor [Malaysian] Chinese, Malays, Indians?" His colleagues nod in agreement. Their emphasis on class highlights the many ways in which there continues to be uneven access—regardless of racial-ethnic background—to resources and opportunities generated by a neoliberal development path.

The syndicate men are proud of how KL has become a world-class city with globally recognized buildings, investors, and tourists from all over the region and the world. However, their ambivalence over large numbers of transnational migrant workers in the city is accompanied at the extreme end by their deep unease with regard to state efforts to market KL as a major tourist, education, and investment site for Gulf countries. One outcome is transformation of what the syndicate men consider spaces occupied by Malaysian Chinese into "foreign" ones, replete with imported Islamized symbols, as if they always have belonged in the city. The men invoke Bukit Bintang's Ain Arabia as an example: "Luckily [the anchor restaurant in little Arabia] closed. That is not their area. They can come and enjoy the girls, study hard, put money in the stock market, but they should not be allowed to buy property that doesn't belong to them."

As the men's discussion of Islamized symbols takes on a gradually agitated tone, one of them looks at his colleague who started to curse and cracks a joke to defuse the tension: "We all know you prefer the young white [backpack tourists] in hot pants and flip-flops in Bukit Bintang. 'Yes, miss, can I help you?'" Indeed, the men are more at ease with "familiar strangers" than "unfamiliar strangers" whose wealth and investments threaten their sense of rootedness.

The syndicate men's emerging cosmopolitan subjectivities, thus, are mediated by intersections of male camaraderie, working-class backgrounds, and the desire to learn and to know of specific Others. In this way, they too exhibit a "mix of atomization and fluid associations." As a world-class city with constant flows of people and ideas, KL is a large contact zone composed of multiple and overlapping smaller ones, in which some people are free to choose where they work, live, and play, while others are restricted or even self-segregated by virtue of their nationality, race-ethnicity, class, occupation, gender, and immigration status. Everyday life in this city nurtures markedly different forms of "actually existing cosmopolitanisms" (Robbins 1998).

CONCLUSION

The analysis in this chapter demonstrates that the cosmopolitan or cosmopolite is more empirically diverse and complex than has been theorized in the main. Besides hypermobile elites, nonelites also can and do evince the characteristics of tolerance, flexibility, and openness to difference. By itself, transnational migration indeed does not necessarily nurture emerging cosmopolitan subjectivities. This is evident in some migrant women's responses to the overall repressive context in which they live and work, for example, the transient superiority in Xiaofan's and Zhenzhen's rhetoric and practice of self-exclusion. On the other hand, syndicate men who have never traveled overseas are able to appreciate and value the Other as demonstrated by their friendships with transnational migrant men workers.

On the whole, migrant women's and syndicate members' encounters with difference reveal that they are not guided solely by utilitarian motives (such as earning income), nor by the narrowness of their upbringing and identity. Even Qing, who refuses to interact with migrants and Malaysians for fear of disclosure as a prostitute, nevertheless desires to do so because of her need for human fellowship. From views on humanity to acts of reciprocity, migrant women and syndicate members express genuine desires to know and appreciate the Other. Their different forms of cosmopolitan sociability manifest along the cognitive, affective, and behavioral dimensions in their acknowledgment of and respect for the coexistence of sameness and difference.

In stratified contexts, however, their cosmopolitan sociabilities are not neutral with regard to gender, race-ethnicity, or class. The gender dimension is inescapable in syndicate men's encounters with migrant women and men. Partly due to syndicate rules and partly due to the nature of their jobs, the men are able to develop more meaningful relationships with migrant men than with the syndicate's migrant women, who invoke income differentials to create even more social distance between them.

Nigerian women, on the other hand, face unique encumbrances wrought from conflation of their nationality, culture, and race-ethnicity. The women's encounters with Malaysian Chinese residents and syndicates are primarily negative. As a result, their cosmopolitan sociability is expressed mostly in encounters with European tourists, expatriates, and Malaysians who are less prejudiced and discriminatory toward them.

The experiences of migrant women who are represented and treated as "white," that is, at the highest tier of sex workers, are bounded by their elite networks. The networks of Ekaterina, Soraya, and Afsar in KL are upper-class Malaysians and expatriates who have common consumption preferences and practices, from place of residence to apparel. In this way, their expressions and experiences of cosmopolitan sociability are limited by a specific nexus of classed and racialized-ethnicized social status.[5] Despite different nationalities and cultures of origin, the women see themselves and are seen as having more in common with elite Malaysians and expatriates than with the other migrant women and working- and middle-class Malaysians. Of the three women, Soraya is the only one who articulates her appreciation of KL's cultural and religious diversity. Afsar is more interested in socializing with men VIPs because of why and how they are able to wield power. Ekaterina pointedly says that she sees no reason to interact with those beyond her elite-of-the-elite social network. The transient superiority inherent in Ekaterina's rhetoric and practice of self-exclusion is unlike that of Xiaofan or Zhenzhen.

The end result is a complex and fragmented picture of how transnational migrant women and syndicate personnel make sense of and negotiate between the parochial and the global in the different contact zones of the global city. Within a largely repressive environment in which the state seeks to rid the city of all irregular transnational migrant workers, as public discourse continues to denigrate if not condemn "foreign prostitutes" and those who assist them, many of the migrant women's and syndicate members' encounters with the Other in KL construct little spaces of hope and empowerment in which there is good in bad and sameness in difference.

CHAPTER 7
Conclusion

Life, moral or physical, is not a completed fact, but is a continual process, depending for its movement upon two contrary forces, the force of resistance and that of expression. Dividing these forces into two mutually opposing principles does not help us, for the truth dwells not in the opposition but in its continual reconciliation.
—Rabindranath Tagore (1921, 32)

Guided by the 3C framework of city, creativity, and cosmopolitanism, this study examines the complexities of and contradictions arising from neoliberal economic restructuring processes that encourage and sustain the phenomenon of women's transnational migration for sex work. Analysis of women's migration and sex work in the global city of KL contextualizes the dimensions of city, creativity, and cosmopolitanism. In all three dimensions, we find the common denominator of classed, gendered, and racialized-ethnicized forces that shape and are shaped by relationships among state policies, public discourse, migrant women, and syndicate personnel.

The in-migration and employment of women sex workers in KL is not a new or unprecedented contemporary phenomenon. During British colonial rule, women from China and India voluntarily and involuntarily migrated to perform sex work in what was a growing trade and mining settlement. They were joined by Malay women, as well as women from Japan and Europe. At independence and with closure of the immigration gates, sex work was performed primarily by Malaysian women from the three major communities of Malays, Chinese, and Indians. By the end of the twentieth century, women from many more nationalities began to arrive in the city for sex work. Their entry and employment came on the heels of postcolonial state policies that successfully guided KL's transformation from a town dominated by the Malaysian Chinese to a global city with a diversified economy and population.

As one key site for the command and control of the new global economy, the global city of KL is connected to its counterparts within and beyond the region by crisscrossing multilane highways: ports and airports, railways, and even fiber-optic cables that make possible flows of capital, goods, information, and services. Some of these highways also serve as migratory pathways for corporate executives, accountants, lawyers, and other categories of global talent required for the world-class city to provide advanced producer services. Notably, the pathways are opened officially to select categories of low-wage temporary, guest, or migrant workers. Migrant women and men who are in search of employment but who cannot (or do not want to) qualify for entry may and will enter on two additional pathways established by ongoing state liberalization of the tourism and education service sectors.

Just as in the colonial past, low-wage transnational migrant workers are indispensable to KL's economic growth. Even though their labor in the manufacturing, agriplantation, construction, and service sectors helps underwrite and maintain KL's competitive identity as a global city, their contributions seldom are acknowledged and affirmed:

> While the presence of the highly skilled is a key indicator of world city status, the presence of low-skilled labor is an equally important indicator of a second labor process underlying world city formation. Migrant workers provide cheap labor to fill the increasing numbers of low-wage jobs that provide services for transnational firms and high-wage professional lifestyles, including maids, gardeners, food-service workers, cleaners and others.
>
> (Malecki and Ewers 2007, 468)

In addition to the much-valorized global talent and these workers' contributions to advanced producer services, global cities such as KL offer personal services, which are performed, more and more, by low-wage migrant workers. KL's growing dependence on services provided by low-wage migrant women and men attests to Sassen's point that migrants are the twenty-first century's "serving classes" in global cities (2002, 262).

This dependence, nevertheless, is mediated by the Malaysian state's migrant diversification strategy that stipulates migrants' placement and employment according to nationality and gender in key economic sectors and industries. Subsequently, public discourse naturalizes ascribed traits specific to migrant men and women from different nationalities. Phrased differently, migrant nationality is conflated with culture, gender, and race-ethnicity.

To be sure, women sex workers from within and beyond the region are members of the serving classes in KL. They provide sexual services as a subcategory of personal services. The women are in all tiers of sex work: their clients range from low-wage migrant and Malaysian workers to middle and upper classes of corporate executives, politicians, state officials, expatriates, tourists, and businessmen. The colonial era's racialized-ethnicized and classed dimension of sex work finds its contemporary expression with women's differential placements in the global city's hierarchy of sex workers. While some women are sex-trafficked, others migrate independently by drawing on their social networks, or with the assistance of syndicates. As noted in this study, nontrafficked women migrate mainly via the tourism and education pathways.

Migratory pathways linking global cities pose tremendous challenges to major receiving states such as Malaysia. They are confronted by the dilemma of keeping external borders open for desired categories of transnational migrants ("highly skilled" workers, certain "unskilled" workers, investors, tourists, and students) and closed entirely to others. With the intensification of public discourse on the myriad ways in which regular and irregular migrants are represented and perceived as threats to the economy, society, and polity, receiving states are compelled to protect internal boundaries of the nation as well.

Constrained yet empowered by the neoliberal ideology that undergirds national, regional, and global economic restructuring processes, major receiving states creatively apply the principle of privatization to processes of securitizing migration. In the case of Malaysia, the state's privatization strategy mostly takes the form of transferring some internal security operations to RELA, the citizen-civilian volunteer corps. For nearly a decade, this volunteer corps has assumed a central role in protecting the world-class city and nation against irregular migrant men and women. Citizen-civilian volunteers uphold the state's 3D approach of detaining, disempowering, and deporting "illegal aliens." Since immigration regulations prohibit entry of the "prostitute," nontrafficked migrant women sex workers then are a major target of RELA and other security agents of the state.

Interviews of the women for this study reveal that their initial decisions to migrate for sex work did not emanate from a sense of "false consciousness" or extreme poverty. With the exception of two women who were sex-trafficked as girls (Siti and Awiti), the women willingly migrated for sex work. The migrant women's decisions were based on their understandings of constraints and opportunities emanating from structural forces that cut across the individual, household, national, and global levels.

From the women's perspectives, sex work in KL and other global cities represents a more viable path to earning higher incomes, and in more acceptable work conditions, than low-wage domestic, factory, and clerical work in sending and receiving contexts. While some women initially were driven by the socioeconomic imperative of assisting family members, others did so to escape patriarchal or religious constraints, as well. Subsequently, transnational migration for sex work offers the women new avenues for life- or self-enhancement, such as unprecedented opportunities to travel and experience the world, to pursue part-time programs of study, to consume the latest couture apparel, to purchase land or homes, and to set up businesses. The women are acutely aware that their transnational migration for sex work has and will continue to elicit the hypocrisy of states and societies that vilify them even as they draw on women's sexualized labor. Migrant women sex workers' experiences in KL are mediated not only by the tier of sex work they are in, but also by specific intersections of nationality, culture, and race-ethnicity.

Despite a hostile environment fueled and endorsed by state policies and regulations, migrant women persist successfully in entering KL for sex work. The women creatively exercise their agentic power to pursue alternative channels of migration and to evade security agents of the state. Migrant women enter as international tourists, as international students, or as authorized migrant workers for other economic sectors and industries. Those who migrate independently and have established social networks in the city rely on migrant and Malaysian friends and acquaintances for protection and for clients. There also are women who migrate and work with the assistance of individual compatriots with local connections in KL and other global cities. The majority of women in this study, however, participate in syndicate-facilitated migration.

The existence of KL's large and small syndicates reflects, as well, the creativity of other people in their responses to constraints and opportunities arising from neoliberal economic restructuring processes. Those who are unable to secure well-paying jobs, those who are marginalized from the formal economy's profit-making activities, and those who want to earn tax-free income and profits, may turn to informal, extralegal economic activities. Their direct and indirect involvement with syndicates facilitating women's transnational migration for sex work is a prime example.

There are different types of syndicates in KL. They vary according to the nature or scope and reach of their activities: there are syndicates that collaborate with transnational counterparts to control all phases of sex trafficking (from recruitment and transportation to work conditions); syndicates that only purchase and control trafficked women; syndicates that operate mainly on members' abilities to lure away migrant women from competitors or persuade migrant women already in the city to be sex workers; and syndicates that collaborate with transnational counterparts to recruit, transport, and employ nontrafficked migrant women. Syndicate X is an example of the last group. During the mid-1990s, the syndicate transformed from a hierarchically structured secret society that controlled Malaysian women sex workers under debt bondage to a more decentralized corporate-like organization that offers the sexual services of contract-based transnational migrant women. Its metamorphosis came about in response to the state's strategy of removing sex workers from city streets and well known sly prostitution sites, amidst the reconfiguration of urban places and spaces.

Under pressure from state policies and regulations, the syndicate's younger generation of leaders identified and pursued opportunities to "professionalize" the secret society. Their philosophy and schema for operating a modern business enterprise prompted a division of labor among four groups: the investment, security-legal, human resources, and miscellaneous divisions. Under this new leadership, the syndicate began investing in legitimate real estate and other businesses and cultivating alliances with transnational and local state and nonstate actors in the migration and ancillary sex industries.

Syndicate X members adamantly insist that their syndicate does not buy or accept sex-trafficked women because of what the leadership acknowledges as the legal, logistical, and moral costs of doing otherwise. Instead, the syndicate enters into contractual exchange relations with migrant women. As part of its efforts to eliminate debt bondage, Syndicate X only charges migrant women the cost of visa applications and airfare prior to arrival in KL. Migrant women then are responsible for paying monthly board and lodging fees in addition to the 40% tax on their income. The syndicate's reputation for treating migrant women well has prompted some women to recruit their compatriots back home, and they are remunerated for doing so.

Syndicate X provides migrant women with the convenience and protection of a one-stop shop. They handle all aspects of women's migration and employment: from travel documents and housing, to personal security, clients, and arrangements for forward journeys to other global cities. In this way, nontrafficking syndicates offer women a more convenient and relatively institutionalized mode (depending on the strength and quality of their transnational alliances) for migrating to global cities within and beyond the region.

Syndicate X's success lies in its leadership's ability to meet existing demands and to adjust operations accordingly, in the pursuit of profits from sex work performed by migrant women. Yet, shifts in the syndicate's transnational alliances as well as strategies to nurture new demands while meeting existing ones (for example, demands for women from specific nationalities and racial-ethnic backgrounds), do not bode well for migrant women's job security. Simply put, migrant women are vulnerable to the vicissitudes of a very fluid, trend-based environment. Southeast Asian women were the preferred nationalities for Syndicate X, its counterparts, and clientele during the early 2000s in KL. Since then, they have been displaced by women from the PRC and women who look "white." Syndicate X, thus, contributes to a gendered, racialized-ethnicized, and classed dimension in the global city's sex industry. The leadership's major decisions pertaining to transnational migrant women cannot but expose self-imposed limits to profit accumulation: the decisions reveal a racial-heterosexual ideology driving their choices with regard to the nationalities and physiognomies of the sex workers.

Despite and because of unequal power relations in the global city, migrant women's and syndicate personnel's encounters with difference evince conceptual, emotional, and behavioral aspects of "cosmopolitan sociability" (Schiller, Darieva, and Gruner-Domic 2011). From views on humanity to acts of reciprocity, many of them acknowledge the coexistence of similarities and differences. They seek to understand and respect alternative ways of living, being, and doing by people born and raised in communities other than their own. At the same time, however, some of them appropriate and endorse deprecating stereotypes, especially those premised on racial-cultural superiority, to rationalize their prejudicial attitudes and discriminatory conduct. Thus, in the global city of KL, migrant women's and syndicate personnel's encounters both challenge and affirm coloniallike ascriptions, ensuing worldviews, and treatments of the Other.

A MURKY WAY FORWARD?

This study raises issues related to policies at the national and international levels. Global or world cities are deeply implicated in contemporary transnational migration for employment, including that for sex work. With the entry of more members into the club of global cities, intercity competition and collaboration will create even more migratory pathways, demands for migrant women sex workers, and modes of organizing their migration and employment. Embedded in webs of interconnectedness, global cities are major junctions or nodes in the global sex frontier.

From this vantage point, receiving states' dominant 3D approach of detaining, disempowering, and deporting irregular migrant women is akin to a dog chasing its own tail. Women travel on the same migratory pathways established between global cities for the movement of executives, investors, authorized low-wage migrant workers, tourists, and students. Even if receiving states are successful in keeping out migrant women, they still are unable to dampen demands for women sex workers. These demands are fueled, organized, and met by a variety of groups, some with transnational alliances and operations straddling the formal and informal economies.

Given the global exigency to combat sex trafficking, receiving states are augmenting the dominant 3D approach with the 3P approach of preventing sex trafficking, protecting victims, and prosecuting or punishing traffickers. The former approach is premised on protection of the receiving economy, society, and polity. The latter approach is premised on protecting trafficked persons, including sex-trafficked women and girls. As a result, protection nets are cast so widely that "[w]omen's own motivations to move, and their diverse experiences of migration are lost" (Crosby 2007, 47). Hence, when some migrant women falsely claim sex-trafficked status to lessen the harsh punishments faced by irregular migrants, this only reinforces states' 3D approach.

Adopted in concert, both approaches convey the notion that receiving states and nations are the true victims. This, subsequently, sanctions ongoing processes of securitizing migration that, depending on the context, can involve citizen-civilians in the protection of their homelands:

> The receiving country is not implicated in their migration phenomenon, and is justified in resorting to methods of containment and confinement. These punitive measures constitute migrant women as outlaws, and compel them to live illegal lives. . . . Her consensual movement is rendered illegal, through the foregrounding of the security of the nation-state, the conservative sexual morality that informs anti-trafficking laws, and the xenophobic responses to global movements that increasingly inform immigration laws.
>
> (Kapur 2003, 6)

Cast as such, the phenomenon of women's transnational migration for sex work is conceptually divorced from structural forces and contradictions of neoliberal globalization that nurture, strengthen, and integrate free-market economies (including states' role in the rise and growth of global cities with their migrant labor markets). This conceals the fact that nontrafficking syndicates and migrant women sex workers emerge from within the larger context of neoliberal globalization: these two major sets of actors also appropriate neoliberal discourse and practice on free-market operations and transactions to achieve their own ends.

Facilitating groups or syndicates are main anchors in global cities' migration and ancillary industries for sex work: they signify localized management of the global sex frontier. Syndicate size, specialization, structure, operations, and transnational alliances are influenced by the political, cultural, economic, and regulatory contexts from which they emerge or transform to organize women's migration and employment for sex work. Despite this diversity, syndicates largely are designated by states and international organizations as "criminal organizations." The blanket designation, to be sure, legitimizes legal action against all groups (trafficking and nontrafficking) that facilitate women's unauthorized migration for employment, as it provides some form of rhetorical assurance with regard to protection of the nation.

Nevertheless, it is impossible to eliminate constantly morphing syndicates and rising cases of irregular migrant women sex workers, in part because of the many stakeholders ranging from agents of the state and legitimate enterprises to a host of workers in "support services" within the informal and formal economies. As the analysis of Syndicate X reveals, such groups provide employment or generate income for many individuals. In an era of constant rapid change, syndicates represent relatively stable economic safety nets for a range of actors. Effective state suppression of these syndicates has to involve, conceivably, the mapping and identification of every domestic and transnational connection (to agents of the state, consulate officers, legitimate businesses, and so forth); the identification and arrests of concealed, powerful interests; and indeed, the full incorporation of marginalized individuals into the formal economy.

Even if all the above measures are viable, at the heart of the issue remain the abiding effects of neoliberal economic restructuring processes on the reconfiguration of everyday life and consciousness. Ostensibly, the new global economy generates more employment and wealth-creation opportunities for many more people. Although this may be the case for specific sectors, industries, and actors, the triad of economic liberalization-privatization-deregulation policies, as implemented in existing political-cultural contexts, continues to differentially marginalize women. Transnational migration for sex work has become a viable opportunity for some women. Their migration for sex work from global city to global city is a hidden-in-plain-sight phenomenon in which "patriarchal ideologies and related gender inequalities are significant, even constitutive, features of the global economy" (Mills 2003, 47).

Women's decisions to migrate for sex work reveal their exercise of agentic power within structural constraints: they choose it over what they consider the limited range of servile, low-wage gendered jobs available to them. Assuredly, migrant women's decisions affirm the resilience of sexualized patriarchal power inherent in sex work, as they elicit contradictions in how the women are perceived and treated:

> Wage work and new modes of commodity consumption open up newly imaginable possibilities of personal autonomy and self-expression that are often targeted most forcefully at women. Nevertheless, these images of modernity often carry a contested moral status: women in particular are vulnerable to accusations of immorality owing to "excessive" modernity and inappropriate commodity consumption. . . . Such charges are only heightened in contexts where economic development relies in part upon the commodification of women's sexual labor.
>
> (Mills 2003, 49–50)

There are sharp differences, to be sure, between the abolitionist and sex worker perspectives, and these perspectives remain pitted against one another in stultifying debates on prostitution's relationship to sex trafficking. Obscured by the debates is the larger context from which emerged both perspectives, that is, the globalized commodification of women's sexual labour. This larger context is what the perspectives have in common, even though they are grounded in different worldviews and they focus on outcomes derived from, and informed by, different empirical realities. Is it possible then to even consider crafting policies that can address meaningfully the range of empirical realities today? This question is important to ask because it prompts us to move beyond an either-or stance. Until we do so, the complexities of women's lives will remain largely obscured, as will viable solutions.

The past few decades of accelerations in the-making-of-the-world-as-a-whole based on and sustained by integrated free-market economies, are naturalizing the commodification of nearly all dimensions of life. To be sure, this can be seen in the ways in which some women are bought and sold into sexual slavery: they are assigned exchange values to be traded and owned within and beyond countries. This can be seen also in the ways in which some women successfully migrate across borders and arrange to exchange their sexual labor for income.

Free markets offer producers the opportunities to sell their products or services, and consumers the opportunities to choose from an ever-growing list. Given the twenty-first century's dominant form of "governance that excuses state retraction from social and job-creation services and places more responsibility on individuals to provide for themselves" (Keough 2006, 433), people then are encouraged to author their own destinies. Free markets putatively expand "the horizons and sites from which individuals can select to shape" their identity and paths in life (Chin 2008a, 109). Freedom of authorship, nonetheless, is circumscribed by intersections of gender, class, education, nationality, and race-ethnicity as evaluated and ranked in different contexts. Indeed, there may be more options, but as demonstrated by the migrant women in this study, the options exist only within specific ranges.

The ever-expanding horizons of neoliberal globalization are accompanied, paradoxically, by a narrowing or recompartmentalization of perspectives, as readily seen in national and global discourses on immigration, the so-called war on terror, elections, and so forth. People are expected to take clear stands, either for or against each issue or controversy. Within a context of constant rapid change, the need to render phenomena easily "legible," that is, in accordance to an either-or perspective, means that there seemingly remains little legitimate space to seriously consider other perspectives without prior or automatic recourse to dismissive attitudes and responses. The irony is that this is unfolding in an era that canonizes freedom, opportunity, and the individual. In theory, these categories contain, encourage, and convey diverse possibilities. Embedded within the structure of a system of nation-states, they are mediated by countervailing pressures to reinscribe order:

> Putting people who move into categories assumes and in fact creates a singularity of experience and opportunity that obscures people's actual lived experiences. The reasons why people move are varied and multifaceted, and belie the categories we have constructed. Categorization fragments, segregates, and creates hierarchy.
>
> (Crosby 2007, 48)

Existing as well within socially stratified contexts, these categories embody and embolden the fight for equality and justice, whether it is the protection of migrant women's rights to be sex workers or the rescue of sex-trafficked migrant women.

What the women in this study tell us is that they have a right to migrate: as Adeola, the Nigerian sex worker claims, "I have a right to be here [Kuala Lumpur] . . . I do not harm anyone." The women also have a right to choose from the limited range of authorized and unauthorized work open to them by neoliberal economic restructuring processes. Lia, the Filipina concierge and part-time sex worker pointedly says,

> Why these women [migrant sex workers] are looked down, I do not agree. Is it worse than being a maid? You read the newspapers . . . some are slapped, punched, and beaten by employers? For a few hundred ringgit, only if employers pay them? Why should this be more acceptable [than sex work] to society? Until we walk in another woman's shoes, we cannot say that we know her life and we cannot judge her.

Lia reminds us that migrant women can and will question what should be defined as acceptable labor, and that their views are just as legitimate. The transnational scope and participation of a range of individuals today expose the fact that transnational migration for sex work increasingly is considered an acceptable economic activity not just by the women, but also by women and men who assist them in sending and receiving cities.

Women's transnational migration for sex work is not an aberration. Criminalizing them—as if to contain the spread of disease—is ultimately counterproductive, because this disease has its pathology in structural constraints and opportunities nurtured by the contemporary marriage of patriarchal power and free-market economies. The phenomenon will persist until and unless this marriage is addressed in ways that account comprehensively and honestly for its intrinsic hypocrisies.

NOTES

CHAPTER 1

1. See especially Mahdavi (2010, 2011), and Andrijasevic (2010). I deliberately employ the term *sex worker* to avoid the negative connotations of the term *prostitute* (see especially Piper 2005). More significant, the women in this study consider sex work as another form of labor that is exchanged for money.

2. Embedded liberalism came about in response to the 1930s global economic depression, that is, by encouraging state intervention in the economy to buffer society against the ravages of unfettered market forces. In the Global North, this gave rise to different forms of the welfare state created by compacts among state, capital, and labor. Following World War II, newly independent countries beyond communist spheres of influence were integrated into an international economic system spearheaded by the Bretton Woods twins. By the late twentieth century, however, structural issues (such as, high unemployment, inflation, and public spending) led to an about-face. In the Global North, the elections of Ronald Reagan in the United States and Margaret Thatcher in the UK marked an ideological shift from the Keynesian approach of state intervention in the economy to the neoliberal approach of liberating capital from all constraints, whether political, social, or regulatory. As a result, policies of deregulation, privatization, and liberalization were hailed as the path to economic growth and prosperity. In the Global South, states that had borrowed heavily (especially from transnational banks flush with petrodollars) could not service their loans when the Organization of Petroleum Exporting Countries (OPEC) raised oil prices again in the late 1970s. The net result was imposition or adoption of structural adjustment programs (SAPs)—an economic menu-based prescription of conditionalities placed on debt restructuring—aimed at removing obstacles to free-market operations.

3. See Sassen (2009) for how global cities are ranked differently depending on a range of criteria, from business and finance indicators to quality of life and freedom.

4. The historical example is the state's role in London's emergence as a major world financial center at turn of the twentieth century (Polanyi 1944).

5. Werbner, for example, calls them "global pathways" (1999).

6. "By managing their location's brand equity, politicians do two things: externally, they aim to attract more clients, charge more for their products/services, and generate overall economic/political advantage for their location; internally, they aim to make their citizens feel better and more confident about themselves by giving them a sense of belonging and a clear self-concept" (van Ham 2002, 253).

7. Given the "place wars" of intercity competition to attract capital and human resources, branding practices have become obligatory, especially for the purposes of differentiation, the creation of emotional ties, and the encouragement of aspirational lifestyles (Yeoh 2005, 946). For reviews of evaluatory frameworks developed to assess the success of states' branding practices, please see Vandewalle (2009). In cities of the Global North for example, we see a reconfigured relationship between tourism promotion, migration, diversity, and place. What used to be much-maligned immigrant enclaves now are promoted as a city's "ethnic advantage" or "diversity dividend": "In downtown or suburban parts of the city, 'ethnic precincts' are essentially clusters of ethnic minority or immigrant entrepreneurs in areas that are designated as ethnic precincts by place marketers and government officials" (Collins 2007, 67). This is similarly the case in Singapore, for example, with state rehabilitation of Little India and Little China. Elsewhere, for example in Shanghai, Dubai, and Kuala Lumpur, multibillion-dollar mega-structures serve as national and global symbols of prominence.

8. GATS's "methodology of the negotiation of services" allows states to determine which of the twelve sectors to open up for foreign investment and which sectors they would like to access overseas. None of the twelve sectors are negotiated separately; rather, "they are negotiated in relation to all the topics covered by the negotiation round" (Verger 2009, 385).

   GATS is governed by three key legal principles: (1) the most favored nation clause (nondiscriminatory treatment); (2) market access (access for all foreign investors identified by GATS); and (3) national treatment (treatment of foreign firms in same way as domestic firms). States can exercise the "general exceptions" clause for exemption from commitments due to negative effects on public morals; on human, animal, or plant life; or on health (for further details, please see World Trade Organization 2011).

9. GATS deals with tourism and travel-related services in the subsectors of hotels and restaurants, travel agency and tour operators, tour guide services, and others. The four modes governed by GATS for the international delivery of services are "consumption abroad," in which tourists travel to where the supplier is located; "cross-border delivery" in which both provider and supplier remain in their respective countries (for example, via the Internet); a "commercial presence" of a foreign provider at a destination site; and "movement of natural persons," in which providers can cross borders to deliver services. Liberalization of tourism sectors opens the door for the entry of foreign firms, labor, and materials, which is required for the provision of services.

10. Akin to the four modes of international service delivery for tourism, consumption abroad refers to the movement of international students; cross-border delivery refers to services such as distance education; commercial presence is related to the establishment of local educational branches overseas; and movement of natural persons refers to the ability of scholars and teachers to cross borders in order to deliver their services (Hanley and Fredriksson 2003, 98). In brief, cross-border education services no longer are bounded exclusively by traditional migratory flows of full-time degree-seeking students from the Global South to the Global North.

11. Critics of liberalizing education argue that education is quickly becoming a major global export commodity, which in turn encourages the restructuring of academic administration according to what have been identified as ideologies of new managerialism (Deem 2001), academic capitalism (Slaughter and Leslie 1997)

and entrepreneurship (as in Clarke's "entrepreneurial university"). Capitalist management principles and modes of assessment increasingly are being adopted within the academy. As such, education no longer is designed to serve the public good: rather it is becoming the handmaiden of global capitalism. Proponents of liberalizing education, nevertheless, argue that it will "bring innovation through new delivery systems and providers and greater student access and economic value" especially given declines in public funding (Knight 2002, 210).

12. The majority of states have not rushed to liberalize their education sectors: in the early 2000s, approximately one-third committed to liberalizing education in general and even fewer committed to liberalizing higher education in particular. During the Uruguay Round of 1986–1998 and the Doha Round of 2001–2009, most states avoided committing education to GATS. The reasons included a low priority assigned to education, the need to balance education's role in national development and identity with that of education as a tradable commodity (Knight 2002, 213), and the complexities of ensuring quality of services and the removal of restrictions on foreign capital (Verger 2009, 383). Gradually, however, more states are beginning to liberalize education, specifically higher education: "From around the world clear signs of changes can be seen in the way education is provided. There is an increased interest for education to be partially or fully provided from the private sector. This is particularly true in the higher education sector and increasingly in vocational education but it is not limited to these sectors" (Hanley and Fredriksson 2003, 99).

13. From the perspective of international students, "the decision to study overseas often [is] a symbolic first step in global career formation" as they "represent an increasingly attractive human resource to governments and employers" (Hawthorne 2010, 94). In some contexts, the desires of students and receiving states intersect: in migration-driven enrollments, students hope to immigrate after their studies, and receiving states hope to transform them into permanent residents. Canada and Australia, for example, have become "dependent on migration for half to one-third of all professional workers." To address workforce supply, "both Canada and Australia have prioritised skilled migration, diversified immigrant source countries, utilised points systems designed to improve selection objectivity while maximising employment outcomes, and in particular enhanced scope for 'two-step' migration (migrants' immediate transition from temporary to permanent resident status)" (Hawthorne 2010, 98).

14. In the Global South, critics warn that local educational systems may be weakened considerably by the establishment of foreign-owned and -operated institutions; national values and priorities may be undermined by foreign providers that do not share similar values; local academics may be exploited by such providers; emphasis on profits will bring about substandard courses; and state control over higher education will be weakened overall (McBurnie and Ziguras 2001, 88). Higher education gradually is being subjected to and governed by commercial or profit motives.

15. The visa is designed to ease families' concerns for children, while fostering "loyalty among regional talent at an early age" (Rubin 2008, 56; see also Sidhu, Ho, and Yeoh 2011).

16. For example, research has shown the diverse causes of women's migration (for example, flight from conflict, sexual violence, familial oppression), and their vulnerabilities in receiving contexts (for example, passports being held by the labor broker, employer-related exploitation and abuse, being subcontracted to

other employers). When captured, irregular migrant women are sent to detention centers or refugee camps in which their specific needs—for example, the needs of pregnant and lactating mothers—are ignored or dismissed by state authorities (see especially Yuval-Davis, Anthias, and Kofman 2005; Binder and Tošić 2005; Trappolin 2005). Detention centers or camps are "zones of exemption" in which the state has no obligation to follow its own laws (Rajaram and Grundy-Warr 2004, 38). Whether the detainees are documented workers who overstayed their contracts, victims of human trafficking, refugees, or asylum seekers, their unapproved and hence unlawful presence casts them outside the parameters of the receiving state's moral responsibility and legal accountability. They are the political, cultural, social, and economic pariahs, who now occupy a transitional space prior to deportation or resettlement. In some countries, sex-trafficked women are given special visas and the right to determine whether or not they wish to assist in the prosecution of traffickers. In other countries, the women are detained in shelters or so-called rehabilitation centers prior to deportation and made to assist in state prosecution of traffickers (Gallagher and Pearson 2010).

17. The abolitionist perspective undergirds the national and global advocacy work of the US-based Coalition Against Trafficking in Women (CATW).

18. See especially the work of the Global Alliance Against Trafficking in Women (GAATW).

19. For a provocative analysis of the cunning of history in which second-wave feminism's critiques (for instance, of the paternalistic state and state intervention in the economy) paradoxically have dovetailed with key tenets of neoliberalism, please see Fraser (2009).

20. By and large, what we do know is that some intermediaries in the migratory process may be friends, acquaintances, or relatives who see themselves as helping women: "[A] great number of people not necessarily tied to crime take advantage of the activities connected to the exportation of migrants and have no interest in stopping it" (Campani quoted in Agustín 2006, 35).

21. Despite the many ways of categorizing a vast body of literature on cosmopolitanism, in general there are two major strands of thought: one is "sociocultural and aesthetic," and the other is political (Kofman 2005, 83). This study focuses on the former. The latter is often associated with the philosopher Immanuel Kant, and his vision of a global political project that would transcend all parochial forms and expressions, including moral and cultural particularities, separating peoples. Kant conceptualized cosmopolitanism along the four dimensions: he conceptualized the political-legal in terms of a world federation; the economic in terms of world trade; the civic in terms of a global public sphere; and the cultural in terms of one humanity (see, for example, Abdelhalim 2010; Archibugi 2003; Delanty 2006; Mignolo 2000).

22. Abdelhalim (2010) and Mignolo (2000) offer analyses of the historical origins of cosmopolitanism from the era of *Orbis Christianus* and its faithful-infidel distinction, to the rise of the nation-state with its citizen-foreigner distinction and that of contemporary neoliberal globalization with its "nativist–cultural relativist" and "secular consumer–religious fundamentalist" distinctions.

23. "All too often it is an 'us'—Westerners, Europeans, humanitarians, etc—who are the cosmopolitans, the champions of justice, human rights, and world order; leaving 'them'—the Third Worlders, the global poor, the "wretched of the earth"—as the abject, the societies and subjects in crisis, the failed states in need of intervention" (Nyers 2003, 1073).

24. Please see Poster (2002) for a literature review of feminist ethnographic studies according to each of the three sets of experiences. See also Wolf (1996).
25. For more detailed discussions of women researchers as "honorary male" in the field, please see especially Ergun and Erdemir (2010); Golombisky (2006); Widerberg (2007); and Wolf (1996).

CHAPTER 2

1. The Golden Triangle originally encompassed only the area of Bukit Bintang. More recently, it has been expanded to cover territory roughly bounded by Jalan Tun Razak, Jalan Ampang, and Jalan Pudu so as to include prime real estate and major landmarks such as PTT and KLCC.
2. MAS is similar to Malay Reservation Land: "It was introduced by the British by virtue of section 6 of the 1897 land enactment. The purpose behind the introduction of this category of land was to cater to the needs of the poorer class of Malays staying in the urban area like Kuala Lumpur. Matters pertaining to Malay Agricultural lands are governed by a special board known as Board of Management created under Notification 21 of the Selangor Gazette 1900. The rule also prescribes that only the Malays can occupy the land and there is no title issued to any individual owner. No dealing can be done involving this land unless with the approval of the Board" (Mohamad 2007, 121). For a good discussion of how the British ignored Malay usufructuary rights in favor of the concept of ownership of private property (following the Torrens system of land administration), please see Yeoh (2001). For more detailed discussions of the Malay Reservation Enactments of 1913 and 1933, please see Kratoska (1985), Nonini (1992) and Roff (1967).
3. Established in 1897, Kampung Baru was gazetted as a Malay Agricultural Settlement (MAS) in 1899. When KL became a FT in the 1970s, Kampung Baru was expanded to include non-MAS areas covering parts of Jalan Chow Kit, Jalan Dang Wangi, Jalan Sultan Ismail, and the Selangor State Development Flats. Consequently, the total area increased from 91 to 153 hectares. Throughout the late twentieth century, the Malaysian state was unsuccessful in redeveloping Kampung Baru because of resistance from the community. In 2010, KL City Hall proposed a renewal plan to transform Kampung Baru into an upmarket commercial and residential area. The proposed project was mired in legal challenges: some lots remained in the original owners' names because beneficiaries had forgotten to register their claims; some lots had multiple owners because of Islamic inheritance laws; some residents rejected giving up control of 40% of the land to non-Malays for redevelopment; the state's proposed rate of approximately RM800 per square foot (due to Kampung Baru's MAS status) was considered substantially below the market rate of RM1200–1500 per square foot; and an administrative oversight had failed to annul the state of Selangor's claim over Kampung Baru when KL was transferred to the federal government. Selangor legally retains jurisdiction over this area (Alhabshi 2010).
4. The Employment (Restriction) Act 1968 allowed the entry of skilled or professional workers.
5. "Bumiputeraism came to stand for a racial condition of political and economic advantage in which Malays could claim unchallenged access to a wide range of resources for advancing their wealth and status" (Lee 2004, 126).
6. Rimmer and Dick (2009) posit that such townships and their latter-day versions were modeled after gated US communities, whereas King (2008) asserts that they were modeled after British town planning.

7. For a discussion of Islamic influences in the architecture of Putrajaya, please see King (2008). For an analysis of the three major phases distinguishing Malaysian architecture in KL, please see Goh and Liauw (2009).

8. The phenomenon of squatter settlements in KL began with its establishment as a colonial trading town. By the 1990s, there were 171 squatter settlements within KL's city limits and many of them were to the east and southeast of the city (Anjomani and Ahmad 1992, 160).

9. W. G. Maxwell, the colonial Resident of Selangor from 1889 to 1892, introduced the Torrens system from South Australia, in which all unregistered land belonged to the state: private ownership was introduced via registration of land with the state (ownership by registration, not by deed). This system would become the basis for the National Land Code in postcolonial Malaysia. The Federal Land Acquisition Act 1960 (revised 1992) gives the Malaysian state the right to acquire land for public purposes and to determine the compensation (see Aiken and Leigh 2011).

10. See especially Yeoh for a historical analysis of the colonial and postcolonial states' squatter policies, particularly how the postcolonial state's efforts to contain expansion of such settlements were mediated simultaneously by the humanitarian approach to make available "communal water stand pipes" to communities "but for a fee" (2001, 112; see also Aiken and Leigh 2011). For discussions of indigenous groups' legal actions to protect their customary land rights (for example, Bukit Tampoi and the dislocation of Temuan people), please see Bunnell and Nah (2004); Fujita (2010); and Nadarajah (2007).

11. "Health tourism in Malaysia has been supported by the government's tourism, health, international trade and industry, and finance ministries, which have helped it grow rapidly over the past few years. The number of private hospitals with over 10,000 beds has risen to 210, compared with only fifty private hospitals with 2,000 beds in 1980. Meanwhile, by the end of 2007, the number of doctors in the private sector had risen to 18,246, while the number of nurses had risen to 68,349. Earlier this year, the Association of Private Hospitals of Malaysia (APHM) forecast that revenues from health tourism will continue to grow at double-digit rates for the next three years" (Global Insight July 15, 2008). Among health tourists from Asia, the Middle East, and Europe, KL is known for its plastic-cosmetic, orthopedic, cardiovascular, and transplant surgeries, and it competes with global cities such as Bangkok, Singapore, New Delhi, and Seoul (The Edge November 30, 2009). Health tourism packages combine such procedures with recuperation periods in luxury apartments or resorts.

12. "Matta deputy president Datuk Khalid Harun said Malaysia currently ranks second to Turkey as the most preferred destination. According to Tourism Malaysia findings, he said, one of the attractions is the promotion of the country as a halal hub. Up to the end of last year, over 200,000 Muslims from West Asia alone visited the country. And Middle Easterners appreciate the country for its stability and Muslim-friendly policies in every industry, including the financial sector. Apart from the food and culture, tour and travel agencies are also using the world-class mosques, infrastructure, and Muslim-friendly accommodations as a selling point" (New Straits Times March 27, 2008).

13. In 2011, there were an estimated 1 million Malaysians overseas and approximately one-third was the result of the "brain drain" (World Bank 2011a, 15).

14. "A different route has been taken by Malaysia, where the growth in graduate and professional education has been led by the business community. Multimedia

University was built by the Malaysian telephone company, while Universiti Teknologi Petronas was originally a wholly owned subsidiary of the national oil company. 'Today these schools attract not just Malaysian students but students from all over South Asia, the Arab world-even European students,' [global education expert] Dr. [Jamil] Salmi said" (International Herald Tribune October 4, 2010).

15. See the Immigration Department of Malaysia's website for more details, particularly in relation to students from specific countries.

16. As of September 2011, students from twenty-seven countries (including Pakistan, Palestine, Sudan, and Japan) were eligible for this international scholarship program. According to MOHE, "By awarding the scholarships, not only it gives the students a chance to further their studies, but it would also strengthen our bilateral relationship with respective countries. Also, it will make Malaysia an excellent hub for higher education at the international level" (New Straits Times September 28, 2011).

CHAPTER 3

1. The Malaysian state has consistently refused to ratify the ILO Convention No. 97 "Migration for Employment' (Revised) 1949" (Sabah is the only state in the federation that ratified this in 1964); the ILO Convention No. 143 "Migrant Workers (Supplementary Provisions) 1975"; and the "UN Convention on the Protection of Rights for All Migrant Workers and Members of Their Families 1990" (Piper 2004a, 2004b; Kabeer 2007; Kaur 2008).

2. Highly skilled migrants, however, are subjected to different rules. They can enter with their spouses and families. State-determined levies amount to only a few hundred ringgit. The maximum length of their work permits used to be five years, before it was revised upward to ten years. In order to attract and retain global talent, state elites proposed the need for an even longer permit period as well as a fast-track system to permanent resident status (National Economic Advisory Council 2010, 123).

3. In 2011, the state increased all levies by RM50 to help pay for the new biometric system implemented to monitor migrants. Employers are responsible for paying the new levies: RM410 for domestic and agricultural workers, RM590 for plantation workers, RM 1250 for manufacturing and construction workers, and RM1850 for services workers (New Straits Times September 6, 2011).

4. Prior to this, Home Affairs already had taken over receipt of levy payments from the Immigration Department. The department's role then focused on visa and permit issuance, and enforcement (Kaur 2006, 26–7).

5. There is no consensus among scholars or politicians as to the meaning of the phrase. For more detailed discussions on the debate, especially between politicians in Malaysia, please see Cheah (2005) and Williamson (2002).

6. Such practices also may be accompanied by "physical and verbal abuse exacted on migrants; and even selective enforcement of more punitive regulations with regard to migrants" (Georges-Abeyie 2001). Mexican migrants' experiences in the United States, for example, attest that "where the law allows policing or enforcement agents any discretion, the tendency is to treat minorities more severely because they are less than human or seen as less deserving" (O'Leary 2007).

7. When one of the major brigades within RELA was alleged to be affiliated with Perkasa, a Malay supremacy group, RELA's director-general as well as the Home

Affairs minister vehemently denied that permission had been given for the group to recruit from RELA's membership (New Straits Times June 24, 2011; The Straits Times June 19, 2011).

8. Although the state refuses to recognize the UN convention, during the 1970s it did work with the United Nations High Commissioner for Refugees (UNHCR) eventually to repatriate and resettle Vietnamese refugees who succeeded in landing on the shores despite real threats of being shot down by the navy. Today, the majority of refugees in Malaysia come from neighboring Southeast Asian countries. Some refugees such as the Christian Chins from Myanmar alleged state discrimination against them (that is, by favoring Muslim Rohinyas from Myanmar and Acehnese from Indonesia) while Rohinyas accused the UNHCR of favoring Christian Chin refugees in the country (Kaur 2007).

9. In 2011, the state entered into negotiations with Australia to pilot an exchange program, in which Malaysia would serve as an offshore processing site on behalf of Australia for 800 asylum seekers, in return for Australia's acceptance of 4000 UN certified refugees from Malaysia (International Herald Tribune July 26, 2011).

CHAPTER 4

1. "In the history of British colonial administration the Chinese Protectorate of Malaya occupies a unique position. . . . It was organized so that Chinese-speaking officers of the Civil Service might be free to deal with specifically Chinese problems such as the suppression of the secret societies and the protection of Chinese immigrants. From the latter activity the protection of women and girls logically followed" (Purcell 1948, 151). In contemporary Singapore, prostitution is legal and it is regulated by the state. For a discussion on the phenomenon of "yellow card girls" (local and transnational migrant women sex workers are legally required to carry yellow identification cards marking them as legal prostitutes), please see Lim (2004).

2. The Po Leung Kuk operated much like "a sort of marriage bureau" for rescued and rehabilitated women and girls (Gullick 2000, 92).

3. See Manderson for a detailed discussion on how STD cases increased as a result of the repeal. The British transferred surveillance of women's bodies to private "medical clubs" that charged women a health exam fee. The colonial authorities also represented sex workers as "vectors" of disease and European men as victims (1997, 50). For an extensive discussion on colonial discourse that racialized and sexualized women on the peninsula, please see Crisnis (2004).

4. Discourse on the white slave traffic (and concomitant representation of women sex workers as victims) culminated in successive White Slave Conventions in 1904, 1910, and 1921 (Crinis 2004; Weitzer 2007).

5. The postcolonial state, in a similar vein, established "rehabilitation" centers for girls: "The programmes in the rehabilitation centres appeared to be geared toward making the girls into good housewives" (Nagaraj and Yahya 1998, 95; see also Gallagher and Pearson 2010, 76–77). The Women and Girls Protection Act 1973 (a latter-day version of the Protection Ordinance) was repealed upon implementation of the Child Act 2001.

6. Although solicitation for prostitution is a criminal offense under the Penal Code, prostitution itself is not a criminal offense (see especially Sections 372 and 373 in Malaysia 2006b). In 2008, an opposition member of Parliament "asked whether the Government would make prostitution a crime because currently

soliciting for prostitution was a crime but not prostitution itself. [Deputy Home Minister] Chor said the current laws were adequate whereby prostitutes or prostitute organizers were charged for the immoral act. However, the Government would consider a change in laws if it becomes a big problem" (The Star November 26, 2008). In 2011, the Malaysian Bar Council's president, in his disagreement with the prime minister's department, stressed the fact that prostitution is not a criminal offense according to the Penal Code: "Prostitution in itself is not a criminal offense," he stressed, though he acknowledged there were certain provisions in the law to prosecute those who offer sex in exchange for money. He pointed to section 372A of the Penal Code, which provides for action against persons living on or trading in prostitution." (The Malaysian Insider April 9, 2011). Indeed, according to Section 372B, "Whoever solicits or importunes for the purpose of prostitution or any immoral purpose in any place shall be punished with imprisonment for a term not exceeding one year or with fine or with both" (Malaysia 2006b, 145), while Section 373(3) criminalizes brothel ownership and operations.

7. *"Alternatif yang mudah bagi membolehkan mereka mencapai taraf hidup yang tinggi"* (Zakaria 1987, 50).

8. This also was the case in Chin and Finckenauer's study on PRC women sex workers in Asian cities (2011).

9. When translated into the English language, the phrase invoked when a man pays for the services of a sex worker is "to call a chicken." According to elderly men (retired members of Chinese secret societies), this phrase originated from Imperial China when farmers threw rice grains to feed their chickens: they "called their chickens." The Cantonese use of the word "goods" can be traced to the colonial era, when wealthy Chinese traders owned warehouses in which they stored their goods, and from which they sold them to retail shops.

10. It was the only small group interview; other women consented only to individual interviews.

11. For a discussion of the three tiers of sex workers in Ho Chi Minh City and the ways in which the highest tier of Vietnamese sex workers perform "relational" or emotional work, please see Hoang (2010).

12. Please see Lévy and Lieber (2008) for how Chinese women navigate the streets in France.

13. This does not imply that young girls (particularly Indonesians) are not sex-trafficked in KL, or that there is an absence of client requests for younger "virginal" women (see, for example, South China Morning Post May 5, 2008). Meizhen elicited hysterical laughs from the group at dinner when she shared what had occurred with a client. She accepted the "fat, ugly, and old" man's request for a "less experienced" sex worker. To play the part, Meizhen ended up feigning sexual ignorance by yelling in pain (such as "Ouch, pain, it hurts . . .") with every thrust on his part.

14. I was not successful in speaking with any African women students who engaged in part-time sex work. A local taxi driver, however, offered some insight into the women. His routes mainly involve Cyberjaya–Putrajaya–Subang Jaya–Shah Alam–KLIA, as he specializes in driving international executives and students back and forth to KLIA. As a side business, he is the intermediary for some African women students and executives who work in the industrial parks. When his executive clients call in advance to "book a girl," he then will call to find out which woman is available at the given day and time. From his perspective, some

African women students perform sex work because they do not have other funding sources and need the extra income. Although African men and women students in KL have a "bad reputation" for being out-of-control and aggressive, "Still you have to pity them because some are very serious students and they are very well brought up. If they don't have enough money for their studies and living expenses, then what else can they do?"

15. She did not volunteer information beyond this, and I did not pursue the matter further.

16. Since Afsar hesitated in speaking further of her logistics job, I chose not to highlight the disparity between her comment about working for a logistics firm and the boredom of a daily shopping and dining routine.

CHAPTER 5

1. Undoubtedly, prostitution's status affects researchers' access to male clients: "Researchers note that customers often refuse to participate in research exercises of an activity which is not condoned by society. . . . A serious lack of systematic survey-based research on the male customer still exists" (Samarasinghe 2009, 38–9).

2. See the edited volume by Ownby and Heidhues (1993) for a radically different contemporary reinterpretation of secret societies.

3. Victor Purcell, who served in the colonial administration, explained this type of indirect rule: "The Government found no effective means of dealing with this menace [secret societies] until 1889. . . . Colonial Cavenagh, the Governor of the Straits from 1859 to 1867, managed however to abate the [secret society] riots by the ingenious device of swearing in the known Lodge Masters of the secret societies as special constables and making them patrol the streets under surveillance to restore order" (1948, 80).

4. Purcell offered the rationale for British intervention: "The British did not interfere with native customs until they forced themselves unpleasantly on their attention. Examples of customs provoking that interference were secret societies, gaming, and the traffic in women and girls" (1948, 82).

5. One syndicate member shared with me what had happened to him when, out of curiosity, he accepted an acquaintance's invitation to view the buying and selling of trafficked women. They drove to a remote jungle site and walked some distance before encountering a group. He saw men in the group standing over numbered trafficked women who were squatting on the ground. Buyers then proceeded to call out numbers and inspect the "property" that they intended to purchase and "rent out" for housework or sex work: "I looked away [so that they could not see his tears] . . . how they treated the girls . . . not like human beings." He vomited on the way back to the car, "I couldn't eat after that. I thought of my daughter and my sisters. I'd kill anyone who treated them this way. . . . I swear on my ancestral altar, [in our syndicate] we don't do this."

6. Chin and Finckenauer found that in KL "many nightclubs, [karaoke bars], and hotels in our research site are actually owned by a small network of wealthy businessmen who are well connected to the local and central authorities" (2011, 477). This similarly is the case in Singapore and Jakarta.

7. For discussions of Soviet and post-Soviet racialization and ethnicization processes in Central Asia, please see Akiner (1997) and Roman (2002).

8. Kim and Fu's research on Russian women sex workers in South Korea also evinces the growing preference for "white" women: "Unlike the way the Third

World Woman has been marketed in developed nations, the emergence of the Western Woman as the new subject of desire and dominance represents a new commodity frontier for men in the emerging economies of the East" (2008, 513).

9. Anti–money laundering laws that require banks to "know your customer" (also known as KYC) tend not to be standardized from one country to another. Neither banks in Singapore nor Malaysia, for example, have a stipulated threshold that automatically flags an account (Shanmugam and Thanasegaran 2008).

10. For the most part, this affirms Shanmugam's study (2004), as well as the Asian Development Bank's finding that *"hawala, padala,* or *hundi* refer to informal channels popular with Indian, Filipino and Bangladeshi nationals. The remitter approaches an identified 'runner' or agent and is given an account number of a bank and a telephone number. He then credits the said money into the said account and informs the individual via telephone of the details. Sometimes it is necessary to fax the deposit slip. Upon confirmation of necessary details, the recipient can receive the cash—sometimes as fast as the same day or the following day. The sender pays no fee, but a tip may be given. The system is perceived as fast, efficient, convenient, cheap, and trustworthy, but there is an element of risk, as this is not an official or legal business. In interviews, the central bank acknowledged the existence of this method, but because the operators are able to camouflage it with a legitimate money changing business, prosecution is difficult. These informal channels are fairly large, with an estimated 30% market share" (Asian Development Bank 2006, 189).

CHAPTER 6

1. The word *cosmopolite* was coined by the ancient Greeks in reference to a "citizen of the world." Even so, it did not refer literally to citizens of the world. The Athenians assumed that man had to belong to a particular state and they denied citizenship to women, slaves, and resident foreigners (see especially Fine and Cohen 2002).

2. The relationship between transnational migrants and cosmopolitans is not as clear-cut as previously conceptualized in the literature on cosmopolitanism. Werbner, in her study of Pakistani migrants writes, "Transnationals are people who move and build encapsulated cultural worlds around them. Cosmopolitans, by contrast, familiarise themselves with other cultures and know how to move easily between cultures. The working-class labour migrants discussed here are primarily transnationals, living in their enclosed cultural worlds wherever they travel, but the paper also shows it is possible to be a working-class cosmopolitan, a person who gains knowledge and familiarity with other cultures" (1999, 19–20; see also Delanty and He 2008). For a more detailed discussion on transnationalism and cosmopolitanism, please see Roudometof: "My argument is that the transnational experience should be conceived as involving several layers ranging from the construction of transnational social spaces to the formation of transnational communities. Hence, transnationalism's relationship to cosmopolitanism is less straightforward than what it might seem at first glance" (2005, 113). He rejects the assignment of "transnational" exclusively to migrants and "cosmopolitan" exclusively to elites, partly because of racial and classed connotations and partly because *transnational* as an adjective often is applied not only to people but to goods, practices, organizations, and so forth.

3. One example is Liebelt's study of Filipina domestic workers in the Middle East. Jerusalem and Amman were some of the transit cities in women's migration from the Philippines to final destinations in Western Europe or North America. In the process of pursuing their strategic economic interests, the women also desired to understand, and some even learned, other cultural-religious practices and beliefs that allowed them symbolically to claim membership in the Holy Land. Their adaptation to receiving households and societies were related closely to their religious self-perceptions as carriers of the word of God: "[Some of the women] become self-proclaimed Middle Eastern experts or politically active Christian Zionists or sentimental Orientalists, who, in spite of their Christianity, miss fasting on Yom Kippur or during Ramadan as they continue their journeys toward Western Europe and North America, where they have hopes of living and perhaps gaining citizenship" (Liebelt 2008, 567).

4. The men are nicknamed after animals, parts of their bodies, numbers, or things. Instead of revealing what he is called by his friends and the syndicate, I have assigned a commonly known and used nickname for him.

5. It is argued that in the contemporary era of neoliberal globalization, hypermobile individuals' lifestyles are affected by capitalism's standardization of experiences. Sami Zubaida's description of elite cosmopolitans in Egypt alludes to the shared experiences of "transnational managerial classes" (Cox 1987) or "transnational capitalist classes" (Sklair 2001), in which members have more in common with one another than with their compatriots back home: "In another global context, international business creates its own uniform milieux, with its executives and personnel travelling the world and residing in diverse centers, but always in the same hotel rooms, apartments, served by Filipina maids, and networks of sociability of colleagues and associates of the same formation. Tourism similarly creates its own milieux: at the level cheaper levels, resorts, hotels, entertainments and food, which strive for standardization from Benidorm to Bodrum" (2002, 39). The point here is that their elite cosmopolitan subjectivity has more to do with their class position and attendant consumption of commodified transnational elite culture, than immersion in and concomitant knowledge of everyday lives in any particular place.

BIBLIOGRAPHY

Abdelhalim, Julten. 2010. "Cosmopolitanism and the Right to Be Legal: The Practical Poverty of Concepts." *Transcience Journal* no. 1(1):63–86.

Acker, Joan. 2004. "Gender, Capitalism and Globalization." *Critical Sociology* no. 30(1):17–41.

Agathangelou, Anna M. 2004. *The Global Political Economy of Sex: Desire, Violence, and Insecurity in Mediterranean Nation States*. New York: Palgrave Macmillan.

Agence France Presse. November 22, 2007. "Malaysia Says Will Keep Controversial Visa on Arrival." Agence France Presse.

Agustín, Laura María. 2005. "Migrants in the Mistress's House: Other Voices in the 'Trafficking' Debate." *Social Politics: International Studies in Gender, State and Society* no. 12(1):96–117.

———. 2006. "The Disappearing of a Migration Category: Migrants Who Sell Sex." *Journal of Ethnic and Migration Studies* no. 32(1):29–47.

———. 2007. *Sex at the Margins: Migration, Labour Markets and the Rescue Industry*. London: Zed Books.

Aiken, S. Robert, and Colin H. Leigh. 2011. "Seeking Redress in the Courts: Indigenous Land Rights and Judicial Decisions in Malaysia." *Modern Asian Studies* no. 45(4):825–75. doi: 10.1017/s0026749x10000272.

Akiner, Shirin. 1997. "Melting Pot, Salad Bowl, Cauldron? Manipulation and Mobilization of Ethnic and Religious Identities in Central Asia." *Ethnic and Racial Studies* no. 20(2):362–98.

Alatas, Syed Hussein. 1977. *The Myth of the Lazy Native: A Study of the Image of the Malays, Filipinos and Javanese from the 16th to the 20th Century and Its Function in the Ideology of Colonial Capitalism*. London: Frank Cass.

Alhabshi, Sharifah Mariam. 2010. "Urban Renewal of Traditional Settlements in Singapore and Malaysia: The Cases of Geylang Serai and Kampung Bharu." *Asian Survey* no. 50(6):1135–61. doi: 10.1525/as.2010.50.6.1135.

Altman, Dennis. 2002. *Global Sex*. Chicago: University Of Chicago Press.

Andrijasevic, Rutvica. 2009. "Sex on the Move: Gender, Subjectivity and Differential Inclusion." *Subjectivity* no. 29:389–406.

———. 2010. *Migration, Agency and Citizenship in Sex Trafficking*. Basingstoke, UK: Palgrave Macmillan.

Anholt, Simon. 2009a. "The Media and National Image." *Place Branding and Public Diplomacy* no. 5:169–79.

———. 2009b. *Places: Identity, Image and Reputation*. New York: Palgrave Macmillan.

Anjomani, Ardeshir, and Faizah Binti Ahmad. 1992. "Squatter Settlement in Kuala Lumpur: Evaluation and Alternatives." *Ekistics* no. 59(354):159–65.

Aoyama, Kaoru. 2009. *Thai Migrant Sex Workers: From Modernisation to Globalisation*. New York: Palgrave Macmillan.

Appiah, Kwame Anthony. 1997. "Cosmopolitan Patriots." *Critical Inquiry* no. 23(3):617–39.

———. 2006. *Cosmopolitanism: Ethics in a World of Strangers*. New York: W. W. Norton.

Archibugi, Daniele. 2003. *Debating Cosmopolitics*. London: Verso.

Asia Times Online. March 3, 2007. "Malaysia Tries to Shackle Foreign Workers." *Asia Times Online*.

Asian Development Bank. 2006. *Workers' Remittance Flows in Southeast Asia*. Manila: Asian Development Bank.

Associated Press. February 26, 2007. "Report: Malaysia May Designate Areas for Foreign Workers over Public Security Concerns." The Associated Press.

———. January 8, 2008. "Malaysian Airports Barred from Recruiting Foreign Workers." The Associated Press.

Atchison, Chris, Laura Fraser, and John Lowman. 1998. "Men Who Buy Sex: Preliminary Findings of an Exploratory Study." In *Prostitution: On Whores, Hustlers and Johns*, edited by James Elias, Vern L. Bullough, Veronica Elias, and Gwen Brewer, 172–203. New York: Prometheus.

Athukorala, Prema-chandra. 2005. "Trade Policy in Malaysia: Liberalization Process, Structure of Protection, and Reform Agenda." *ASEAN Economic Bulletin* no. 22(1):19–34.

Banderet, Christoph, and Thomas Weder. 2004. *Destination Schweiz: Migration und Asyl in der Schweiz* [Destination Switzerland: Migration and Asylum in Switzerland]. Bern: Bundesamt für Flüchtlinge.

Barry, Kathleen L. 1984. *Female Sexual Slavery*. Updated ed. New York: New York University Press.

Baxstrom, Richard. 2008. *Houses in Motion: The Experience of Place and the Problem of Belief in Urban Malaysia*. Stanford: Stanford University Press.

BBC. January 3, 2007. "Incidents May Mar Malaysia's Tourism Bid." *BBC News*.

———. August 9, 2010 "Malaysian Rights Group Wants Separate Law for Migrant Smuggling." *BBC Monitoring Asia Pacific*.

———. February 24, 2010. "Malaysia Puts Burden of Monitoring Foreign Workers on Industries." *BBC Monitoring International Reports*.

Berman, Jacqueline. 2003. "(Un)Popular Strangers and Crises (Un)Bounded: Discourses of Sex-Trafficking, the European Political Community and the Panicked State of the Modern State." *European Journal of International Relations* no. 9(1):37–86.

Bernama. August 18, 2004. "Prostitutes Moving to City Outskirts—Cop." *Malaysian National News Agency*.

———. February 13, 2007. "Foreign Workers' Bill Goes to Parliament Next Month—Radzi." *Malaysian National News Agency*.

———. November 25, 2008. "Over 7,000 Prostitutes Busted in 'OPS NODA' since 2003." *Malaysian National News Agency*.

———. April 23, 2010. "Malaysia Set to Capture Greater Share of International Mice Market." *Malaysian National News Agency*.

———. March 31, 2010. "Call to Turn Malaysia into Islamic Education Hub." *Malaysian National News Agency*.

Bigo, Didier, and Elspeth Guild. 2005. *Controlling Frontiers: Free Movement Into and Within Europe*. Aldershot: Ashgate.

Binder, Susanne, and Jelena Tošić. 2005. "Refugees as a Particular Form of Transnational Migrations and Social Transformations: Socioanthropological and Gender Aspects." *Current Sociology* no. 53(4):607–24.

Bishop, Ryan, John Phillips, and Wei-Wei Yeo. 2003. *Postcolonial Urbanism: Southeast Asian Cities and Global Processes*. New York: Routledge.

Block, Alan A., and William J. Chambliss. 1981. *Organizing Crime*. New York: Elsevier.

Bowen, John. 2000. "Airline Hubs in Southeast Asia: National Economic Development and Nodal Accessibility." *Journal of Transport Geography* no. 8(1):25–41. doi:10.1016/s0966-6923(99)00030-7.

Brennan, Denise. 2004. "Women Work, Men Sponge, and Everyone Gossips: Macho Men and Stigmatized/ing Women in a Sex Tourist Town." *Anthropological Quarterly* no. 77(4):705–33.

Brett, Judith, and Anthony Moran. 2011. "Cosmopolitan Nationalism: Ordinary People Making Sense of Diversity." *Nations and Nationalism* no. 17(1):188–206.

Briones, Leah. 2008. "Beyond Trafficking, Agency and Rights: A Capabilities Perspective on Filipina Experiences of Domestic Work in Paris and Hong Kong." *Wagadu: A Journal of Transnational Women's and Gender Studies* no. 5:49–72.

Brunovskis, Anette, and Rebecca Surtees. 2010. "Untold Stories: Biases and Selection Effects in Research with Victims of Trafficking for Sexual Exploitation." *International Migration* no. 48(4):1–37. doi: 10.1111/j.1468-2435.2010.00628.x.

Bunnell, Tim, Paul A. Barter, and Sirat Morshidi. 2002. "Kuala Lumpur Metropolitan Area: A Globalizing City—Region." *Cities* no. 19(5):357–70.

Bunnell, Tim, and Alice M. Nah. 2004. "Counter-global Cases for Place: Contesting Displacement in Globalising Kuala Lumpur Metropolitan Area." *Urban Studies* no. 41(12):2447–67.

Burawoy, Michael. 2001. "Manufacturing the Global." *Ethnography* no. 2(2):147–59.

Burawoy, Michael, Joseph A. Blum, Sheba George, Zsuzsa Gille, Millie Thayer, Teresa Gowan, Lynne Haney, Maren Klawiter, Steve H. Lopez, and Sean Riain. 2000. *Global Ethnography: Forces, Connections, and Imaginations in a Postmodern World*. Berkeley: University of California Press.

Cabezas, Amalia L. 2004. "Between Love and Money: Sex, Tourism, and Citizenship in Cuba and the Dominican Republic." *Signs: Journal of Women in Culture & Society* no. 29(4):987–1015.

Calavita, Kitty. 2006. "Gender, Migration, and Law: Crossing Borders and Bridging Disciplines." *The International Migration Review* no. 40(1):104–32.

Calcutt, Lyn, Ian Woodward, and Zlatko Skrbis. 2009. "Conceptualizing Otherness: An Exploration of the Cosmopolitan Schema." *Journal of Sociology* no. 45(2):169–86.

Capous-Desyllas, Moshoula. 2007. "A Critique of the Global Trafficking: Discourse and U.S. Policy." *Journal of Sociology & Social Welfare* no. 34(4):57–79.

Carstens, Sharon A. 1993. "Chinese Culture and Polity in Nineteenth-Century Malaya: The Case of Yap Ah Loy." In *"Secret Societies" Reconsidered: Perspectives on the Social History of Modern South China and Southeast Asia*, edited by David Ownby and Mary Somers Heidhues, 120–52. Armonk, NY: M. E. Sharpe.

Castles, Stephen, and Mark J. Miller. 2009. *The Age of Migration: International Population Movements in the Modern World*. Fourth ed. New York: Guilford Press.

Cerny, Philip G. 1997. "Paradoxes of the Competition State: The Dynamics of Political Globalisation." *Government and Opposition* no. 32(2):251–74.

Ceyhan, Ayse, and Anastassia Tsoukala. 2002. "The Securitization of Migration in Western Societies: Ambivalent Discourses and Policies." *Alternatives: Global, Local, Political* no. 27(1 (Suppl)):21–39.

Chan, Kwok-Bun, and Vivien Wai-Wan Chan. 2010. "The Return of the Native: Globalization and the Adaptive Responses of Transmigrants." *World Futures* no. 66(6):398–434.

Cheah, Boon Kheng. 2005. "Ethnicity in the Making of Malaysia." In *Nation-Building: Five Southeast Asian Histories*, edited by Gungwu Wang, 91–116. Singapore: Institute of Southeast Asian Studies.

Chin, Christine B. N. 1998. *In Service and Servitude: Foreign Female Domestic Workers and the Malaysian "Modernity" Project*. New York: Columbia University Press.

———. 2000. "The State of the 'State' in Globalization: Case Study of Economic Restructuring in Malaysia." *Third World Quarterly* no. 21(6):1035–57.

———. 2002. "The 'Host' State and the 'Guest' Worker in Malaysia: Public Management and Migrant Labour in Times of Economic Prosperity and Crisis." *Asia Pacific Business Review* no. 8(4):19–40.

———. 2003. "Institutionalisierte Diskriminierung als Staatliche Politik: Frauen und Migration in Südostasien [Institutionalized Marginality as State Policy: Women and Migration in Southeast Asia]." In *Leviathan: Migration im Spannungsfeld von Globalisierung und Nationalstaat [Migration in the Area of Conflict of Globalization and the National State]*, edited by Dietrich Thränhardt and Uwe Hunger, 313–33. Wiesbaden: Westdeutscher Verlag.

———. 2008a. *Cruising in the Global Economy: Profits, Pleasure and Work at Sea, The International Political Economy of New Regionalisms*. Aldershot, Hampshire: Ashgate.

———. 2008b. "'Diversification' and 'Privatisation': Securing Insecurities in the Receiving Country of Malaysia." *The Asia Pacific Journal of Anthropology* no. 9(4): 285–303.

Chin, Ko-lin, and James O. Finckenauer. 2011. "Chickenheads, Agents, Mommies, and Jockeys: The Social Organization of Transnational Commercial Sex." *Crime, Law and Social Change* no. 56(5):463–84.

Chu, Yiu-kong. 2000. *The Triads as Business*. Routledge Studies in the Modern History of Asia. London: Routledge.

Chuang Tzu. 1994. *Wandering on the Way: Early Taoist Tales and Parables of Chuang Tzu*. Translated by Victor H. Mair. New York: Bantam Books.

Clifford, James. 1992. "Traveling Cultures." In *Cultural Studies*, edited by Lawrence Grossberg, Cary Nelson, and Paula Treichler, 96–116. London: Routledge.

Cohen, Robin. 2004. "Chinese Cockle-pickers, the Transnational Turn and Everyday Cosmopolitanism: Reflections on the New Global Migrants." *Labour, Capital and Society* no. 37(1–2):130–49.

Collins, Jock. 2007. "Ethnic Precincts as Contradictory Tourist Spaces." In *Tourism, Ethnic Diversity and the City*, edited by Jan Rath, 67–85. New York: Routledge.

Cox, Robert W. 1987. *Production, Power, and World Order: Social Forces in the Making of History*. New York: Columbia University Press.

Crinis, Vicki D. 2004. *The Silence and Fantasy of Women and Work*. Doctoral dissertation, History and Politics Program and CAPSTRANS Research Institute, University of Wollongong (Australia). http://ro.uow.edu.au/theses/236.

———. 2005. "The Devil You Know; Malaysian Perceptions of Foreign Workers." *Review of Indonesian and Malaysian Affairs* no. 39(2):91–111.

———. 2010. "Sweat or No Sweat: Foreign Workers in the Garment Industry in Malaysia." *Journal of Contemporary Asia* no. 40(4):589–611.

Crosby, Alison. 2007. "People on the Move: Challenging Migration on NGOs, Migrants and Sex Work Categorization." *Development* no. 50(4):44–9. doi: 10.1057/palgrave.development.1100424.

Datta, Ayona. 2009. "Places of Everyday Cosmopolitanisms: East-European Construction Workers in London." *Environment and Planning A* no. 41(2):353–70.

DeBernardi, Jean. 1993. "Epilogue: Ritual Process Reconsidered." In *"Secret Societies" Reconsidered: Perspectives on the Social History of Modern South China and Southeast Asia*, edited by David Ownby and Mary Somers Heidhues, 212–33. Armonk, NY: M. E. Sharpe.

Deem, Rosemary. 2001. "Globalisation, New Managerialism, Academic Capitalism and Entrepreneurialism in Universities: Is the Local Dimension Still Important?" *Comparative Education* no. 37(1):7–20.

Delanty, Gerard. 2006. "The Cosmopolitan Imagination: Critical Cosmopolitanism and Social Theory." *The British Journal of Sociology* no. 57(1):25–47.

Delanty, Gerard, and Baogang He. 2008. "Cosmopolitan Perspectives on European and Asian Transnationalism." *International Sociology* no. 23(3):323–44.

Derudder, Ben, Frank Witlox, James Faulconbridge, and Jon Beaverstock. 2008. "Airline Data for Global City Network Research: Reviewing and Refining Existing Approaches." *GeoJournal* no. 71(1):5–18.

Deutsche Presse-Agentur. August 20, 1998. "Malaysia Upset over ILO Survey on Malaysian Prostitutes." *Deustche Presse-Agentur.*

Devadason, Evelyn S., and Wai Meng Chan. 2011. *A Critical Appraisal of Policies and Laws Regulating Migrant Workers in Malaysia*. World Business and Social Science Research Conference. http://www.wbiconpro.com/210-DEVADASON.pdf.

Diouf, Mamadou. 2000. "The Senegalese Murid Trade Diaspora and the Making of a Vernacular Cosmopolitanism." *Public Culture* no. 12(3):679–702.

Dobrowolsky, Alexandra. 2007. "(In)Security and Citizenship: Security, Im/migration and Shrinking Citizenship Regimes." *Theoretical Inquiries in Law* no. 8(2):629–62.

Douglass, Mike. 2006. "Local City, Capital City or World City? Civil Society, the (Post-) Developmental State and the Globalization of Urban Space in Pacific Asia." *Pacific Affairs* no. 78(4):543–58.

Duyne, Petrus C. 1996. "Organized Crime, Corruption and Power." *Crime, Law and Social Change* no. 26(3):201–38.

Dyer, Sarah, Linda McDowell, and Adina Batnitzky. 2010. "The Impact of Migration on the Gendering of Service Work: The Case of a West London Hotel," *Gender, Work and Organization* no. 17(6): 635–657.

Economic Planning Unit. 2011a. *Number of Foreign Workers in Malaysia by Country of Origin, 1999-2008*. Official Portal: Economic Planning Unit, Prime Minister's Department, Government of Malaysia. http://www.epu.gov.my/html/themes/epu/images/common/pdf/eco_stat/pdf/1.4.1.pdf

———. 2011b. *Number of Foreign Workers in Malaysia by Sector, 1999-2008*. Official Portal: Economic Planning Unit, Prime Minister's Department, Government of Malaysia. http://www.epu.gov.my/html/themes/epu/images/common/pdf/eco_stat/pdf/1.5.1.pdf

The Edge. November 30, 2009. "Cover Story: Borderless Medicine." The Edge.

Enloe, Cynthia H. 2000. *Bananas, Beaches and Bases: Making Feminist Sense of International Politics*. Updated ed. Berkeley: University of California Press.

Equitable Tourism Options. 2000. *Continuing Saga of Marginalisation: A Dossier on Women and Tourism*. Bangalore: Equations.

Ergun, Ayça, and Aykan Erdemir. 2010. "Negotiating Insider and Outsider Identities in the Field: "Insider" in a Foreign Land; "Outsider" in One's Own Land." *Field Methods* no. 22(1):16–38.

Fine, Robert, and Robin Cohen. 2002. "Four Cosmopolitanism Moments." In *Conceiving Cosmopolitanism: Theory, Context and Practice*, edited by Steven Vertovec and Robin Cohen, 137–62. New York: Oxford University Press.

Forsyth, Peter, John King, and Cherry Lyn Rodolfoc. 2005. "Open Skies in ASEAN." *Journal of Air Transport Management* no. 12(3):143–52.

Fraser, Nancy. 2009. "Feminism, Capitalism, and the Cunning of History." *New Left Review* no. 56:97–117.

Freedman, Maurice. 1960. "Immigrants and Associations: Chinese in Nineteenth-Century Singapore." *Comparative Studies in Society and History* no. 3(1):25–48.

Fu, Xiaowen, Tae Hoon Oum, and Anming Zhang. 2010. "Air Transport Liberalization and Its Impacts on Airline Competition and Air Passenger Traffic." *Transportation Journal* no. 49(4):24–41.

Fujita, Mari Anna. 2010. "Forays into Building Identity: Kampung to Kampong in the Kuala Lumpur Metropolitan Area." *Journal of Architectural Education* no. 63(2):8–24.

Gallagher, Anne, and Elaine Pearson. 2010. "The High Cost of Freedom: A Legal and Policy Analysis of Shelter Detention for Victims of Trafficking." *Human Rights Quarterly* no. 32(1):73–114.

Garcés-Mascareñas, Blanca. 2010. "Legal Production of Illegality in a Comparative Perspective. The Cases of Malaysia and Spain." *Asia Europe Journal* no. 8(1):77–89.

Geoffroy, Christine. 2007. "'Mobile' Contexts/'Immobile' Cultures." *Language and Intercultural Communication* no. 7(4):279–90.

Georges-Abeyie, Daniel E. 2001. Foreword to *Petit Apartheid in the U.S. Criminal Justice System: The Dark Figure of Racism*, edited by Dragan Milovanovic and Katheryn K. Russell, ix–xiv. Durham, NC: Carolina Academic Press.

Gill, Saran Kaur. 2005. "The Implications of WTO/GATS on Higher Education in Malaysia." In *Country Paper on Malaysia: The Implications of WTO/GATS on Higher Education in Asia & the Pacific*, 86–113. Seoul, Korea: UNESCO Forum Occasional Paper Series Paper no. 9.

Gille, Zsuzsa, and Seán Ó Riain. 2002. "Global Ethnography." *Annual Review of Sociology* no. 28:271–95.

Global Insight. July 15, 2008. "Sharp Rise in Health Tourism Boosts Private Sector in Malaysia." Global Insight.

Globalization and World Cities Research Network. 2011. *Globalization and World Cities Research Network*. Loughborough University. http://www.lboro.ac.uk/gawc/.

Goh, Beng-Lan, and David Liauw. 2009. "Post-Colonial Projects of a National Culture: Kuala Lumpur and Putrajaya." *City* no. 13(1):71–79.

Golombisky, Kim. 2006. "Gendering the Interview: Feminist Reflections on Gender as Performance in Research." *Women's Studies in Communication* no. 29(2):165–92.

Gozdziak, Elzbieta M., and Micah N. Bump. 2008. *Data and Research on Human Trafficking: Bibliography of Research-Based Literature*. Washington, D.C.: Institute for the Study of International Migration, Walsh School of Foreign Service, Georgetown University.

Gribble, Cate. 2008. "Policy Options for Managing International Student Migration: The Sending Country's Perspective." *Journal of Higher Education Policy and Management* no. 30(1):25–39.

Grosfoguel, Ramón. 2004. "Race and Ethnicity or Racialized Ethnicities? Identities within Global Coloniality." *Ethnicities* no. 4(3):315–36.

Grubesic, Tony H., Timothy C. Matisziw, and Matthew A. Zook. 2008. "Global Airline Networks and Nodal Regions." *GeoJournal* no. 71(1):53–66.

Gullick, J. M. 2000. *A History of Kuala Lumpur, 1857–1939*. Kuala Lumpur: Malaysian Branch of the Royal Asiatic Society.

Gustafson, Per. 2002. *Place, Place Attachment and Mobility: Three Sociological Studies*. Gothenburg, Sweden: Department of Sociology, Göteborg University.

———. 2009. "More Cosmopolitan, No Less Local: The Orientations of International Travellers." *European Societies* no. 11(1):25–47.

Hage, Ghassan. 1998. *White Nation: Fantasies of White Supremacy in a Multicultural Society*. London: Pluto Press.

Hall, C. Michael, and Jan Rath. 2007. "Tourism, Migration and Place Advantage in the Global Cultural Economy." In *Tourism, Ethnic Diversity and the City*, edited by Jan Rath, 1–24. London: Routledge.

Hamzah, Sendut. 1965. "The Structure of Kuala Lumpur: Malaysia's Capital City." *The Town Planning Review* no. 36(2):125–38.

Hanley, Sheena, and Ulf Fredriksson. 2003. "Effects of the General Agreement on Trade in Services on the Education Systems in Europe." *Education Review* no. 16(2):97–102.

Hannerz, Ulf. 1990. "Cosmopolitans and Locals in World Culture." In *Global Culture: Nationalism, Globalization and Modernity*, edited by Mike Featherstone, 237–52. London: SAGE.

———. 2004. 'Cosmopolitanism.' In *Companion to the Anthropology of Politics*, edited by David Nugent and Joan Vincent, 69–85. Oxford: Blackwell.

Harris, Linda Craig. 1993. "Xinjiang, Central Asia and the Implications for China's Policy in the Islamic World." *China Quarterly* (133):111–29.

Harun, Hiswani. 2010. *Policy Priorities for Malaysia in the Area of Services Trade*. Permanent Mission of Malaysia to the WTO, Ministry of International Trade and Industry. http://www.oecd.org/dataoecd/32/1/46658257.pdf.

Harvey, David. 2005. *A Brief History of Neoliberalism*. New York: Oxford University Press.

Hasan, Haryati. 2005. "Malay Women and Prostitution in Kota Bharu, Kelantan, 1950s–1970s." *Journal of the Malaysian Branch of the Royal Asiatic Society* no. 78(1):97–120.

Hawthorne, Lesleyanne. 2010. "Demography, Migration and Demand for International Students." In *Globalisation and Tertiary Education in the Asia-Pacific: The Changing Nature of a Dynamic Market*, edited by Christopher Findlay and William G. Tierney, 93–119. Singapore: World Scientific Publishing Company.

Healey, Lucy. 2000. "Gender, 'Aliens,' and the National Imaginary in Contemporary Malaysia." *Sojourn: Journal of Social Issues in Southeast Asia* no. 15(2):222–54.

Hedman, Eva-Lotta E. 2008. "Refuge, Governmentality and Citizenship: Capturing 'Illegal Migrants' in Malaysia and Thailand." *Government and Opposition* no. 43(2):358–88.

Henry, Marsha Giselle. 2003. "'Where Are You Really From?': Representation, Identity and Power in the Fieldwork Experiences of a South Asian Diasporic." *Qualitative Research* no. 3(2):229–42.

Hesford, Wendy S., and Wendy Kozol. 2005. Introduction to *Just Advocacy? Women's Human Rights, Transnational Feminisms, and the Politics of Representation*, edited by Wendy S. Hesford and Wendy Kozol, 1–32. New Brunswick, NJ: Rutgers University Press.

Hiebert, Daniel. 2002. "Cosmopolitanism at the Local Level: The Development of Transnational Neighbourhoods." In *Conceiving Cosmopolitanism: Theory, Context, and Practice*, edited by Robin Cohen and Steven Vertovec, 209–23. New York: Oxford University Press.

Hing, A.Y. 2000. "Migration and the Reconfiguration of Malaysia." *Journal of Contemporary Asia* no. 30(2):221–45.

Hirschman, Charles. 1986. "The Making of Race in Colonial Malaya: Political Economy and Racial Ideology." *Sociological Forum* no. 1(2):330–61.

———. 1987. "The Meaning and Measurement of Ethnicity in Malaysia: An Analysis of Census Clarification." *Journal of Asian Studies* no. 40(3):555–82.

Hoang, Kimberly Kay. 2010. "Economies of Emotion, Familiarity, Fantasy, and Desire: Emotional Labor in Ho Chi Minh City's Sex Industry." *Sexualities* no. 13(2):255-272.

Hoffstaedter, Gerhard. 2009. "Contested Spaces: Globalization, the Arts and the State in Malaysia." *Ethnicities* no. 9(4):527–45.

Hubbard, Phil. 2011. "Gender, Power & Sex in the World City Network." *L'espace politique* no. 13(1):2–38.

Hughes, Donna M. 2000. "The 'Natasha' Trade: The Transnational Shadow Market of Trafficking in Women." *Journal of International Affairs* no. 53(2):625–51.

Hughes, Gordon. 2006. "Community Cohesion, Asylum Seeking and the Question of the Stranger: Towards a New Politics of Public Safety." *Cultural Studies* no. 21(6):931–51.

Ibrahim, Maggie. 2005. "The Securitization of Migration: A Racial Discourse." *International Migration* no. 43(5):163–87.

Immigration Department of Malaysia. 2011. *'Permohonan Pembantu Rumah Asing' [Foreign Domestic Application]*. Government of Malaysia. http://www.imi.gov.my/index.php?option=com_content&view=article&id=230&Itemid=67&lang=bm.

International Herald Tribune. December 10, 2007. "A Campaign of Brutality; Foreign Laborers Hunted Down in Malaysia." International Herald Tribune.

———. October 4, 2010. "Traffic Picks Up in Global University Race; Flow of Foreign Students Grows More Complex as 'Brain Exchange' Develops." International Herald Tribune.

———. July 26, 2011. "Malaysia and Australia Agree on Refugee-Exchange Program." International Herald Tribune.

International Labour Office. 2010. *Women in Labour Markets: Measuring Progress and Identifying Challenges*. Geneva: International Labour Organization.

Jeffreys, Sheila. 1997. *The Idea of Prostitution*. North Melbourne: Spinifex.

———. 2006. "The Traffic in Women: Human Rights Violation or Migration for Work?" In *Migrant Women and Work*, edited by Anuja Agrawal, 194–217. New Delhi: SAGE.

———. 2009. *The Industrial Vagina: The Political Economy of the Global Sex Trade*. New York: Routledge.

Kabeer, Naila. 2007. *"Footloose" Female Labour: Transnational Migration, Social Protection and Citizenship in the Asia Region*. IDRC Working Papers on Women's Rights and Citizenship, International Development Research Centre, Ottawa. http://www.idrc.ca/EN/Programs/Social_and_Economic_Policy/Womens_Rights_and_Citizenship/Documents/WRC-WP1-Kabeer-Migration.pdf.

Kapur, Ratna. 2003. "The "Other" Side of Globalization: The Legal Regulation of Cross-Border Movements." *Canadian Woman Studies* no. 22 (3/4):6–15.

Karyotis, Georgios. 2007. "European Migration Policy in the Aftermath of September 11: The Security-Migration Nexus." *Innovation: European Journal of Social Sciences* no. 20(1):1–17.

Kassim, Azizah. 1987. "The Unwelcome Guests: Indonesian Immigrants and the Malaysian Public Responses." *Southeast Asian Studies* no. 25(2):265–78.

Kaur, Amarjit. 2006. *Managing the Border: Regulation of International Labour Migration and State Policy Responses to Global Governance in Southeast Asia*. 16th Biennial Conference of the Asian Studies Association of Australia, Wollongong. http://coombs.anu.edu.au/SpecialProj/ASAA/biennial-conference/2006/Kaur-Amarjit-ASAA2006.pdf.

———. 2007. Refugees and Refugee Policy in Malaysia. *University of New England Asia Centre, UNEAC Papers* No. 18. http://www.une.edu.au/asiacentre/PDF/No18.pdf.

———. 2008. International Migration and Governance in Malaysia: Policy and Performance. *University of New England Asia Centre, UNEAC Papers* No. 22. http://www.une.edu.au/asiacentre/PDF/No22.pdf.

———. 2010. "Labour Migration in Southeast Asia: Migration Policies, Labour Exploitation and Regulation." *Journal of the Asia Pacific Economy* no. 15(1):6–19.

Kaur, Kiranjit. 2005. "The Media and Migrant Labour Issues in Malaysia: A Content Analysis of Selected Malaysian Newspapers." *Review of Indonesian and Malaysian Affairs* no. 39(2):69–90.

Kelly, Liz. 2005. "'You Can Find Anything You Want': A Critical Reflection on Research on Trafficking in Persons within and into Europe." In *Data and Research on Human Trafficking: A Global Survey*, edited by Frank Laczko and Elzbieta M. Gozdziak, 235-265. Geneva: International Organization for Migration.

Kempadoo, Kamala, Jyoti Sanghera, and Bandana Pattanaik. 2005. *Trafficking and Prostitution Reconsidered: New Perspectives on Migration, Sex Work, and Human Rights*. Boulder: Paradigm.

Keough, Leyla J. 2006. "Globalizing 'Postsocialism': Mobile Mothers and Neoliberalism on the Margins of Europe." *Anthropological Quarterly* no. 79(3):431–61.

Khoo, Gaik Cheng. 2008. "Urban Geography as Pretext: Sociocultural Landscapes of Kuala Lumpur in Independent Malaysian Films." *Singapore Journal of Tropical Geography* no. 29(1):34–54.

Kim, Joon K., and May Fu. 2008. "International Women in South Korea's Sex Industry: A New Commodity Frontier." *Asian Survey* no. 48(3):492–513.

King, Ross. 2008. *Kuala Lumpur and Putrajaya: Negotiating Urban Space in Malaysia*. Honolulu: University of Hawai'i Press.

Kitiarsa, Pattana. 2008. "Thai Migrants in Singapore: State, Intimacy and Desire." *Gender, Place & Culture: A Journal of Feminist Geography* no. 15(6):595–610.

Kleemans, Edward R. 2007. "Organized Crime, Transit Crime, and Racketeering." *Crime and Justice* no. 35(1):163–215.

Knight, Jane. 2002. "Trade Talk: An Analysis of the Impact of Trade Liberalization and the General Agreement on Trade in Services on Higher Education." *Journal of Studies in International Education* no. 6(3):209–29.

Kofman, Eleonore. 2004. "Family-Related Migration: A Critical Review of European Studies." *Journal of Ethnic & Migration Studies* no. 30(2):243–62.

———. 2005. "Figures of the Cosmopolitan: Privileged Nationals and National Outsiders." *Innovation: The European Journal of Social Science Research* no. 18(1):83–97.

Kofman, Eleonore, and Parvati Raghuram. 2006. "Gender and Global Labour Migrations: Incorporating Skilled Workers." *Antipode* no. 38(2):282–303.

Kothari, Uma. 2008. "Global Peddlers and Local Networks: Migrant Cosmopolitanisms." *Environment and Planning D: Society and Space* no. 26(3):500–516.

Kratoska, Paul H. 1985. "The Peripatetic Peasant and Land Tenure in British Malaya." *Journal of Southeast Asian Studies* no. 16(1):16–45.

Ku, Samuel C.Y. 2008. "China's Changing Political Economy with Malaysia and Southeast Asia: A Comparative Perspective." *Journal of Asian and African Studies* no. 43(2):155–71.

Kuala Lumpur City Hall. 2002. *Kuala Lumpur Structure Plan 2020*. http://www.dbkl.gov.my/pskl2020/english/index.htm.

Kurasawa, Fuyuki. 2004. "A Cosmopolitanism from Below: Alternative Globalization and the Creation of a Solidarity without Bounds." *European Journal of Sociology* no. 45(2):233–55.

Kusow, Abdi M. 2003. "Beyond Indigenous Authenticity: Reflections on the Insider/Outsider Debate in Immigration Research." *Symbolic Interaction* no. 26(4):591–99.

Kyle, David J., and Rachel Goldstein. 2011. "Migration Industries: A Comparison of the Ecuador-US and Ecuador-Spain Cases." Research Report. EU-US Immigration Systems 2011/15. San Domenico di Fiesole, Italy: Robert Schuman Centre for Advanced Studies, European University Institute. http://cadmus.eui.eu/handle/1814/17845

Lahav, Gallya. 2000. "The Rise of Non-State Actors in Migration Regulation in the United States and Europe: Changing the Gatekeepers or 'Bringing Back the State'?" In *Immigration Research for a New Century: Multidisciplinary Perspectives*, edited by Nancy Foner, Ruben G. Rumbaut, and Steven J. Gold, 215–41. New York: Russell Sage.

Lai, Ah Eng. 1986. Peasants, Proletarians and Prostitutes: A Preliminary Investigation into the Work of Chinese Women in Colonial Malaya. *Research Notes and Discussion Papers No. 59.* Singapore: Institute for Southeast Asian Studies.

Lamont, Michèle, and Sada Aksartova. 2002. "Ordinary Cosmopolitanisms: Strategies for Bridging Racial Boundaries among Working-Class Men." *Theory, Culture & Society* no. 19(4):1–25.

Landau, Loren B., and Iriann Freemantle. 2010. "Tactical Cosmopolitanism and Idioms of Belonging: Insertion and Self-Exclusion in Johannesburg." *Journal of Ethnic and Migration Studies* no. 36(3):375–90.

Lee, Raymond L. M. 2004. "The Transformation of Race Relations in Malaysia: From Ethnic Discourse to National Imagery, 1993–2003." *African and Asian Studies* no. 3(2):120–43.

Lees, Lynn Hollen. 2011. "Discipline and Delegation: Colonial Governance in Malayan Towns, 1880–1930." *Urban History* no. 38(1):48–64.

Lefebvre, Henri. 1991. *The Production of Space*. Oxford: Blackwell.

Lehtinen, Terhi. 2004. "Lion and the Orchid Cosmopolitan Cities, Transnational Networks, Community Narratives and Identities of the African Community in South East Asia—The Case of Bangkok." Paper read at International Studies Association, Annual Convention, at Montreal, Quebec, Canada.

Lerner, Gerda. 1979. *The Majority Finds Its Past: Placing Women in History*. New York: Oxford University Press.

Lévy, Florence, and Marylène Lieber. 2008. "Northern Chinese Women in Paris: The Illegal Immigration-Prostitution Nexus." *Social Science Information* no. 47(4):629–42.

Liebelt, Claudia. 2008. "On Sentimental Orientalists, Christian Zionists, and Working Class Cosmopolitans: Filipina Domestic Workers' Journeys to Israel and Beyond." *Critical Asian Studies* no. 40(4):567–85.

Lim, Gerrie. 2004. *Invisible Trade: High-Class Sex for Sale in Singapore*. Singapore: Monsoon Books.

Lim, Lin Lean. 1998. *The Sex Sector: The Economic and Social Bases of Prostitution in Southeast Asia*. Geneva: International Labour Organization.

Lim, Tin Seng. 2009. "Renewing 35 Years of Malaysia-China Relations: Najib's Visit to China." *Background Brief No. 460.* Singapore: East Asia Institute, National University of Singapore.

Liow, Joseph. 2003. "Malaysia's Illegal Indonesian Migrant Labour Problem: In Search of Solutions." *Contemporary Southeast Asia* no. 25(1):44–64.

Liow, Joseph Chinyong. 2006. "Malaysia's Approach to Indonesian Migrant Labor: Securitization, Politics, or Catharsis?" In *Non-Traditional Security in Asia: Dilemmas in Securitization*, edited by Mely Caballero-Anthony, Ralf Emmers and Amitav Archarya, 40–65. Aldershot, Hampshire: Ashgate.

Lyman, Stanford M., W. E. Willmott, and Berching Ho. 1964. "Rules of a Chinese Secret Society in British Columbia." *Bulletin of the School of Oriental and African Studies, University of London* no. 27(3):530–39.

Mahdavi, Pardis. 2010. "Race, Space, Place: Notes on the Racialisation and Spatialisation of Commercial Sex Work in Dubai, UAE." *Culture, Health & Sexuality* no. 12(8):943–54.

———. 2011. *Gridlock: Labour, Migration and Human Trafficking in Dubai.* Stanford: Stanford University Press.

Mahler, Sarah J., and Patricia R. Pessar. 2006. "Gender Matters: Ethnographers Bring Gender from the Periphery toward the Core of Migration Studies." *The International Migration Review* no. 40(1):27–63.

Mak, Lau Fong. 1981. *The Sociology of Secret Societies: A Study of Chinese Secret Societies in Singapore and Peninsular Malaysia.* Kuala Lumpur: Oxford University Press.

Malay Mail. August 13, 2010. "Malaysia Abolishes Visa-on-Arrival Effective August 16." The Malay Mail.

———. February 21, 2012. "Visa Clampdown to Curb Student Prostitution." The Malay Mail.

Malaysia, Government of. 2006a. Laws of Malaysia, Immigration Act 1959/1963: Act 155 (incorporating all amendments up to January 1, 2006). Edited by The Commissioner of Law Revision. Kuala Lumpur: Percetakan Nasional Malaysia, Government of Malaysia.

———. 2006b. Laws of Malaysia, Penal Code: Act 574 (incorporating all amendments up to January 1, 2006). Edited by The Commissioner of Law Revision. Kuala Lumpur: Percetakan Nasional Malaysia, Government of Malaysia.

Malaysia Tourism Promotion Board/Tourism Malaysia. 2011a. *Advertising* Campaign. Government of Malaysia.Research. Tourism Malaysia, Government of Malaysia. http://corporate.tourism.gov.my/images/Malaysia%20Truly%20Asia/Domestic_1.pdf.

———. 2011b. *Facts & Figures.* Tourism Malaysia, Government of Malaysia. http://corporate.tourism.gov.my/research.asp?page=facts_figures.

———. 2012. *Research: Tourist Arrivals to Malaysia for Jan-Dec 2011.* Tourism Malaysia, Government of Malaysia. http://corporate.tourism.gov.my/images/research/pdf/2011/TouristArrivals_JanDec_2011.pdf.

Malaysian Investment Development Authority. 2011. *Immigration Procedures: Employment of Foreign Worker.* Malaysian Investment Development Authority, Government of Malaysia. http://www.mida.gov.my/env3/index.php?page=employment-of-foreign-workers.

Malaysia Economy. 2010. "Wilayah Persekutuan Kuala Lumpur: Total Population According to Age and Ethnicity" Malaysia Economy. http://www.malaysiaeconomy.net/english/index.php?option=com_content&view=article&id=188:population-of-kuala-lumpur-19801990&catid=38:population&Itemid=53.

The Malaysian Insider. May 20, 2010. "Foreign Worker Levy Hike in 2011." The Malaysian Insider.

———. April 9, 2011. "No Need RCI on Sex Video, Prostitution Not Criminal, Say Lawyers." The Malaysian Insider.

Malecki, Edward J., and Michael C. Ewers. 2007. "Labor Migration to World Cities: With a Research Agenda for the Arab Gulf." *Progress in Human Geography* no. 31(4):467–84.

Manderson, Lenore. 1997. "Migration, Prostitution and Medical Surveillance in Early Twentieth-Century Malaya." In *Migrants, Minorities and Health: Historical and Contemporary Studies,* edited by Lara Marks and Michael Worboys, 49–69. London: Routledge.

Martin, Bill. 1998. "Knowledge, Identity and the Middle Class: From Collective to Individualised Class Formation?" *The Sociological Review* no. 46(4):653–86.

Massey, Douglas S., Joaquin Arango, Graeme Hugo, Ali Kouaouci, Adela Pellegrino, and J. Edward Taylor. 2005. *Worlds in Motion: Understanding International Migration at the End of the Millennium, International Studies in Demography.* Oxford: Oxford University Press.

Mathur-Helm, Babita. 2002. "Expatriate Women Managers: At the Crossroads of Success, Challenges and Career goals." *Women in Management Review* no. 17(1):18–28.

May, Jon, Jane Wills, Kavita Datta, Yara Evans, Joanna Herbert, and Cathy McIlwaine. 2007. "Keeping London Working: Global Cities, the British State and London's New Migrant Division of Labour." *Transactions of the Institute of British Geographers* no. 32(2):151–67.

McBurnie, Grant, and Christopher Ziguras. 2001. "The Regulation of Transnational Higher Education in Southeast Asia: Case Studies of Hong Kong, Malaysia and Australia." *Higher Education* no. 42(1):85–105.

McIllwain, Jeffrey Scott. 1999. "Organized Crime: A Social Network Approach." *Crime, Law and Social Change* no. 32(4):301–23.

Mignolo, Walter D. 2000. "The Many Faces of Cosmo-polis: Border Thinking and Critical Cosmopolitanism." *Public Culture* no. 12(3):721–48.

Mills, Mary Beth. 2003. "Gender and Inequality in the Global Labor Force." *Annual Review of Anthropology* no. 32(1):41–62.

Milovanovic, Dragan, and Katheryn K. Russell. 2001. *Petit Apartheid in the U.S. Criminal Justice System: The Dark Figure of Racism.* Durham, NC: Carolina Academic Press.

Ministry of Higher Education. 2011. *Statistics of Higher Education of Malaysia 2010.* Putrajaya: Ministry of Higher Education, Government of Malaysia.

———. 2012a. *Malaysia Higher Education Statistics 2011: Private Higher Education Institutions (Chapter 2).* Ministry of Higher Education, Government of Malaysia. http://www.mohe.gov.my/web_statistik/perangkaan2011/BAB2-IPTS.pdf.

———. 2012b. *Malaysia Higher Education Statistics 2011: Public Higher Education Institutions (Chapter 1).* Ministry of Higher Education, Government of Malaysia. http://www.mohe.gov.my/web_statistik/perangkaan2011/BAB1-IPTA.pdf.

Ministry of Home Affairs. 2010. *InfoRELA.* Ministry of Home Affairs, Government of Malaysia, November. http://www.moha.gov.my/images/stories/pdf/Buletin_RELA/INFO_NOVEMBER_%202010.pdf.

———. 2011. *Roles and Functions of RELA.* Ministry of Home Affairs, Government of Malaysia. http://www.moha.gov.my/index.php?option=com_content&view=article&id=110&Itemid=146&lang=en.

Mohamad, Nor Asiah. 2007. "Buying Properties in Malaysia? Highlight on Laws, Policies and Their Implication on Foreign Land Ownership." Paper read at International Law and Trade: Bridging the East-West Divide, May 10–11, 2007, Ankara, Turkey.

Mok, Ka Ho. 2008. "Singapore's Global Education Hub Ambitions: University Governance Change and Transnational Higher Education." *International Journal of Educational Management* no. 22(6):527–46.

Molz, Jennie Germann. 2006. "Cosmopolitan Bodies: Fit to Travel and Travelling to Fit." *Body & Society* no. 12(3):1–21.

Moon, Katharine H. S. 1997. *Sex Among Allies: Military Prostitution in U.S.-Korea Relations.* New York: Columbia University Press.

Morshidi, Sirat. 1997. "Globalization of Economic Activity and the Changing Landscape of Kuala Lumpur Central Planning Area." *Asian Geographer* no. 16(1–2):37–58.

———. 2000. "Globalising Kuala Lumpur and the Strategic Role of the Producer Services Sector." *Urban Studies* no. 37(12):2217–40. doi:10.1080/00420980020002788.

Morshidi, Sirat, Ahmad Abdul Razak, and Yew Lie Koo. 2009. "Trade in Services and Its Policy Implications: The Case of Cross-Border/Transnational Higher Education in Malaysia." *Journal of Studies in International Education* no. 20(10):1–20.

Muller, Benjamin J. 2004. "(Dis)qualified Bodies: Securitization, Citizenship and 'Identity Management.'" *Citizenship Studies* no. 8(3):279–94.

Nadarajah, Yaso. 2007. "Life Under the Freeway in Malaysia: Community Resilience amidst Modernization in Contemporary Malaysia." *Local-Global: Identity, Security, Community* no. 4:70–81.

Nagaraj, Shyamala, and Siti Rohani Yahya. 1998. "Prostitution in Malaysia." In *The Sex Sector: The Economic and Social Bases of Prostitution in Southeast Asia*, edited by Lin Lean Lim, 67–99. Geneva: International Labour Organization.

Nagel, Joane. 2000. "States of Arousal/Fantasy Islands: Race, Sex and Romance in the Global Economy of Desire." *American Studies* no. 41(2–3):159–81.

Najib, Tun Abdul Razak. 2010. Speech introducing the motion to table the Tenth Malaysian Plan, June 10, 2010. http://www.pmo.gov.my/dokumenattached/speech/files/RMK10_Speech.pdf.

Nambiar, Shankaran. 2009. "Revisiting Privatisation in Malaysia: The Importance of Institutional Process." *Asian Academy of Management Journal* no. 14(2):21–40.

Narayan, Kirin. 1993. "How Native Is a 'Native' Anthropologist?" *American Anthropologist* no. 95(3):671–86.

Narayanan, Suresh, and Yew-Wah Lai. 2005. "The Causes and Consequences of Immigrant Labour in the Construction Sector in Malaysia." *International Migration* no. 43(5):31–57.

The Nation (Thailand). August 20, 2010. "Malaysia Boosts Security Corps Accused of Abuses." The Nation (Thailand).

National Economic Advisory Council. 2010. *New Economic Model for Malaysia Part 1: Strategic Policy Directions*. Putrajaya: National Economic Advisory Council, Government of Malaysia.

New Straits Times. August 15, 1997. "Warning to Colleges to Vet Intake of Foreigners." New Straits Times.

———. February 10, 2002. "Easy Pickings in Malaysia." New Straits Times.

———. June 15, 2002. "Vice Syndicates Bringing in Viets and Cambodians." New Straits Times.

———. September 20, 2004. "'555' Book and the Oldest Profession." New Straits Times.

———. March 13, 2006. "A Suspicious Love of English." *New Straits Times*.

———. December 5, 2006. "MP: Pimps Rule the Streets of Bukit Bintang." New Straits Times.

———. February 24, 2007. "Ministries in Turf War over New Bill." New Straits Times.

———. March 9, 2007. "Syed Hamid: We Won't Recognise Refugees." New Straits Times.

———. March 13, 2007. "Suhakam: Rela Volunteers Must be Strictly Vetted." New Straits Times.

———. May 10, 2007. "Rela 'Should Not Be Disbanded because of a Few Bad Hats.'" New Straits Times.

———. May 11, 2007. "Give Us Your Support." New Straits Times.

———. June 6, 2007. "When 'Little Dragon Ladies' Strike Fear." New Straits Times.

———. February 12, 2008. "4 Star Hotel with Foreign Frontline Workers under Fire." New Straits Times.

———. March 27, 2008. "Out to Make Malaysia Top Muslim Tourist Destination." New Straits Times.

———. April 27, 2008. "Foreign Workers Trapped in a 'No-Win' Situation." New Straits Times.

———. May 4, 2008. "Have Letter Will Travel." New Straits Times.

———. March 21, 2009. "Majority of Those Caught from China." New Straits Times.

———. June 26, 2009. "Foreign Students Worth RM4b to Us." New Straits Times.

———. September 27, 2009a. "Lure of Rich Pickings in Malaysia." New Straits Times.

———. September 27, 2009b. "Trafficked Women Too Afraid to Tell the Truth." New Straits Times.

———. November 19, 2009. "Panel to Review Monitoring of Foreign Students." New Straits Times.

———. November 28, 2009. "Student Visa Abuse Cases on the Rise." New Straits Times.

———. January 31, 2010. "Students Not Told of Work Rules." New Straits Times.

———. February 7, 2010. "'They Make Me Feel like a Man.'" New Straits Times.

———. February 20, 2010. "Alien Horde's Love Affair with the Promised Land." New Straits Times.

———. March 23, 2010. "Hubbies for Hire at RM5,000." New Straits Times.

———. May 23, 2010. "African Alienation." New Straits Times.

———. June 6, 2010. "Education Ministry Weeding Out Below-Par Institutions." New Straits Times.

———. October 19, 2010. "Huge Returns." New Straits Times.

———. November 6, 2010. "Ekuinas to Take Control of Education Group." New Straits Times.

———. April 17, 2011. "Golfers' Angry Wives Come Out Swinging." New Straits Times.

———. May 26, 2011. "CATS to Help Lower Crime Rate." New Straits Times.

———. June 4, 2011. "Top Cop: 'X' Serves as Identification." New Straits Times.

———. June 9, 2011. "Agents to Help Register, Legalise Foreign Workers." New Straits Times.

———. June 24, 2011. "Rela Will No Longer Round Up Illegals on Its Own." New Straits Times.

———. July 7, 2011. "Pay Minimum Wage or Risk Fine." New Straits Times.

———. September 6, 2011. "Levy Hike Well Received." New Straits Times.

———. September 28, 2011. "Grants for Foreign Students." New Straits Times.

———. October 5, 2011. "1.3m Aliens in 'Wrong Jobs.'" New Straits Times.

New York Times. December 10, 2007. "A Growing Source of Fear for Migrants in Malaysia." The New York Times.

———. December 20, 2009. "36 Hours: Kuala Lumpur." The New York Times.

Nonini, Donald M. 1992. British Colonial Rule and the Resistance of the Malay Peasantry, 1900–1957. Monograph Series no. 38. New Haven: Southeast Asia Studies, Center for International and Area Studies, Yale University.

Nyers, Peter. 2003. "Abject Cosmopolitanism: The Politics of Protection in the Anti-Deportation Movement." Third World Quarterly no. 24(6):1069–1093.

Obi, Cyril I. 2010. "African Migration as the Search for a Wonderful World: An Emerging Trans-global Security Threat?" African and Asian Studies no. 9(1–2):128–48.

Olds, Kris. 2007. "Global Assemblage: Singapore, Foreign Universities, and the Construction of a 'Global Education Hub.'" World Development no. 35(6):959–75.

O'Leary, Anna Ochoa. 2007. "Petit Apartheid in the U.S.-Mexico Borderlands: An Analysis of Community Organization Data Documenting Work Force Abuses of the Undocumented." *Forum on Public Policy: A Journal of the Oxford Round Table.* http://forumonpublicpolicy.com/archive07/oleary.pdf.

Ong, Aihwa. 1999. *Flexible Citizenship: The Cultural Logics of Transnationality.* Durham: Duke University Press.

Ownby, David. 1993. Introduction to *"Secret Societies" Reconsidered: Perspectives on the Social History of Modern South China and Southeast Asia*, edited by David Ownby and Mary Somers Heidhues, 3–33. Armonk, NY: M. E. Sharpe.

Ownby, David, and Mary Somers Heidhues. 1993. *"Secret Societies" Reconsidered: Perspectives on the Social History of Modern South China and Southeast Asia.* Armonk, NY: M. E. Sharpe.

Parreñas, Rhacel Salazar. 2011. *Illicit Flirtations: Labor, Migration, and Sex Trafficking in Tokyo.* Stanford: Stanford University Press.

Penttinen, Elina. 2007. *Globalization, Prostitution and Sex Trafficking: Corporeal Politics.* Routledge Advances in International Relations and Global Politics. New York: Routledge.

Phongpaichit, Pasuk. 1982. *From Peasant Girls to Bangkok Masseuses.* Geneva: International Labour Office.

Pickering, Sharon. 2001. "Common Sense and Original Deviancy: News Discourses and Asylum Seekers in Australia." *Journal of Refugee Studies* no. 14(2):169–86.

Piper, Nicola. 2004a. "Gender and Migration Policies in Southeast and East Asia: Legal Protection and Sociocultural Empowerment of Unskilled Migrant Women." *Singapore Journal of Tropical Geography* no. 25(2):216–31.

———. 2004b. "Rights of Foreign Workers and the Politics of Migration in South-East and East Asia." *International Migration* no. 42(5):71–97.

———. 2005. "A Problem by a Different Name? A Review of Research on Trafficking in South-East Asia and Oceania." *International Migration* no. 43(1–2):203–33. doi: 10.1111/j.0020-7985.2005.00318.x.

Piper, Nicola, and Keiko Yamanaka 2008. "Feminised Migration in East and Southeast Asia and the Securing of Livelihoods." In *New Perspectives on Gender and Migration: Livelihood, Rights and Entitlements*, edited by Nicola Piper, 159-188. London: Routledge.

Platt, Leah. 2001. "Regulating the Global Brothel." *The American Prospect.* http://prospect.org/article/regulating-global-brothel.

Polanyi, Karl. 1944. *The Great Transformation: The Political and Economic Origins of Our Time.* Boston: Beacon Press.

Poster, Winifred. 2002. "Racialism, Sexuality, and Masculinity: Gendering 'Global Ethnography' of the Workplace." *Social Politics: International Studies in Gender, State and Society* no. 9(1):126–58.

Pratt, Mary Louise. 2008. *Imperial Eyes: Travel Writing and Transculturation.* 2nd ed. New York: Routledge.

Price, Marie, and Lisa Benton-Short. 2007. "Immigrants and World Cities: From the Hyper-Diverse to the Bypassed." *GeoJournal* no. 68(2–3):103–17.

———. 2008. *Migrants to the Metropolis: The Rise of Immigrant Gateway Cities, Cultural and Ethnic Studies.* Syracuse: Syracuse University Press.

Purcell, Victor. 1948. *The Chinese in Malaya.* London: Geoffrey Cumberlege for Oxford University Press.

Pyle, Jean L., and Kathryn B. Ward. 2003. "Recasting Our Understanding of Gender and Work During Global Restructuring." *International Sociology* no. 18(3):461–89.

Rajaram, Prem Kumar, and Carl Grundy-Warr. 2004. "The Irregular Migrant as Homo Sacer: Migration and Detention in Australia, Malaysia and Thailand." *International Migration* no. 42(1):33–64.

Raymond, Janice G. 2004. "Prostitution on Demand: Legalizing the Buyers as Sexual Consumers." *Violence Against Women* no. 10(10):1156–86.

Rimmer, Peter J., and Howard Dick. 2009. *The City in Southeast Asia: Patterns, Processes and Policy*. Honolulu: University of Hawai'i Press.

Robbins, Bruce. 1998. "Introduction Part I: Actually Existing Cosmopolitanism." In *Cosmopolitics: Thinking and Feeling Beyond the Nation*, edited by Pheng Cheah and Bruce Robbins, 1-19. Minneapolis: University of Minnesota Press.

Robertson, Philip S. Jr. 2008. Migrant Workers in Malaysia—Issues, Concerns and Points for Action. Fair Labor Association. http://www.alfea.org/img/OutsourcingCompanies.pdf.

Robinson, Jennifer. 2002. "Global and World Cities: A View from off the Map." *International Journal of Urban and Regional Research* no. 26(3):531–54.

Robinson, Lillian S. 2006. "Sex in the City: Prostitution in the Age of Global Migrations." *Labour, Capital & Society* no. 39(2):48–77.

Roff, William R. 1967. *The Origins of Malay Nationalism*. New Haven: Yale University Press.

Roman, Meredith L. 2002. "Making Caucasians Black: Moscow Since the Fall of Communism and the Racialization of Non-Russians." *Journal of Communist Studies and Transition Politics* no. 18(2): 1-27.

Romero, Mary. 2006. "Racial Profiling and Immigration Law Enforcement: Rounding Up of Usual Suspects in the Latino Community." *Critical Sociology* no. 32(2):447–73.

———. 2008. "Crossing the Immigration and Race Border: A Critical Race Theory Approach to Immigration Studies." *Contemporary Justice Review: Issues in Criminal, Social, and Restorative Justice* no. 11(1):23–37.

Roudometof, Victor 2005. "Transnationalism, Cosmopolitanism and Glocalization." *Current Sociology* no. 53(1):113–35.

Rubin, Kyna. 2008. "Singapore's Push for Foreign Students." *International Educator* no. 17(1):56.

Ruhne, Renate, and Martina Löw. 2009. "Domesticating Prostitution: Study of an Interactional Web of Space and Gender." *Space and Culture* no. 12(2):232–49.

Sadiq, Kamal. 2005. "When States Prefer Non-Citizens Over Citizens: Conflict Over Illegal Immigration into Malaysia." *International Studies Quarterly* no. 49(1):101–22.

Samarasinghe, Vidyamali. 2009. "'Two to Tango': Probing the Demand Side of Female Sex Trafficking." *Pakistan Journal of Women's Studies: Alam-e-Niswan* no. 16(1–2):33–54.

Sanders, Teela. 2008. "Selling Sex in the Shadow Economy." *International Journal of Social Economics* no. 35(10):704–16.

Sardar, Ziauddin. 2000. *The Consumption of Kuala Lumpur*. London: Reaktion Books.

Sassen, Saskia. 2000. "The Global City: Strategic Site/New Frontier." *American Studies* no. 41(2–3):79–95.

———. 2001. The Global City: New York, London, Tokyo. 2nd ed. Princeton: Princeton University Press.

———. 2002. "Women's Burden: Counter-Geographies of Globalization and the Feminization of Survival." *Nordic Journal of International Law* no. 71(2):255–74.

———. 2005. "The Global City: Introducing a Concept." *Brown Journal of World Affairs* no. 11(2):27–43.

———. 2008. "Nurturing Asia's World Cities." *Far Eastern Economic Review*, no. 171(4):57–59.

———. 2009. "Cities in Today's Global Age." *SAIS Review* no. 29(1):3–34.

Schiller, Nina Glick, and Ayse Cağlar. 2009. "Towards a Comparative Theory of Locality in Migration Studies: Migrant Incorporation and City Scale." *Journal of Ethnic & Migration Studies* no. 35(2):177–202.

Schiller, Nina Glick, Tsypylma Darieva, and Sandra Gruner-Domic. 2011. "Defining Cosmopolitan Sociability in a Transnational Age. An Introduction." *Ethnic and Racial Studies* no. 34(3):399–418.

Scholte, Jan Aart. 2000. *Globalization: A Critical Introduction*. Basingstoke, UK: Palgrave Macmillan.

Schram, Tom. 1994. "Sense Making across Disciplines: The Spindlers, Adaptation, and the Self That Never Left." *Anthropology and Education* no. 25(4):463–72.

Scott, James C. 1999. *Seeing Like a State: How Certain Schemes to Improve the Human Condition Have Failed*. New Haven: Yale University Press.

Shanmugam, Bala. 2004. "Hawala and Money Laundering: A Malaysian Perspective." *Journal of Money Laundering Control* no. 8(1):37–47.

Shanmugam, Bala, and Haemala Thanasegaran. 2008. "Combating Money Laundering in Malaysia." *Journal of Money Laundering Control* no. 11(4):331–44.

Shatkin, Gavin. 2007. "Global Cities of the South: Emerging Perspectives on Growth and Inequality." *Cities* no. 24(1):1–15.

Sheller, Mimi. 2010. "Air Mobilities on the U.S.-Caribbean Border: Open Skies and Closed Gates." *The Communication Review* no. 13(4):269–88. doi: 10.1080/10714421.2010.525469.

Shelley, Louise. 2003. "Trafficking in Women: The Business Model Approach." *Brown Journal of World Affairs* no. 10(1):119–31.

Shin, Kyoung-Ho, and Michael Timberlake. 2000. "World Cities in Asia: Cliques, Centrality and Connectedness." *Urban Studies* no. 37(12):2257–85. doi: Doi:10.1080/00420980020002805.

Sidhu, Ravinder, K.-C. Ho, and Brenda Yeoh. 2011. "Emerging Education Hubs: The Case of Singapore." *Higher Education* no. 61(1):23–40. doi: 10.1007/s10734-010-9323-9.

Simonovsky, Yamila, and Malte Luebker. 2011. "Global and Regional Estimates on Domestic Workers." Domestic Work Policy Brief Series, No. 4, International Labour Organization: Geneva, Switzerland. http://www.ilo.org/travail/whatwedo/publications/WCMS_155951/lang--en/index.htm

Sinclair, M. Thea. 1997. *Gender, Work and Tourism*. London: Routledge.

Sklair, Leslie. 2001. *The Transnational Capitalist Class*. Malden: Blackwell.

Skrbis, Zlatko, and Ian Woodward. 2007. "The Ambivalence of Ordinary Cosmopolitanism: Investigating the Limits of Cosmopolitan Openness." *The Sociological Review* no. 55(4):730–47.

Slaughter, Sheila, and Larry L. Leslie. 1997. *Academic Capitalism: Politics, Policies, and the Entrepreneurial University*. Baltimore: Johns Hopkins University Press.

Soderlund, Gretchen. 2005. "Running from the Rescuers: New U.S. Crusades against Sex Trafficking and the Rhetoric of Abolition." *NWSA Journal* no. 17(3):64–87.

Soni-Sinha, Urvashi. 2008. "Dynamics of the 'Field': Multiple Standpoints, Narrative and Shifting Positionality in Multisited Research." *Qualitative Research* no. 8(4):515–37. doi: 10.1177/1468794108093898.

South China Morning Post. December 9, 2006. "Nightclubs Ban 'China Dolls' in Clampdown: Mainland Sex Workers Barred, but NGOs Say They Are Victims." South China Morning Post.

———. May 5, 2008. "Jungle's Dirty Secret." South China Morning Post.

———. July 14, 2008. "Chinese Prostitutes in Quandary as Malaysian Visa Racket Busted." South China Morning Post.

Spaan, Ernst, Ton van Naerssen, and Gerard Kohl. 2002. "Re-imagining Borders: Malay Identity and Indonesian Migrants in Malaysia." *Tijdschrift voor Economische en Sociale Geografie* no. 93(2):160–72.

Spanger, Marlene. 2002. "Black Prostitutes in Denmark." In *Transnational Prostitution: Changing Patterns in a Global Context*, edited by Susanne Thorbek and Bandana Pattanaik, 121-133. London: Zed.

Spindler, George, and Louise Spindler. 1989. "The Self and Instrumental Model in the Study of Cultural Change and Modernization." *Kroeber Anthropological Society Papers* no. 69–70:109–16.

———. 1992. "The Enduring, Situated, and Endangered Self in Fieldwork: A Personal Account." *The Psychoanalytic Study of Society* no. 17:23–28.

Standing, Guy. 1999. "Global Feminization Through Flexible Labour: A Theme Revisited." *World Development* no. 27(3):583–602.

———. 2011. *The Precariat: The New Dangerous Class*. New York: Bloomsbury Academic,

The Star. November 26, 2006. "Bukit Bintang not Patpong." The Star.

———. June 6, 2007. "Hourly Allowance to Replace RM80 Rela Incentive." The Star.

———. September 28, 2007. "Foreign Help, Local Strength. Why Not?" The Star.

———. November 26, 2008. "Chor: Current Laws on Prostitution Adequate." The Star.

———. July 26, 2009. "Tricked by Sex Syndicates." The Star.

———. February 3, 2011. "Rebranding Exercise as Rela Membership Exceeds 2 Million." The Star.

———. February 20, 2011. "Marrying for Money." The Star.

———. June 24, 2011. "Rela Stops War Against the Illegals." The Star.

Stark, Jan. 2006. "'Snow Leopard' meets 'Asian Tiger': Shaping Malaysia's relations with Central Asia." *The Round Table: The Commonwealth Journal of International Affairs* no. 95(385):455–71.

Stoler, Ann Laura. 1992. "Sexual Affronts and Racial Frontiers: European Identities and the Cultural Politics of Exclusion in Colonial Southeast Asia." *Comparative Studies in Societies and History* no. 34(3):514–51.

The Straits Times. July 17, 2001. "Uzbeki Women in Sex Trade Prove Elusive." The Straits Times.

———. July 4, 2004. "KL Scraps Rule on China Women; 'Suspicious' Tourist Visa Applicants Need Not Be Accompanied by Male Kin but Will Be Interviewed." The Straits Times.

———. August 1, 2009. "Malaysians on Guard against Crime; Many Are Turning to Private Security to Keep Homes Safe." The Straits Times.

———. June 26, 2010. "Malaysia: Foreign and Local Undergrads Targeted." The Straits Times.

———. June 19, 2011. "KL Volunteer Corps' Ranks Jump Sharply; Rela Includes Brigade Linked to Malay Supremacy Group Perkasa, Raising Opposition's Concerns." The Straits Times.

SUARAM. 2006. *Memorandum to SUHAKAM: Violence, Brutality, Theft and Abuse of Power by RELA Personnel in Government's Ongoing Operations*, November 1, 2006. http://www.suaram.net/?option=com_content&task=view&id=298&Itemid=29. Accessed July 3, 2008.

Tagliacozzo, Eric. 2008. "Morphological Shifts in Southeast Asian Prostitution: The Long Twentieth Century." *Journal of Global History* no. 3(2):251–73.

Tagore, Rabindranath. 1921. *Thought Relics*. New York: Macmillan Company.

Tan, Beng Hui. 2003. "'Protecting' Women: Legislation and Regulation of Women's Sexuality in Colonial Malaya." *Gender, Technology and Development* no. 7(1): 1–30.

Taylor, Jacqueline Sánchez. 2001. "Dollars Are a Girl's Best Friend? Female Tourists' Sexual Behaviour in the Caribbean." *Sociology* no. 35(3):749–64.

Teodosio, Virginia A. 2007. "The Informal Sector, Women and Class." *Philippine Journal of Labor and Industrial Relations* no. 27(1–2): 113–31.

ter Haar, Barend J. 1998. *The Ritual and Mythology of the Chinese Triads: Creating an Identity Brill's Scholars' List*. Leiden: Brill.

Ting-Toomey, Stella. 2005. "The Matrix of Face: An Updated Face Negotiation Theory." In *Theorizing about Intercultural Communication*, edited by William B. Gudykunst, 71–92. Thousand Oaks: SAGE.

Trappolin, Luca. 2005. "Gender Victims and Cultural Borders: The Globalization of Prostitution in Italy." *Dialectical Anthropology* no. 29(3–4):335–48.

Trocki, Carl A. 1993. "The Rise and Fall of the Ngee Heng Kongsi in Singapore." In *"Secret Societies" Reconsidered: Perspectives on the Social History of Modern South China and Southeast Asia*, edited by David Ownby and Mary Somers Heidhues, 89–119. Armonk, NY: M. E. Sharpe.

Trường, Thanh-Dạm. 1990. *Sex, Money, and Morality: Prostitution and Tourism in Southeast Asia*. Atlantic Highlands, NJ: Zed Books.

Turner, Bryan S. 2010. "Enclosures, Enclaves, and Entrapment." *Sociological Inquiry* no. 80(2):241–60. doi: 10.1111/j.1475-682X.2010.00329.x.

Turner, Jackie, and Liz Kelly. 2009. "Trade Secrets: Intersections between Diasporas and Crime Groups in the Constitution of the Human Trafficking Chain." *The British Journal of Criminology* no. 49(2):184–201.

United Nations Office on Drugs and Crime. 2010a. *The Globalization of Crime: A Transnational Organized Crime Threat Assessment*. New York: United Nations Office on Drugs and Crime.

———. 2010b. Issue Paper: Organized Crime Involvement in Trafficking in Persons and Smuggling of Migrants. New York: United Nations Office on Drugs and Crime. http://www.ungift.org/doc/knowledgehub/resource-centre/UNODC_Issue_Paper_Organized_Crime_Involvement.pdf.

United States Department of States. 2010. Annual US Trafficking in Persons Report (USTIP). United States Department of State. http://www.state.gov/g/tip/rls/tiprpt/2010/index.htm

van Eyck, Kim. 2003. *Flexibilizing Employment: An Overview*. SEED Working Paper No.24. Geneva: International Labour Organization.

van Ham, Peter. 2002. "Branding Territory: Inside the Wonderful Worlds of PR and IR Theory." *Millennium-Journal of International Studies* no. 31(2):249–69.

van Munster, Rens. 2005. "The EU and the Management of Immigration Risk in the Area of Freedom." In *Security and Justice: Political Science Publications* no. 12/2005. Odense: University of Southern Denmark.

Vandewalle, Ian. 2009. *Critical Points in City Branding*. Liverpool: Liverpool Hope University. http://www.kavalagreece.gr/wp-content/uploads/2008/10/kavala-paper-ian-vandewalle-liverpool.doc.

Vaughn, Bruce, and Michael Martin. 2007. "Malaysia: Political, Security, Economic, and Trade Issues Considered." In *CRS Report for Congress*. Washington DC, Congressional Research Service, Library of Congress. http://www.dtic.mil/dtic/tr/fulltext/u2/a480762.pdf

Verger, Antoni. 2009. "The Merchants of Education: Global Politics and the Uneven Education Liberalization Process within the WTO." *Comparative Education Review* no. 53(3):379–402.

Vina, Stephen R., Blas Nunez-Neto, and Alyssa Bartlett Weir. 2006. "Civilian Patrols Along the Border: Legal and Policy Issues." In *CRS Report for Congress*. Washington, D.C.: Congressional Research Service, Library of Congress.

Wakefield, Alison. 2003. *Selling Security: The Private Policing of Public Space*. Portland: Willan.

Ward, J. S. M., and W. G. Stirling. 1925. *The Hung Society Or the Society of Heaven and Earth*. London: Baskerville.

Warren, James. 1990. "Prostitution in Singapore Society and the Karayuki-san." In *The Underside of Malaysian History: Pullers, Prostitutes, Plantation Workers . . .*," edited by Peter J. Rimmer and Lisa M. Allen, 161–78. Singapore: Singapore University Press.

Weitzer, Ronald. 2007. "The Social Construction of Sex Trafficking: Ideology and Institutionalization of a Moral Crusade." *Politics & Society* no. 35(3):447–75.

Werbner, Pnina. 1999. "Global Pathways. Working Class Cosmopolitans and the Creation of Transnational Ethnic Worlds." *Social Anthropology* no. 7(1):17–35.

———. 2006. "Vernacular Cosmopolitanism." *Theory, Culture & Society* no. 23(2–3):496–8.

Westwood, R. I., and S. M. Leung. 1994. "The Female Expatriate Manager Experience: Coping with Gender and Culture." *International Studies of Management & Organization* no. 24(3):64–85.

Widerberg, Karin. 2007. "Among 'The Others': Migration and Gender and the Ethnographic Approach." York: The University of York. http://www.york.ac.uk/res/researchintegration/Integrative_Research_Methods/Widerberg%20Ethnography%20April%202007.pdf

Williamson, Thomas. 2002. "Incorporating a Malaysian Nation." *Cultural Anthropology* no. 17(3):401–30.

Wilson, Edward O. 1998. *Consilience: The Unity of Knowledge*. New York: Vintage Books.

Wolf, Diane L. 1996. *Feminist Dilemmas In Fieldwork*. Boulder: Westview Press.

Wonders, Nancy A., and Raymond Michalowski. 2001. "Bodies, Borders, and Sex Tourism in a Globalized World: A Tale of Two Cities—Amsterdam and Havana." *Social Problems* no. 48(4):545–71.

Wong, Lin Ken, and C. S. Wong. 1960. Review of "Chinese Secret Societies in Malaya: A Survey of the Triad Society from 1800–1900." *Journal of Southeast Asian History* no. 1(1):97–114.

Wong, Tai Chee. 1991. "From Spontaneous Settlement to Rational Land Use Planning: The Case of Kuala Lumpur, Malaysia." *Sojourn: Journal of Social Issues in Southeast Asia* no. 6(2):240–62.

World Bank. 2011a. *Malaysia Economic Monitor Brain Drain*. The World Bank. http://web.worldbank.org/WBSITE/EXTERNAL/COUNTRIES/EASTASIAPACIFICEXT/MALAYSIAEXTN/0,contentMDK:22900721~pagePK:1497618~piPK:217854~theSitePK:324488,00.html.

World Bank. 2011b. *World Development Report 2012: Gender Equity and Development*. Washington, DC: The World Bank.

World Trade Organization. 2011. *The General Agreement on Trade in Services (GATS): Objectives, Coverage and Disciplines*. World Trade Organization. http://www.wto.org/english/tratop_e/serv_e/gatsqa_e.htm.

Wynne, Mervyn Llevelyn. 1941. *Triad and Tabut: A Survey of the Origin and Diffusion of Chinese and Mohamedan Secret Societies in the Malay Peninsula, A.D. 1800–1935*. Singapore: Government Printing Office.

Yeoh, Brenda S. A. 2005. "The Global Cultural City? Spatial Imagineering and Politics in the (Multi)cultural Marketplaces of South-east Asia." *Urban Studies* no. 42(5–6):945–58.

Yeoh, Brenda S. A., and Shirlena Huang. 2011. "Introduction: Fluidity and Friction in Talent Migration." *Journal of Ethnic and Migration Studies* no. 37(5):681–90.

Yeoh, Brenda S. A., and Katie Willis. 2005. "Singaporean and British Transmigrants in China and the Cultural Politics of 'Contact zones.'" *Journal of Ethnic and Migration Studies* no. 31(2):269–85.

Yeoh, Seng Guan. 2001. "Creolized Utopias: Squatter Colonies and the Post-Colonial City in Malaysia." *Sojourn: Journal of Social Issues in Southeast Asia* no. 16(1):102–24.

Yuval-Davis, Nira, Floya Anthias, and Eleonore Kofman. 2005. "Secure Borders and Safe Haven and the Gendered Politics of Belonging: Beyond Social Cohesion." *Ethnic and Racial Studies* no. 28(3):513–35.

Zakaria, Abdul Hadi. 1987. "Pelacuran di kalangan Wanita Dan Gadis [Prostitution among Women and Girls]." *Jurnal Antropologi Dan Sosiologi* [*Journal of Anthropology and Sociology*] no.15:41–62.

Zhang, Sheldon X., Ko-Lin Chin, and Jody Miller. 2007. "Women's Participation in Chinese Transnational Human Smuggling: A Gendered Market Perspective." *Criminology* no. 45(3):699–733.

Ziguras, Christopher. 2003. "The Impact of the GATS on Transnational Tertiary Education: Comparing Experiences of New Zealand, Australia, Singapore and Malaysia." *Australian Educational Researcher* no. 30(3):89–109.

Ziguras, Christopher, and Siew-Fang Law. 2006. "Recruiting International Students as Skilled Migrants: The Global 'Skills Race' as Viewed from Australia and Malaysia." *Globalisation, Societies and Education* no. 4(1):59–76.

Zubaida, Sami. 2002. "Middle Eastern Experiences of Cosmopolitanism." In *Conceiving Cosmopolitanism: Theory, Context, and Practice*, edited by Steven Vertovec and Robin Cohen, 32–41. New York: Oxford University Press.

INDEX

controlled violence, punishments for transgressions, 132

corporate funding of public universities, 55

corporate universities, 12, 13, 56

cosmopolitanism and cosmopolitans, 25–27, 146–172
    emerging cosmopolitan subjectivities of sex workers, 150–162
    etymology *cosmopolite*, 25, 170, 195n1
    respect as element of, 149, 155, 157, 171, 178
    syndicates' effect on cosmopolitan behavior, 138, 162–170
    tolerance, flexibility, and openness, 25, 26, 170

Cote D'Ivoire, 74, 159

couriers delivering "packages" overseas, 114, 115

creativity in managing and facilitating sex worker migration, 14–24
    "traffickers" *vs.* facilitators, 23, 24
    See also syndicates

crime, 15, 76
    arrests. *See* arrests
    "courier" and "logistics" jobs, 116
    criminalization of sex work, 20, 88, 123, 128, 183
    within Golden Triangle, 75
    "insiders" *vs.* "outsiders," 47
    "organized crime," 23, 124
    perception of migrants as cause of, 76
    RELA, combating urban crime, 81, 82

cruise industry, 29

"crusade ideology," 20

cultural diplomacy, 13

cultural issues, 60, 68, 76, 77, 111, 144
    immigrant enclaves promoted for diverse ethnic advantage, 186n7
    intercultural communicative practices, 151–153
    specific threats associated with specific migrant nationalities, 68, 69
    worldviews, differences in, 60, 147–149, 152, 153, 157, 161, 168, 178

cultural tourism park, 48

"culture of suspicion" or surveillance, 38

currency exchange rates, 143

"*cuti cuti Malaysia*" (vacation in Malaysia), 48, 49

Cyberjaya, 44, 75

Dangerous Societies Ordinance of 1869, 129

databases with biographical information, travel profiles, arrest records, 17

de facto employers, 62

debt bondage. *See* indentured servitude

debt bondage/indentured servitude, 38, 92, 105, 124, 125, 129, 132, 133, 136, 177

decisions to migrate for sex work. *See* goals and plans for the future

deforestation, 42

degradation, status of sex work as, 98

"demand" for sex, 121–125

deportation, 20
    3D approach, 16, 20, 73, 175, 179
    workers' complaints against employers, 63

detention. *See* arrest and detention

"differential inclusion," 9

dignity of sex work, 98

diplomats as cosmopolitan travelers, 25

"discrepant" cosmopolitanism, 26

Doha, 3, 13, 109, 110

dress. *See* clothing

drivers, 30, 115, 134, 165
    ancillary industry for sex work, 123
    syndicates, 108, 120, 123, 134–136, 138–140, 144

drugs, 69, 75, 86, 102, 112, 119, 128

Dubai, 109, 110

earnings of sex workers, 89–96, 98, 101, 104, 106, 111–113, 176
    aging, effect on earnings, 110
    condom-less experience, 99
    hierarchical differentials, 90
    refusal of clients to pay, 112
    and syndicates, 120, 137

Eastern Europe, migratory pathways, 108–112

education, 12–14, 55, 58, 107, 108
    branch campuses, 13, 55
    corporate funding of public universities, 55
    corporate universities, 12, 13, 56
    cross-border movements of students and faculty, 12
    distance learning, 13

education brokers, 13
fly-by-night "shophouse" colleges, 57
franchising of educational
   institutions, 13
GATS (General Agreement on Trade in
   Services), 12–14, 23
international education (IE), 13
as "internationally traded service," 12
Kuala Lumpur's world-class
   universities, 54–58
migratory path to sex work, 12–14, 23,
   57, 74, 75, 112
Muslim countries, students from,
   58
part-time certification courses, 14
private education market, 54, 55
sex workers with university degrees,
   99
state liberalization of, 54–58
subsidization of student expenses via
   sex work, 57, 107
syndicate payment of tuition and fees,
   108
women's goals and plans for the future
   building school for girls, 110
   education of siblings, 113
elderly women
   help in abduction, 86
   "mamees," 23, 90, 132, 133, 135, 137
election clashes between Malays and
   Chinese in Kuala Lumpur, 40
elites *vs.* nonelites, 3, 170, 171
   sophisticated *vs.* crude clients and
      women, 99, 140, 144, 162
   See also cosmopolitanism
"embedded liberalism," 3, 185n2
Emergency (Essential Powers) Act 1964,
   78
Employment Act 1955, 63
employment agencies, 123
   "migration industries," 22, 122
   state regulation of, 62
employment set-aside policy, 48
"enduring self," 21, 118, 119
"enemy No. 2," 81
English language, 14, 89, 99, 101, 102,
   106, 107, 138, 148, 153, 163,
   193n6
entrapment, internal border
   management, 61, 76

escort agencies, 23
Essential Regulations 1966, 78, 79
ethnicity issues, 67, 68, 116
   brothels as racialized-ethnicized
      spaces, 86, 87
   gendered, racialized, and classed
      cosmopolites, 146–172
   Malay supremacy group, 78, 191n7
   "petit apartheid," 17, 71, 83
   threats associated with specific
      migrant nationalities, 68, 69
   See also racial issues
"everyday" cosmopolitanism, 26
evictions, 38, 45
executive assistant, 106
experienced (sexually) women, 102, 103,
   109, 135, 137
explorers as cosmopolitan travelers, 25
export-oriented production, 18, 19, 41
eye contact, 105

facials
   courses on, 102
   salons, "sly" prostitution sites, 88,
      92–95, 116, 131, 177
facilitation of in-migration and
   employment
   creativity in managing and facilitating
      sex worker migration, 14–24
   "traffickers" versus facilitators, 23, 24
   See also syndicates
families
   encouraging migration, 85
   painful relationships, 109, 116
   remittance of earnings, 110, 114,
      141–143
   response to women's choices, 101, 100,
      110
   responsibilities to, 93, 98, 102, 103, 117
   strained relationships with, 92, 116
   See also children and child care;
      parents of sex workers
Federal Territory (FT), 35, 41–44, 78, 90,
   108, 131, 189n3
fees
   entrance via formal channels, 64, 65
   men willing to marry migrant women
      Asian countries, 69
   of syndicates, 24, 96, 103, 108, 109,
      115, 125, 132, 136, 143

hierarchy within Chinese secret societies, 130
hierarchy within Kuala Lumpur, 59
hierarchy within syndicates, 133
Hire Indonesians Last policy, 47, 52
homosexuality and bisexuality
    female clients, 93, 138
    Syndicate X heterosexual ideology, 139–141, 144
Hong Kong, 55, 86, 96, 100, 102, 113, 114, 162, 164
    syndicate circuit of Hong Kong, KL, Singapore, Sydney, Auckland, and Taipei, 138
honorary males, 30
hospitality workers, sex workers categorized as, 11
hotels and restaurants, 44, 132
    budget hotels and inns, 95
    low-wage positions, 11, 68
    pelacur hotel, 88
    "sly" prostitution sites (massage parlors, restaurants, etc.), 88, 92–95, 116, 131, 177
    syndicates, assistance to, 120, 123, 144
housing, 45, 54, 96, 109
    kongsi, 76
    within "migration industries," 122
    raids, 80
    See also condominiums and apartments
hui, 126
    See also secret societies
hygiene of clients, 93
hypocrisy and power imbalances, 155, 158, 176, 183

ikan bilis ("anchovy") syndicates, 131
Ikatan Relawan Rakyat Malaysia (RELA), 17, 18, 29, 77–82, 85
Immigration Act 1956/1963, 63
Immigration Act 1959/1963, 88
Immigration Ordinance of 1953, 39
immigration quotas, 65
immigration-labor categories, 22
"incipient democracy," 127
indentured servitude/debt bondage, 38, 62, 86, 92, 105, 124–125, 129, 132–133, 136, 177

independent workers
    freelancers, 88, 89, 96, 103, 105, 112, 137, 153
    pelacur bebas, 88
India and Indian workers, 14, 37–40, 50, 53, 58, 67, 68, 70, 74, 86, 150, 173, 195n10
    colonial policies shaping Malay relationship with Chinese and Indian migrant workers, 14, 38–41
    citizenship in Malaya, 40
    Malaysia as sanctuary, 67
    syndicate operations by Malaysians of Indian descent, 131
    Tamil women, 86, 87
indigenization of urban areas and employment sectors previously 'sinicized,' 41
Indonesia and Indonesian workers, 42, 45, 46, 47, 67
    diplomat spouse's arrest 81
    domestic workers, 28, 42, 53
    migrant women golf caddies, 72
    migrant women displaced by Chinese sex workers, 106
    Hire Indonesians Last policy Malaysia, 47
    Malaysia as sanctuary, 67
    shift in Malay perceptions and treatment of Indonesians, from "insiders" to "outsiders," 47
Indonesians identified with Islamic militancy in Southeast Asia, 47
induction courses and surveillance
    migrants, 65
informal *vs.* formal channels of migration, 8, 19, 22
informal economies, 4
    Kuala Lumpur, 59
information technology. *See* technology
internal border control, 60–83
international education (IE), 12, 57
International Labour Organization (ILO), 4, 5, 70
International Monetary Fund structural adjustment programs (SAPs), 6, 19
Iran and Iranian workers, 50, 51, 56, 114, 115, 116, 161, 162

race riots, 40
segregation, 38, 39
self-declared prostitutes, 39
skyline photo, 35
sporting events, 50
squatter settlements, 45
Structure Plans, 43, 49
syndicates working within, 130
    See also syndicates
tourism, 49–64
traffic, 34
"unity out of diversity," 51
volunteer corps. See RELA (Ikatan
    Relawan Rakyat Malaysia)
as world-class, 6, 32–59
zoning and demolition of small, older
    business establishments, 132
Kuala Lumpur City Centre. See KLCC
Kuala Lumpur International Airport. See
    KLIA

labor brokers, 22, 23, 29, 30, 54, 73, 92,
    104, 122, 136
labor flexibilization process, 4, 63–4
labor unions, 66
Lagos, 109
lawyers
    "migration industries," 123
    outsourcing, 36
Liberia, 74
licensing and registration of sex
    workers by colonial state, 86, 87
little Arabia, 52, 170
Little India, 88

Mafia, 23
Malay Agricultural Settlement (MAS),
    37, 189n3
Malay identity, 40, 189n5
Malay Reservation Enactment 1913, 38
Malay reservation land, 40
Malay supremacy group, 78
Malayan Communist Party (MCP), 39
Malay-Muslim ethos, 51
Malaysia, 32–59
    advanced producer services, 14, 36,
        44, 45, 48, 54, 174
    agricultural heritage, 41
    apocalyptic vision of Malaysia overrun
        by outsiders, 68

appropriation of privately owned land
    for megastructural projects, 45
bilateral trade relations with PRC, 51
blueprint for "developed" status, 43
borders, reestablishment, 60–83
"brain drain," 55
citizen volunteerism, 78
colonial history, 14, 37–41, 85–88,
    127–129
"competition state," 47, 48
education, liberalization of, 54–58
emerging middle classes, 41
employment set-aside policy, 48
"foreigner management and
    monitoring," 65
Hire Indonesians Last policy, 47
Home Affairs, centralization of migrant
    worker administration, 65, 66
indigenization of urban areas and
    employment sectors previously
    'sinicized,' 41
internal border control, 60–83
Kuala Lumpur
    role of state in making world-class,
        7, 10, 32–59
    See also Kuala Lumpur
legacies of colonial rule, 40, 58
migrant workers
    by country of origin, 2000–2010
        (table), 46
    by economic sector, 2000–2010
        (table), 46
    migratory pathways. See migratory
        pathways
minimum-wage system, 64
New Economic Model (NEM), 48
New Economic Policy of 1971–1990
    (NEP), 41
planned townships, 42, 44
as Promised Land, 67
public transportation system, 48
repressive state strategies concerning
    borders, 60–83
as sanctuary, 67
sovereignty, 17
state agencies, ancillary industry for
    sex work, 123
state as competitive corporation, 48
state securitization of migration,
    15–18

traffic congestion in Kuala Lumpur, 34

trafficked women, 3, 5, 6, 54, 86, 108, 124, 125, 131
  Anti-Trafficking in Persons Act 2007 (ATPA), 73
  inspection of "property," 194n
  internal border control, 62, 67, 69, 70, 80
  murky relationship between migrant women and sex trafficking, 72, 73, 104–5, 114
  trafficking *vs.* migration, 9, 19–24, 27, 72, 73, 104, 108, 122

"transit crime" *vs.* "organized" crime, 124

transnational banking services, 141–143

transportation firms as "migration industries," 22, 122–123

travel agents, ancillary industry for sex work, 123

Triads, 23, 24, 126, 127
  See also secret societies

trickery, recruitment by, 3, 19, 38, 86

tuition, 13, 57, 108

Ukrainian workers, 70, 112, 113, 156

United Nations Convention Relating to the Status of Refugees, 80

United Nations Protocol to Prevent, Suppress, and Punish Trafficking in Persons, 20

United States Trafficking in Persons Report (USTIP), 73

Universal Declaration of Human Rights, 15

universities. *See* education

"unskilled" migrant workers, 16, 25, 175
  See also guest workers

urbanization, 38, 41, 42, 88

Uruguay Round on trade agreements, 10, 187n12

Uzbekistan and Uzbekistan workers, 53, 70, 74, 112, 113, 139, 140, 144, 145

"vernacular" cosmopolitanism, 26

vice syndicates. *See* syndicates

vice-raids. *See* raids

victim-perpetrator relationship, complexity of, 72–73, 114

Vietnamese migrants, 54, 67–69, 94, 106, 121, 139, 150, 168, 192n8

vigilante groups, 17, 79

VIPs, 98, 113–115, 138, 140, 144, 172

visas, 16, 19, 64, 96, 102–104, 112, 134, 136, 138, 177, 188n16, 191n4
  student visas, 13, 69, 75, 95, 108, 114, 117

visa-on-arrival (VOA), 74

Vision 2020, 43, 48, 58, 66

wages. *See* earnings of sex workers

warrantless searches for irregular migrants, 79

Wawasan 2020, 43, 48, 58, 66 *See also* Vision 2020

weak *vs.* robust migration industries, 123

Western Union, remittance of earnings, 141

white skinned women. *See* skin color

Wilayah Persekutuan, 35
  See Federal Territory

Women and Girls Protection Ordinance of 1888, 86, 87

working-class clients, 89–93

World Bank structural adjustment programs (SAPs), 6, 19, 185n

World Trade Organization (WTO), 10, 12

worldviews, differences in, 6, 25–27, 60, 147–149, 152, 153, 157, 161, 168, 178

"writing" on bodies of sex workers, 71, 72

Yakuza, 23

Yap Ah Loy, 37, 39, 128

"yellow card girls," 192

zoning in Kuala Lumpur, 132, 192n